Japan-China Relations
through the Lens of Chinese Politics

Japan-China Relations through the Lens of Chinese Politics

KOKUBUN Ryosei

Japan Publishing Industry Foundation for Culture

NOTE ON JAPANESE AND CHINESE NAMES:
Japanese and Chinese names in this book are given in customary order, surname first. Japanese names are spelled in accordance with the bearer's wishes where known; otherwise they are romanized according to the Hepburn system, with long vowels indicated by macrons. An exception has been made for the author's given name. Mainland Chinese names are romanized using the Hanyu Pinyin system, simplified Chinese romanization, with surnames separated by a space; Taiwanese names are romanized and hyphenated according to general usage.

Japan-China Relations through the Lens of Chinese Politics
Kokubun Ryosei. Translated by the Japan Institute of International Affairs (JIIA).

Published by Japan Publishing Industry Foundation for Culture (JPIC)
2-2-30 Kanda-Jinbocho, Chiyoda-ku, Tokyo 101-0051, Japan
First English edition: March 2021

Originally published in Japanese under the title of *Chūgoku seiji kara mita Nicchū kankei* by Iwanami Shoten, Publishers, in 2017.
English publishing rights arranged with Iwanami Shoten, Publishers, Tokyo.

This publication is the result of a collaborative effort between the Japan Institute of International Affairs (JIIA) and Japan Publishing Industry Foundation for Culture (JPIC).

Jacket and cover design: Fukazawa Kohei

Printed in Japan
ISBN 978-4-86658-127-9
https://www.jpic.or.jp/

Contents

Preface

"Fortune and misfortune are intertwined like the strands of a rope," as the saying goes. In other words, things are good at times and bad at times, and the good and bad are like the two sides of the same coin.

Japan-China relations since 1972, when the two countries normalized diplomatic ties, have seen both good times and bad. All in all, relations were relatively good until the first half of the 1990s but have taken a downward trajectory from the latter half of the 1990s onward, especially since the beginning of the twenty-first century. Needless to say, problems have occasionally surfaced and put a strain on bilateral relations even in the best of times, and there have likewise been moments of improvement even in the midst of deteriorating relations.

The objective of this book is to explore the factors that have contributed to the ups and downs in Japan-China relations. Most prior studies have considered this topic chiefly in the context of Japanese foreign policy; viewing it from a Japanese standpoint provides access to a far greater wealth of materials and enables a pluralistic approach. This has inevitably led to the prevalence of studies that focus on issues of history between Japan and China, a trend that of late has been noticeable among American and European researchers in particular. When studies put the history issues front and center, it draws the world's attention to Japan's stance on these issues. This is because different views abound in Japan, including ones that are extreme, and are being openly debated. By contrast, Chinese attitudes toward Japan are ostensibly monolithic, owing in part to its political system, and analyses of opinions within China have consequently taken a back seat.

Other arguments also exist with regard to the variables affecting Japan-China relations, including those about the power shift or power transition that occurred as China became the world's second largest economy after the United States, overtaking Japan in GDP, in 2010; those that zero in on the rise of nationalism in both countries, a phenomenon that also relates to historical issues; and others that look at economic fluctuations on a global level. But while these all make sense as situational factors accounting for the backdrop to the vicissitudes in bilateral ties, none of them can hardly be considered direct factors involved in the decisions of policymakers.

This book adopts the basic approach taken by area studies, which endeavors to understand the thinking and workings of a region by way of elucidating the unique characteristics found within that region and to abstract therefrom the explanatory variables that close in on the root of phenomena. With regard to the various situations that arise in international politics and diplomacy as well, this standpoint stresses those factors related to domestic politics.

The chief object of analysis in this volume is Chinese domestic politics. This book is grounded in the hypothesis that the causes of changes in Japan-China relations are primarily to be found in Chinese domestic politics. Economic growth and the advancement of the market economy in China of late have undoubtedly contributed to greater diversity and pluralism in Chinese society and to significant changes in Chinese attitudes. As far as the political system is concerned, though, the one-party dictatorship by the Chinese Communist Party (CCP) remains largely unchanged, and pluralism is absent from the political sphere. The basis of politics being power, fierce power politics is constantly being waged behind the scenes between the various factions of the CCP. In the average country or society, public opinion is gauged in accordance with the rules of open debate and elections under the rule of law, and these processes determine whether power remains in the same hands or is handed over to a successor. If a political party loses an election, it is only to be expected that the party will give up the reins of government. But in China, where no mechanisms or rules exist for a transfer of power between parties, the Communist Party simply cannot relinquish power.

The intentions, relationships, and actions of the supreme leader and other top-level leaders remain crucial in understanding Chinese politics. This is why politics in China is called the "rule of men" (*jinchi/renzhi*) as opposed to the "rule of law" (*hōchi/fazhi*). Moreover, it is easy to imagine the substantial influence that the course of the power game in domestic politics must exert on China's foreign policy, and this book assumes that these effects are particularly pronounced when it comes to the country's policy toward Japan. Because the CCP grounds the historical legitimacy of its power in its victory in the "Anti-Japanese War" (Second Sino-Japanese War, 1937–45), its relations with Japan have always inherently involved a delicate aspect. In a nutshell, the CCP emphasizes principle in Sino-Japanese relations when playing up the party's historical legitimacy but views the same relations in more pragmatic terms when asserting that its legitimacy lies in the daily lives of Chinese citizens today. China's policy toward Japan, then, is a subject that directly correlates with the CCP's party line.

Based on the above understanding, I will begin by surveying the current topology of research on Chinese politics while casting an eye back over the historical development of area studies in the United States and Japan. Following the introductory chapter, Part I will shed light on the Chinese political system by analyzing each decade from the 1980s—when the policies of reform and opening up began in earnest—to the present day. Part II will elucidate how China's domestic politics and its policy toward Japan are closely connected by examining the various affairs that have arisen between Japan and China in each era. I will conclude the book with a final chapter that sums up Parts I and II, which are organically linked.

Introduction

Chinese Politics as Area Studies

1. Area Studies: From the United States to Japan

What is area studies? The answer to this question depends on the person responding to it. Although there is an overall framework to which all would agree, individual researchers have their respective thoughts and positions on their field. The answer also hinges on the academic discipline in which individual researchers conduct their work, such as cultural anthropology, sociology, economics, or political science. Hence, the term "area studies" has a variety of definitions.

Area studies was originally born in the United States during World War II. Numerous debates have ensued about its definition, and I too have made my case on a number of occasions. The crux of the issue comes down to whether or not area studies can be called a discipline in its own right. Can it rightly claim its place as a science—an "ology"—on a par with, say, economics, political science, or sociology?[1] It has often been argued that area studies is not so much a stand-alone discipline as a methodology that supports other more legitimate ologies. This is precisely why the field has yet to achieve mainstream recognition.

To summarize the gist of arguments that have been made in the past, area studies involves selecting an area of the world and seeking to understand the personality thereof. The question then is what criteria are used in delimiting a certain part of the world: is it by country, by geographical region, by culture, or perhaps by religion? This too depends on the awareness of the individual researcher. Area studies is generally seen to concern itself with characterizing different cross sections of a given slice of the world—which brings us to the next question of what scholarly approaches are to be used to achieve that end. Again, the response will vary from one scholar to the next. For me it is political science.

---

1 Kokubun Ryosei, "Chiiki kenkyū to kokusai seiji no aida" [Between Area Studies and International Politics], in *Nihon no kokusai seijigaku 3: Chiiki kara mita kokusai seiji* [Japan's International Politics, vol. 3: International Politics Viewed from Areas], eds. Kokubun Ryosei, Sakai Keiko, and Endō Mitsugi (Tokyo: Yūhikaku, 2009).

Turning to the question of what the components of area studies are, learning the local language invariably ranks at the top of the list. Thus equipped, researchers are then advised to conduct fieldwork if at all possible. But whereas fieldwork is a minimum requirement in such disciplines as cultural anthropology, it is often not feasible in political science and the like. As such, scholars of political science commonly employ interview-based surveys, but even such methods meet serious limitations in the face of a political system like China's.

After language and fieldwork, emphasis is placed on collaborative research. This is because the unique features of a region cannot be fully unraveled without interdisciplinary dialogue between diverse fields. But universities tend to be compartmentalized, and many academics are not even acquainted with colleagues outside their own department. As a case in point, I once belonged to a department that had some 5,000 students and a full-time faculty of about 120. Given this state of affairs within a single department, knowing about other departments is even more difficult. This is partly why area studies was born; the barriers created by compartmentalization needed to be taken down. It follows that area studies must necessarily be interdisciplinary and comprehensive.

Because of its very nature, though, area studies has always been dogged by one problem: the potential absence of a sweeping gaze that addresses how to position individual studies—each of which looks into the character of an individual area—into a theoretical whole, or how to place them within a larger historical context. A political scientist conducting area studies, for instance, must analyze the characteristics of a region in a manner relevant to the discipline of political science; but in practice this is extremely difficult. And so it goes that area studies and established disciplines have come to be seen as being in perpetual rivalry.[2] How to close this divide and theorize on a broader scale is a

2 Lucian W. Pye, ed., *Political Science and Area Studies: Rivals or Partners?* (Bloomington: Indiana University Press, 1975).

chronic question for area studies scholars—and one that continues to be debated today.

A similar situation exists between international relations and area studies, two fields that could be said to differ in orientation from the outset. Researchers in area studies actively place themselves in the local scene through fieldwork. This approach is difficult to reconcile with international relations, which seeks to view things within the greater context of the overarching international system or relations between countries. Interestingly, international relations and area studies enjoy a relatively close relationship in Japan, unlike in the United States. This stems from differences in how area studies developed in the two countries. In the United States the field is usually not included in international relations, but this is not the case in Japan. In the following section, I will substantiate this assertion by reviewing the history of area studies in the United States.

Area Studies in the United States: Characteristics and Development
As noted above, area studies—also known as regional studies—was born in the United States during World War II. The chief objects of study at the time were Germany and Japan. In short, area studies was based on the very pragmatic question of how to defeat America's enemies; it was all-out war, and the Americans were intent on learning about the languages and cultures of the enemies. To that end, cultural anthropologists and other scholars were mobilized to gain insight into conditions in hostile countries. This was the origin of area studies. Ruth Benedict's *The Chrysanthemum and the Sword* (1946), which is cited as required reading when a student in the United States begins studying Japan, was among the fruits of this wartime effort.

There is no denying that area studies developed in part to answer the demands of war. After World War II, the focus of area studies turned to the Soviet Union and China, reflecting a rapid shift in the United States' real-world concern as the Cold War took hold. Against the backdrop of the Cold War, considerable funds were funneled into

USSR-related research in order to better know the hypothetical enemy and inform decisions in line with US policy. When the People's Republic of China was founded in 1949, dollars flowed into the field of China studies. The same occurred in the 1960s, when substantial money and interest were diverted to Southeast Asian studies during the Vietnam War (1955–75). In this respect, it can be argued that area studies in the United States had a strong affinity with real politics and government policy by virtue of its very origin.

In the United States, government funds frequently go to foundations, and while this still holds true, the total dollars that once went into area studies is almost unimaginable today. American research in area studies received massive funding from the 1950s to 1960s, after which budgets began to dwindle and continue to do so today. But it is not solely in response to politics and government policy that area studies flourished in the United States; the flow of funds and talent into academic societies and universities confronted academia with the question of how to establish area studies as a discipline.

Perhaps due in part to these origins, area studies in the United States has tended to focus largely on such fields as political science, history, and cultural anthropology. The roots of area studies as an academic field lie in generating data for use by disciplines like these. In its earliest stages, it mostly played the auxiliary role of material and data provision, uncovering regional characteristics and feeding back those findings to the respective disciplines. And because of its humble beginnings as a material provider, there has always been a pecking order of sorts between area studies and these disciplines.

In political science, the key concern lies in how to theorize the knowledge gleaned from analyzing individual regions, leading area studies to be accepted and utilized in the domain of comparative politics. The primary object of interest in this subfield was developing countries; when independent states were newly born in places like Asia, Africa, and Latin America, the American attention—whether of policymakers or of researchers—was directed toward where these countries were headed. Amid the Cold War, there was an underlying political imperative to contemplate how the United States could keep these fledgling countries from being won over by communism.

A case in point is Walt Whitman Rostow's highly influential book, *The Stages of Economic Growth: A Non-Communist Manifesto* (1960), in which he laid out a phased process for growing young countries into societies along the lines of the US model. As this work exemplifies, area studies of the time had real-life policy implications, addressing the creation of a program, as it were, for the development of these countries. This was a natural corollary of the Cold War climate. Rostow's ideas later drew heavy criticism, as modernization theory itself came under attack. The point of contention, in a nutshell, was that the theory was based on Eurocentric thinking. This critique emerged against the backdrop of the Vietnam War and out of honest doubts about why American youths had to die in Vietnam. As people sought to learn where Vietnam was and what the situation was there, it became blatantly clear that no research was being conducted on Vietnam itself. This fueled a scathing assault on area studies in its conventional form, which had been conducted within the paradigm of modernization theory. Modernization theory was predicated on the assumption that all emerging countries of the world were headed along a predictable trajectory of development that culminated in an American-style society. The anti-Vietnam War movement gave prominence to the view that different regions were meant to develop in different ways, and area studies continued to face such criticisms until the late 1970s.

When the Vietnam War came to an end, the United States was burned out. It quickly lost interest in the outside world, and on the domestic front it was severely plagued by a slow economy and unemployment until the 1980s. Having been studying in the United States right around this time, I vividly recall the country's social climate toward the war. People skirted around the topic, and as for youths, they hardly knew anything about it. When a course titled "The Vietnam War" was inaugurated in 1984 at the University of Michigan, where I was at the time, the classroom was packed with students—a testament to the simmering curiosity that young people harbored within them about the war, a subject that grownups were reluctant to talk about.

In the 1980s, the United States began to slowly recover from the economic stagnation that it had suffered earlier in the decade. Meanwhile, interest in area studies waned from around that time, as did criticism of modernization theory. The various research funds that went into area studies also decreased. These trends became more pronounced in the 1990s, as the progress of globalization and the recovery of the domestic economy paved the way to US hegemony. Francis Fukuyama's *The End of History and the Last Man* (1992) represented one of the intellectual currents of the era, which purported that the wave of globalization was pushing the world toward convergence. On these grounds, the view spread in the United States that the need to study individual regions had become obsolete.

As a result, US society grew even more introverted, giving rise in the 1990s to a state of affairs in which many students of area studies found difficulty landing research jobs at academic institutions; scholars now needed to be well versed in theory to find employment. Particularly in the field of economics, even some outstanding scholars at the forefront of research on the Chinese economy lost their places in academia, causing a stir. A similar trend was also seen in political science and other fields. Although some research funding has come to be diverted to Middle East and China studies since the turn of the millennium—owing to such events as the multiple terrorist attacks of September 11, 2001, and the Iraq War, as well as China's rise to power—a return to the glory of the 1950s and 1960s appears unlikely. We must keep in mind that the changing circumstances of area studies in the United States have always been linked to the times.

Genealogy of Area Studies in Japan

Area studies in Japan followed a very different course from that of its American counterpart. Although the field as practiced in Japan after

World War II was introduced from the United States, something akin to it already existed prior to the war. In prewar Shanghai, for instance, Japan established an institute of higher learning called the Tō-A Dōbun Shoin (East Asia Common Culture Academy, or Tung Wen College). This, Douglas R. Reynolds argues, served as the model for area studies worldwide, having included in its curriculum language study, fieldwork, and interdisciplinary research—all of which are defining characteristics of area studies.[3] By that token, the South Manchuria Railway Research Department might also qualify as a research institution of a similar nature.

Keio University, where I worked for many years, likewise had a research institution before the war that engaged in something resembling area studies. This was the Asia Research Institute. The activities of the institute can be glimpsed from records dating to the last few years of the war, and they strongly reflect the times in which they took place. In the same period, Tokyo Imperial University—the predecessor of the University of Tokyo—set up the Institute of Oriental Culture, the charter of which is also heavily tinged with the atmosphere of wartime Japan. History mirrors the times, and there is no escaping it. Both the Tō-A Dōbun Shoin and the South Manchuria Railway Research Department conformed to Japan's policy orientation at the time, a fact reminiscent of the genesis of area studies in the United States. This all goes to show that, as I have asserted, something that could be labeled as area studies existed in Japan even before the concept came into being.

Nonetheless, area studies is generally viewed as having entered Japan from the United States only after World War II. At Keio University, Ishikawa Tadao founded a course on "regional studies" in the Department of Political Science in the late 1950s after returning from his studies in the United States, where he had witnessed the flowering of area studies. This course endures to this day as a core component of the department's curriculum. American studies at the University

---

3 Douglas R. Reynolds, "Chinese Area Studies in Prewar China: Japan's Tō-A Dōbun Shoin in Shanghai, 1900–1945," *Journal of Asian Studies* 45, no. 5 (November 1986): 945–70.

of Tokyo and equivalent programs at other schools also began in like manner, when young academics who had studied in the United States established research centers or launched new courses.

These were followed in 1958 by the Institute of Developing Economics and in 1959 by the Japan Institute of International Affairs, which were set up under the jurisdiction of the Ministry of International Trade and Industry and the Ministry of Foreign Affairs, respectively. As university-affiliated institutions go, the 1963 founding of the Center for Southeast Asian Studies at Kyoto University was significant. A look at the prospectuses of these entities reveals an interesting commonality: they all strove to stay at arm's length from actual politics by imbuing their guiding principles with a nonpolitical character. This was most likely motivated by a desire to articulate their renunciation of prewar ways, scholarship included; prewar scholarship was deemed to have been used for war purposes, and these organizations were eager to highlight how the postwar world had made a clean break from this legacy. It thus appears that when area studies made its way to postwar Japan from the United States, an unspoken consensus existed among Japanese scholars to see to it that the field took root in a form free of political elements.

Setting aside the particular leanings of area studies in Japan, the field as a whole fit in well with the country's intellectual climate. Following the introduction of area studies at Keio University by Ishikawa and others in the late 1950s, area studies groups at the university published the fruits of joint research over the next two decades. Meanwhile, the rapid rise of Japan's economy from the 1970s on piqued international interest in research on the country itself, making Japan studies one of the main focuses of area studies worldwide. Against this backdrop, the field enjoyed significant growth in Japan in the 1980s, thanks in large part to the need for Japan's internationalization.

The word *kokusaika* (internationalization) gained currency in Japan in the 1980s, a time when many Japanese corporations expanded overseas in the face of increasing domestic costs and the appreciation of the yen against the US dollar. After *Japan as Number One: Lessons for America* by Harvard sociologist Ezra F. Vogel came out in 1979, the world's interest turned to the why and how of Japan's miraculous rise from the ashes of war. The 1980s saw many fine young researchers across the world, including the United States and China, flock to the study of Japan. As the tide of internationalization lifted the country to greater prominence, the question of how best to interact with the wider world came to loom large in Japan, prompting voices that urged the importance of advancing domestic research in international relations and area studies. The 1984 creation of the Keio Center for Area Studies, the precursor of the current Keio Institute of East Asian Studies, was a reflection of these conditions. International relations and area studies were treated more or less synonymously as they took root in Japan; this is one point that differs from the United States, as I will discuss later.

We have seen above that area studies in postwar Japan was strongly inclined to keep a distance from politics in an effort to set itself apart from its prewar equivalent. This was the principal difference with area studies in the United States. Looking at subsequent developments, there is no denying that in some respects, area studies in Japan progressed in step with political or policy-related concerns. But the researchers nonetheless had a penchant for steering clear of these interests. Ensuring neutrality meant focusing as much as possible on empirical analysis, and on this score, area studies in Japan was not too oriented toward theorization. Empirical research leveraging historical materials is the forte of Japanese scholars, and Japan's academic climate tends to place the highest premium on the careful accumulation of facts. Every detail is scrutinized and brought into fine relief. This kind of approach being the specialty of Japanese scholarship overall, the importance of formulating theory inevitably pales by comparison. In research on developing regions, there is a deeply rooted view that area studies is about expounding on how a widely accepted theory does not accord with the realities of a region, but the discussion does not extend to the issue of how to overturn the conventional theory and construct a new one. Area studies exists in a vacuum, whereby researchers content themselves with thoroughly elucidating the particularities of a specific region.

Another aspect of area studies in Japan is that it is often integrated with international relations. In the United States, by contrast, it developed an affinity with comparative politics, due to a greater interest in comparing the characteristics of a country with those of US politics or of other countries than in looking at the relationships between them as a means of working toward a theory. Thus, in the domain of political science, area studies in the United States became affiliated with comparative politics, whereas in Japan it found a place with international relations.

2. Postwar Research on Chinese Politics: The United States and Japan

Research Trends in Postwar America: Debates over the Chinese Revolution

Before looking back over the development of research on Chinese politics in postwar Japan, I would first like to consider the course that it took in the United States—a subject about which I wrote a substantial essay based on my studies there.[4]

The Cold War was already underway when the PRC was born in 1949. The United States saw the fledgling state as "communist China," not to mention a hostile country. In the academic community, interest initially focused on what the new China was like as a state. What was its relationship with the Soviet Union, with which it had forged an alliance, and were their systems identical in nature? These were some of the key questions at stake regarding communist China.

---

4 Kokubun Ryosei, "Amerika no Chūgoku kenkyū" [China Research in the United States], *Iwanami kōza gendai Chūgoku bekkan 2: Gendai Chūgoku kenkyū annai* [Iwanami Lectures on Contemporary China, supplementary vol. 2: Introduction to Research on Contemporary China] (Tokyo: Iwanami Shoten, 1990).

The China Quarterly, the most authoritative journal in the field of modern China studies, was inaugurated in 1960, and the first several issues featured a debate between Benjamin I. Schwartz of Harvard University and Karl A. Wittfogel.[5] Wittfogel was widely known for his theory on Oriental despotism, which held that Eastern (Chinese) society was a "hydraulic society" and that the rise and fall of successive dynasties hinged on how they dealt with agricultural water rights. The crux of the Schwartz-Wittfogel controversy was whether or not China and the Soviet Union were the same in their substance. The overriding theme of the debate at the time had to do with the nature of the Maoist Revolution initiated by Mao Zedong: did it replicate the Soviet experience or not? Schwartz contended that the Chinese Communist Party was a group of ethnocentrists with strong nationalistic overtones, which set the revolution qualitatively apart from the Russian revolution, whereas Wittfogel asserted that China was downright communistic and thus comparable to the Soviet Union. Schwartz's position was later vindicated by the Sino-Soviet split that reared its head soon thereafter.

The Vietnam War provided the major turning point for China studies in the postwar United States. This came in the form of the above-mentioned critique of modernization theory, which posed an antithesis to the conventional notion that all countries would follow in the footsteps of the United States by countering that each region may have its own respective path of development. In so doing, young academics driven by the anti-war movement were taking establishment scholars to task. But the upshot was that they unconditionally extolled the Cultural Revolution—which was raging in China at the time—in an extension of their opposition to modernization theory. These young scholars preached the importance of traveling on one's own two feet

---

5 Benjamin Schwartz, "The Legend of the 'Legend of "Maoism"'," *The China Quarterly*, (vol. 2, April–June 1960); Karl Wittfogel, "The Legend of 'Maoism'," Part 1 and Part 2, *The China Quarterly* (vol. 1, January–March and April–June 1960); Wittfogel and Schwartz, "Controversy," *The China Quarterly* (vol. 4, October–December 1960).

around China in the throes of the Cultural Revolution and trying to understand it from within. Some of the chief proponents of this view met Zhou Enlai in person and, moved by the experience, came to praise everything that China said and did. By taking their critique of modernization theory too far, they had fallen into the trap of accepting the PRC's official line at face value.

The biggest debate in the China field at the time concerned the nature of the Chinese revolution, or Maoist revolution: Was the revolution communist or nationalist at its core? Was it the result of the Chinese peasantry rising up in an agrarian revolution to undermine the class-based society that clearly existed in the old agricultural villages, or was it about the CCP's appeal to Chinese nationalism in the struggle against Japan during the Anti-Japanese War? Chalmers A. Johnson of the University of California, Berkeley, took the view that the essence of the Chinese revolution was nationalism, inviting a backlash from younger scholars.[6] By contrast, Mark Selden maintained that the revolution was an agrarian one and thus communist in its nature and became the darling of the American China studies community.[7] Incidentally, this period saw fairly frequent exchanges between the China studies communities of Japan and the United States. This was largely because gaining entry to China was not easy for researchers of both countries, and Japanese and American scholars often compared notes on their assessments of what went on behind the "bamboo curtain." But as China opened up to the outside world, enabling researchers to actively conduct fieldwork within its borders and to dialogue firsthand with Chinese society, Japan-US exchanges in turn decreased.

Alongside the debate about the essence of the Chinese revolution, there was another related controversy. The United States had developed numerous ties with the communists during World War II, leading to the

---

6 Chalmers Johnson, *Peasant Nationalism and Communist Power: The Emergence of Revolutionary China, 1937–1945* (Stanford: Stanford University Press, 1962).

7 Mark Selden, *The Yenan Way in Revolutionary China* (Boston: Harvard University Press, 1970).

speculation that this may have represented a "lost chance" to forge good relations with the new government that later took power in Beijing. A significant number of Americans, including some members of the US State Department and military—not to mention the journalist Edgar P. Snow, whose 1937 book *Red Star over China* gave a firsthand account of the Chinese communist movement—had built a rapport with the CCP. Critics questioned why these ties were neglected. Although one detects a bit of hindsight there, now-inconceivable debates like this were carried on in all seriousness from the late 1970s through the 1980s.

Trends in China Studies after the Tiananmen Square Incident
It was the Tiananmen Square Incident of 1989 that put an end to these debates. The brutal quashing of the students' demands for democracy by tanks of the People's Liberation Army was telecast live around the world, pushing the issues of human rights and democracy in China to the forefront of discourse in the United States and demythologizing the country. Other preexisting debates about why the CCP was victorious or what prevented the United States from recognizing the new China were also swept away in one fell swoop.

In the wake of the incident, China studies worldwide shifted attention to such theories as comparative socialism, civil society, and the transformation of authoritarian regimes, all anticipating the emergence of democracy in China. But as the hope for democratization proved futile over time, the focus of research turned to state corporatism—to the question of what accounted for the resilience of the CCP. Many researchers came to draw on the theory of corporatism, postulating that the party was skillfully co-opting the Chinese populace to support the system. The problem with this approach is that while it may be able to explain current realities, it offers little insight into the future. As such, in recent years it has been replaced by state-society relations, which considers the present state of Chinese society on the basis of its distance from the state, as the mainstream approach.

As is clear from this retrospective review, the study of Chinese politics has been heavily influenced by the circumstances of each era, and its story illustrates the difficulty of maintaining a consistent awareness of and perspective on the issues in the face of such changes. That is indeed the greatest challenge of studying contemporary history. From the 1980s onward, as China opened its doors to the world, articles and dissertations not based on fieldwork ceased to be appreciated in the United States. More than that, though, in regard to employment in academia, there has been a growing proclivity to value only those scholars who attempt a theory in their work by drawing on such approaches as comparative politics—evidence, it would seem, that area studies is on the wane in the United States. This may parallel the country's declining role as the police of the world and the greater tendency of American society to look inward. In Japan, meanwhile, theory development has risen in importance, but it remains the case that the true worth of an area studies scholar is often judged by the quality of his or her empirical analysis of a region.

In Postwar Japan: The Impact of the Cultural Revolution and the Tiananmen Square Incident

Let us now turn to Japan. As noted above, research on Chinese politics in Japan after World War II fundamentally began by rejecting prewar scholarship. Postwar academics concerned themselves with the question of how to distance themselves from Japanese area studies of the past, which they regarded as having been conducted to serve the war effort. But while it is true that postwar area studies was largely characterized by a conscious effort to stand aloof from political affairs, Chinese politics was one area of research that in some respects became politically charged by way of overcompensation. This can be attributed to the growing influence of certain ideologies and a particular political party.

Any consideration of the academic climate in postwar Japan must take into account the role of Marxism. While it is rarely discussed these days, Marxism held great sway for a time, to the extent that the bulk of Japanese scholars in the social sciences and humanities were likely under its influence. Being a socialist regime that had been established by a communist revolution, the PRC was a research subject that Marxists naturally found approachable. As such, the field of China studies in postwar Japan was heavily populated with researchers who embraced or sympathized with Marxism.

The Cultural Revolution brought about a rift among the Japanese Marxists engaged in China studies. This mirrored the split between China and the Soviet Union: Soviet-biased scholars speculated that the Maoist revolution was no more than an indigenous revolution by peasants and had little to do with orthodox Marxism, while pro-China researchers countered by pointing the finger of revisionism at Soviet socialism, which they claimed was a far cry from the ideals of genuine socialism. This dispute in turn set off a polemic about how to assess the Cultural Revolution that was in progress in China under Mao Zedong. The controversy was such that it led to some violent incidents in Japan. These developments, spanning the late 1960s and early 1970s, took place in parallel with domestic student protests, which in effect emulated China's Red Guard movement.[8]

Throughout this period, Japanese researchers who based their study of Chinese politics on US-style area studies did not involve themselves deeply in political movements or ideological debates like the above. Although they, too, occasionally came under attack as being reactionary or pro-establishment, the fierce wrangling among the Marxists during the Cultural Revolution largely kept them out of the critical cross hairs. Thanks to this, those scholars who engaged themselves in research on Chinese politics in the realm of area studies were evidently able to maintain a dispassionate analytical eye, free from the politicized atmosphere of the Cultural Revolution. In addition to Keio University's

---

8 For analysis of this matter, see Baba Kimihiko, *Sengo Nihonjin no Chūgoku zō: Nihon haisen kara bunka daikakumei, Nicchū fukkō made* [The Image of China Held by Postwar Japanese: From Japan's Defeat to the Cultural Revolution and Reestablishment of Japan-China Diplomatic Relations] (Tokyo: Shin'yōsha, 2010).

Ishikawa Tadao, such figures as Etō Shinkichi, Uno Shigeaki, Okabe Tatsumi, and Nakajima Mineo comprised the core of the Japanese academic cadre carrying out area-studies-based research on China.

The impact of the Tiananmen Square Incident on China studies in Japan was immense. Through live broadcasts, the Japanese witnessed in real time an inexorable reality underlying the Chinese political system that they had hitherto either not seen or refused to see. Until then, perhaps owing to prewar circumstances, there had been a certain atmosphere in Japanese society of refraining from negative commentary on China, but this quickly dissipated after the events of June 4, 1989. In that sense, the end of the Cold War and the Tiananmen Square Incident played a major part in lifting the political and ideological shroud that had quietly hung over China. Today the tendency to shine the spotlight only on China's negative aspects seems to be growing stronger, possibly in reaction to past attitudes or due to the worsening of Japan-China relations. At any rate, along with these real-world developments, research on Chinese politics in the tradition of postwar Japanese area studies naturally grew in importance, and the approach came to be widely accepted as a methodology. As was the case in the United States, in the wake of the Tiananmen Square Incident the study of Chinese politics in Japan became more deeply informed by political system theories premised on eventual democratization and by state-society theory. Yet the inclination to value historical empiricism—the forte of area studies in Japan—over theory has not essentially changed, nor has its affinity for international relations rather than for comparative politics. It is worth noting, however, that some recent studies of contemporary Chinese politics by young scholars indicate ambitious efforts to make their work more relevant to the field of comparative politics.

3. Challenges in the Study of Chinese Politics

The first challenge in the study of Chinese politics is how to approach and address real-world problems. China is rife with issues on all fronts, and Japan-China relations are highly strained as well. How should researchers face up to these realities? It is not the job of a scholar to take to political commentary or to political action of some kind. It is possible and indeed imperative, though that we scholars offer some sort of message or sense of direction through our research by presenting a theoretical or historical perspective. Those who make use of this may be politicians or policymakers outside academia. Individuals tasked with actual policymaking lead busy lives consumed by day-to-day concerns, leaving them little room to maintain a long-term viewpoint, and the fruits of scholarly research could prove meaningful here. But to that end, scholars must strive to provide realistic perspectives in plainer language, while policymakers and persons and organizations charged with handling current issues need to have a willingness and effort to be receptive to such broader perspectives.

Today China-related issues are no longer the exclusive province of experts. Ordinary people discuss them as everyday topics, and Japanese citizens everywhere are engaging in debate over China as if they are all pseudo-experts. This brings us to ask ourselves what experts like us should be communicating, and how. At times we must set forth arguments that run counter to public opinion, and at times we must confront matters with considerable will and determination. There is a widespread preconception that the China experts at the Ministry of Foreign Affairs of Japan—dubbed the "China school"—are a bunch of Sinophiles who are busy advocating for China. China scholars are also sometimes framed in similar terms. That image in itself is of course bi-ased, but the fact remains that scholars are faced with a major challenge given the current situation.

The second issue is the ability to reach international audiences. Younger China scholars in Japan have studied in China, and their Chinese language ability is markedly better than that of older generations. In the days when researchers could not enter China, they frequently interacted with colleagues in the United States and other countries, and English was often more useful to them than Chinese. It goes without saying that Japan's China experts need to be proficient in both languages going forward. Today, due to demand in Japanese society, China studies experts face no shortage of requests for articles and lectures in the domestic market, so that they can afford to focus their activities on Japan alone. In area studies on most other parts of the world, by contrast, smaller domestic demand forces scholars to keep international standards in mind as they go about their research. On this score, China scholars in Japan may be somewhat spoiled. They certainly cannot publish all of their research in English, nor do they need to. But it is vital nonetheless that they do not lose sight of these aspirations and keep up an effort to make their research results available in English or Chinese or both, if only a part or essence thereof. They should take pride in the fact that Japan has developed its own empirical brand of China area studies and should put more energy into sharing the fruits of that research with the international community.

The third issue is the need for a more theoretical orientation. Area studies scholars can be something of a geek: the more deeply they study an area, the more they become absorbed in it and come to relish the characteristic appeal of area studies. That in itself is not a bad thing, but from there it is all too easy for scholars to sink into the depths of their subject matter and confine themselves to their own little world, unable to see the forest for the trees. The key is striking a balance between empiricism and theory. Harking back to the primary purpose of scholarship, the charge of a researcher is to provide scientific explanations about a particular subject. That being the case, area studies scholars should be unstinting in their efforts to reframe their research in the context of larger theories and broader histories. For students of Chinese politics, this translates to the need for a deeper dialogue with comparative politics.

The fourth and final issue is a donut phenomenon lately befalling Chinese political studies, wherein analyses of the power center are decreasing on the one hand and those of related areas, such as political and social conditions, are becoming mainstream on the other. For the longest time, it sufficed for studies on Chinese politics to home in on the CCP's leadership and nothing else. The entrenched one-party dictatorship, coupled with the limited availability of data owing in part to the impossibility of conducting fieldwork, meant that China's power center and political system themselves were the focus of most studies. But as the CCP loosened its totalitarian grip on the country, opening the doors to fieldwork, the diversity and pluralism of Chinese society grew evident, and the breadth of research greatly expanded. Today, it has become difficult for aspiring young academics to get a degree in Chinese political studies unless their research extends into these other areas.

Alongside these developments, though, the view spread even in academia that analyzing the Communist Party's top leadership was the job of journalists and pundits. As a result, analysis of the power structure began to fall through the cracks in the research world, and studies of Chinese politics lost some of their substance without their requisite attention to political and social conditions. The challenge going forward is to reverse the donut phenomenon and, through extensive empirical research, get down to the nitty-gritty of the power center, the political and social landscape, and the intermediate domain linking the two: the political structure.

On one final note, I would like to point out the importance of not getting caught up in historical materials. While it is perfectly commendable for young scholars of today to put their energy into unearthing new materials, preoccupation with this task could cause them to lose sight of their actual research. The point of excavating new data and historical materials is to seek new interpretations; but this can also be done to some extent by rereading the basic documents that were previously available. The unexpected may well lurk in nooks and crannies that prior research has overlooked.

Part I

The Chinese Political System: Legitimacy Gone Astray

Chapter 1

The Implementation and Failure of Political Reform:
The Deng Xiaoping, Hu Yaobang, and Zhao Ziyang Eras

To all outward appearances, the discussion of political reform has been forgotten in today's China; the issue is almost never openly debated. But the fact of the matter is that the subject is being intentionally avoided by China's top leadership. This stems from a shared awareness that reform is the most dangerous policy for the continuation of the system of one-party rule by the Chinese Communist Party (CCP). Even amid the relentless factional struggle that defines Communist Party politics, there appears to be a tacit consensus among the factions that this is a line that must not be crossed. Efforts have instead been made to cleanse the political system of the corruption plaguing it by launching anti-corruption campaigns and the like. But these campaigns invariably prey on those who have lost the power struggles, and the winners survive no matter how corrupt they might be. That is the reality of Chinese politics.

Looking back, though, there was a time in China when political reform was being actively debated and politics was beginning to take on a luster. Needless to say, this was the period from the end of the 1970s to the 1980s, following the end of the Cultural Revolution. It was the so-called Deng Xiaoping era, when Chinese society was at its most dynamic even as the policy of reform and opening up encountered stiff resistance. That climate quickly withered with the Tiananmen Square Incident of 1989 and the collapse of the Soviet Union in 1991. Subsequently, while the words "political reform" did not disappear altogether from discourse in the 1990s and 2000s, the eyes of not only China but also the entire world were drawn to the dazzling world of money and goods amid the country's rapid economic growth. Meanwhile, the market economy under the CCP's dictatorship slowly eroded the political structure, and as the twenty-first century drew on, "political reform" gradually became a dead letter both in word and in actual policy.

This chapter turns back the pages to the era when there still were glimmers of hope for political reform. By returning to that point, I will sort out what things were being debated regarding political reform and in what manner. To give my conclusion first, even though the various problems relating to the Chinese political system and arguments about how to go about reforming it were discussed exhaustively during this era, the reforms were ultimately sidestepped as Chinese leaders guarded against the possibility that such reforms could undermine the dominance of the Communist Party.

1. The Origins of Political Reform

A vision for reforming the political system in China was first set forth in the wake of the Third Plenum of the Eleventh Central Committee of the CCP, held in December 1978, which declared that China would pursue modernization across the board. Already at this early time, the plenum's communiqué noted such problems as nonseparation between party and government administration and a bloated administrative machinery, and preached the need to reform not only the "base," which in Marxist theory refers to the economic structure, but also the political and legal "superstructure" into forms conducive to modernization: "Carrying out the four modernizations requires great growth in the productive forces, which in turn requires diverse changes in those aspects of the relations of production and the superstructure not in harmony with the growth of the productive forces, and requires changes in all methods of management, actions and thinking which stand in the way of such growth."[1]

What is widely recognized as the first proposition of political reform, though, is Deng Xiaoping's August 1980 address titled "On the Reform of the System of Party and State Leadership."[2] In his speech, Deng pointed out a number of problems—including excessive concentration of power, the proliferation of concurrent and deputy posts,

---

1 "Communiqué of the Third Plenary Session of the Eleventh Central Committee of the Communist Party of China," *Peking Review* 21, no. 52 (December 29, 1978): 11.
2 Deng Xiaoping, "On the Reform of the System of Party and State Leadership," in *Selected Works of Deng Xiaoping*, vol. 2 (1975–1982) (Beijing: Foreign Languages Press, 1984), 302–25.

the mixing of party and government business, and the deinstitutional-ization of leadership transition and succession—and urged reforms to tackle these personnel and administrative problems. By raising these issues, he clearly aimed at eliminating the evils that arose during the years of the Cultural Revolution under Mao Zedong's command. At the same time, it would appear that he was implicitly criticizing the fact that Hua Guofeng, Mao's successor, simultaneously held the top posts of both the CCP and the government. Sure enough, Hua lost his post as premier at the Third Session of the Fifth National People's Congress (NPC), which took place on the heels of Deng's speech.

How did these moves to reform the state of political leadership relate to the so-called Beijing Spring seeking political democratization and liberalization, which was born out of the atmosphere of ideological emancipation and the "crises of faith, confidence, and trust" (the crises of faith in socialism, in the CCP leadership, and in Marxism-Lenin-ism and Mao Zedong Thought) that followed the Third Plenum of the Eleventh Central Committee of the CCP? Deng himself did not perceive reform from above as leading directly to democratization or liberalization. As history shows, he had by this time already implement-ed policies aimed at resolutely containing moves from below toward democratization—which had been labeled anti-socialist—by cracking down on the Beijing Spring movement, including the arrest of Wei Jingsheng, its central figure.

In March 1979, as if to provide a theoretical basis for these ac-tions, Deng formulated the "Four Cardinal Principles" as an effective political and ideological framework for China. These principles were: (1) upholding the socialist road, (2) upholding the dictatorship of the proletariat, (3) upholding the leadership of the Communist Party, and (4) upholding Marxism-Leninism and Mao Zedong Thought.[3] The reasoning in Deng's mind, in a nutshell, was that "stability" and "unity" were essential to achieving a modern economy, and any "objec-

---

3 Deng, "Uphold the Four Cardinal Principles," in *Selected Works*, vol. 2, 144.

tions" from below had to be dismissed to that end. He presumably also harbored renewed fears about the kind of social chaos that the "Great Democracy" (*Daminzhu*) of the Cultural Revolution had caused.

Notwithstanding these political limits, the real-life demands that arose following the Third Plenum of the Eleventh Central Committee of the CCP, namely ideological emancipation and proposals for political reform, served to fuel the development of the hitherto-immature field of political science and invigorate scholarly debates about political reform. In December 1980 the Chinese Association of Political Science was formally instituted—the first of its kind since the founding of the People's Republic of China—and embarked on the work of establishing political science as an academic discipline, unlike the preexisting politics course (*zhengzhike*) taught in schools, the purpose of which was the study of Marxism-Leninism and Mao Zedong Thought. Shortly before that, moreover, in October 1980 Liao Gailong of the Party History Research Center proposed his "Gengshen reforms," which envisioned a plan for democratizing the party and state. In it Liao advocated the necessity of bold reforms in the political structure, such as undertaking constitutional revisions to divide the NPC into two chambers—a regional chamber representing regional interests and a social chamber representing class and corporate interests—and systemically guaranteeing criticisms of party and state organs by the people, on the premise that it is conducted under party guidance.[4] These were revolutionary proposals, even from today's perspective.

One notable point regarding debates about political reform in that period is that the expression *zhengzhi tizhi gaige* (reform of the political structure or political regime) had hardly taken root; the preferred phrase was *zhengzhi zhidu gaige* (reform of the political system). For example, in October 1980 the editorial department of the *Guangming Daily* sponsored a "discussion meeting about the issues of the political

---

4 Liao Gailong, "Lishi de jingyan he women de fazhan daolu" [The Experience of History and Our Development Path], *Zhonggong yanjiu* 15, no. 9 (September 1981): 108–177.

system and economic reform" in Beijing. At this meeting Yan Jiaqi—
an assistant researcher at the Institute of Philosophy of the Chinese
Academy of Social Sciences, who would go on to become a theoretical
leader of democratization at the time of the 1989 Tiananmen Square
Incident—advanced the critique that China's state system strongly
retained its feudal nature, as could be seen in the personal authoritarian rule and lifelong tenure by supreme leaders during the Cultural
Revolution, and pressed for radical reform of these problems. Prior to
this Yu Haocheng, the then editor in chief of the Masses (*Qunzhong*)
Publishing House whose statements later led him to bear the brunt
of criticism after Tiananmen, had already asserted that "the object of
political system reform is to realize democratization."[5]

A discussion may be in order here of the Chinese terms *zhengzhi
zhidu* and *zhengzhi tizhi*, which were translated above as "political
system" and "political structure," respectively. According to subsequent
analyses of the use of these words in China, the former refers to the
fundamental properties of the state—specifically, in China's case, the
people's democratic dictatorship based on a worker-peasant alliance under CCP leadership and, in terms of state organizations, the system of
the NPC. The latter refers to the scaffolding that supports an existing
political system, namely, such components as the administrative and
judicial apparatuses, the civil servant system, and the electoral system.[6]
In other words, reform of the "system" (*zhidu*) would amount to altering the foundations of the socialist political edifice, while reform of the
"structure" (*tizhi*) would chiefly involve organizational and personnel
issues and would not extend to the fundamental components of the
system. Even today, official documents in China apparently distinguish

---

5 "Taolun woguo zhengzhi zhidu he jingji tizhi gaige de wenti" [Discussing the Problem of Reforming China's Political System and Economic System], *Guangming Daily*,
October 16, 1980.

6 Chi Fulin et al., eds., *Zhengzhi tizhi gaige jiben wenti tantaolun* [Exploratory Essays
on the Fundamental Problems of Political Structure Reforms] (Beijing: Chunqiu
Publishing House, 1988), 11–12.

between the "socialist political *zhidu* (system)" or "socialist economic *zhidu* (system)," which are considered permanent, and the "socialist political *tizhi* (structure)" or "socialist economic *tizhi* (structure)," which are treated as variable.

At the time, though, no hard-and-fast concepts about political reform likely existed. As far as the economy was concerned, reform of the structure had already been accepted as the way to go; the socialist system of the economy was not to be tampered with, and reforms were to be strictly limited to the supporting machinery. Why, then, was reform of the system advocated when it came to politics? One reason may be that, based on the fundamental principles of Marxism, the economic base was believed to determine the superstructure, including politics. Even if political reforms were labeled "systemic," Chinese politics would not be straying outside the bounds of socialism as long as the economic system remained socialist—so the thinking likely went.

Another practical reason may be that Deng Xiaoping himself used the phrase "reform of the system of party and state leadership," possibly in light of the above distinction between politics and economics. The fact that Deng went with "leadership system" rather than "leadership structure" at this point may imply that he originally had in mind reforms of fundamental aspects of the political fabric, even though he drew a sharp line between his own ideas and democratization demands like those seen in the Beijing Spring. The rather extreme arguments of Liao Gailong, Yan Jiaqi, and Yu Haocheng appear to have been developed in line with Deng's calls for reform. That said, reforms of the political system had the potential to come in conflict with the Four Cardinal Principles, and to keep such problems in check, efforts gradually got underway to standardize the use of the term "structure" or "regime" for reform (*tizhi gaige*) in politics as well.

The term "political structural reform" became fully entrenched in China only after Deng repeatedly invoked it in 1986, but it began to overtake "political system reform" as the more popular term from around 1982. The phrasing chosen by Hu Yaobang in his report to the Twelfth National Congress of the CCP in September of that year was "reforms of the state's political structure and leadership structure." Moreover, Deng used the expression "political structural reform" in his speech at the Second Plenum of the Twelfth Central Committee of the CCP in October 1983. In this manner, the reform of politics—like that of the economy—came to be framed as "structural reform," and Chinese leaders grew more and more explicit in indicating that such reforms would not involve the basic "political system."

Let us look at how actual policies progressed after debates about reform of the leadership system were launched in 1980 by Deng Xiaoping and others. The first half of 1980s was the era of economic reform: first came the introduction of the production responsibility system in rural areas, after which the focus shifted to reforms of the factory and enterprise management structures in the cities. Reforms in the area of politics thus tended to go on the back burner, but some measures were still implemented. From 1982 to 1983, for instance, Premier Zhao Ziyang and others spearheaded structural reforms of the State Council, which included reducing the number of departments, commissions, and offices directly under its control, cutting back on vice-premier posts, and establishing new state councilor positions. In reality, though, efforts to streamline the state machinery led to its renewed bloating in a variety of ways, such as the creation of new posts to replace defunct ones. And as the separation of party and government was proceeding at a snail's pace, functional improvements to the State Council itself could not be achieved either. The Twelfth National Congress of the CCP held in September 1982 proclaimed its decision to abolish the post of party chairman and the rejuvenation of party cadres, and the new constitution adopted at the National Congress shortly thereafter mandated the scrapping of lifelong tenure for key posts in state organs. But CCP elders of the first revolutionary generation continued to cling to power, and this "rule of individuals" (*renzhi*) symbolized the dark clouds hanging over the future of political reform.

2. The 1986 Student Movement and the Democratization Issue

As noted above, the focus in the first half of the 1980s was on economic reform, and discussions of political reform almost never came into the limelight, save for those at the start of the decade. This was probably due in part to the political retrenchment led by conservatives in the CCP, such as Wang Zhen, Hu Qiaomu, and Deng Liqun—instances of which include the anti-bourgeois-liberalization campaign, which among other things criticized Bai Hua's literary work *Kulian* (Bitter Love) in 1981, and the anti-spiritual-pollution campaign against Western influences in the autumn of 1983. The greater emphasis that was placed on the Four Cardinal Principles may also have been a factor. Behind the scenes of these developments, General Secretary Hu Yaobang, who was relatively open to measured "liberalization" of the press, frequently registered his objections to offensives by those of the conservative camp and was in turn criticized by the conservatives in various ways.[7]

Debates about political reform regained momentum from the spring of 1986 onward—particularly from around June of that year, when Deng Xiaoping began to talk actively about political reform. "It does not seem likely that we will be able to adapt to the situation unless we undertake reform of the political structure," Deng stated on June 10. "Political structure should be included in the reforms, and it should be regarded as one of the hallmarks of reform."[8] On June 28 he further said, "The question of whether all our reforms ultimately succeed depends on political reform. After all, it is human beings who

---

7 Zhao Ziyang, *Chō Shiyō gokuhi kaisōroku: Ten'anmon jiken "daidan'atsu" no butaiura* [The Secret Memoir of Zhao Ziyang: Behind the Stage of the "Big Crackdown" in the Tiananmen Square Incident], eds. Bao Pu et al., trans. Kōno Junji (Tokyo: Kōbunsha, 2010), chap. 1, pt. 4.

8 Deng Xiaoping, "Keizai jōkyō no hōkoku o chōshu shita sai no danwa" [Remarks on Hearing Report about Economic Conditions," in *Gendai Chūgoku no kihon mondai ni tsuite* [Fundamental Issues in Present-day China] (Beijing: Foreign Languages Press, 1987), 245.

get things done."[9] From this time on, remarks related to political reform dramatically increased in Deng's speeches.

Why did political reform emerge as a subject of debate in this period? The first factor is that, as Deng himself noted, economic reforms encountered numerous obstacles as they shifted from the countryside to the cities and progressed in the latter, and political reform became critical to eliminating these hindrances. In Deng's own words: "What is significant is that the political structure is not adapted to the demands of economic reform. For this reason, if we do not reform the political structure, we cannot guarantee results from economic reform, nor can we continue to move ahead with economic reform."[10] The second factor was that—again, as Deng himself admitted—despite his having raised the issue of leadership system reform in 1980, no such reforms were effectively implemented, as is illustrated by the fate of the aforementioned reforms to the State Council. According to Deng, "I proposed reforming the political structure as early as 1980, but it did not lead to any concrete measures; now is the time to put it on the agenda."[11] As for what specifically Deng had in mind around this time regarding the substance of reforms to the political structure, it can be summarized as follows: separating the roles of party and government for the sake of greater efficiency, devolving administrative authority to the regions to encourage their initiative, streamlining the bloated organization and machinery, and making the cadres younger and more specialized. In other words, Deng's definition of political reform was limited to administrative reform of those areas in politics that were relevant to promoting economic reform.

---

9 Deng, "Seiji taisei no kaikaku to hō ishiki no kyōka" [Reform of the Political System and Strengthening of Legal Consciousness], in *Gendai Chūgoku*, 252.

10 Deng, "Seiji taisei o kaikaku shinakereba seisanryoku no hatten ga samatagerareru" [If the Political System Is Not Reformed, the Development of the Productive Forces Will Be Hindered], in *Gendai Chūgoku*, 255.

11 Deng, "Keizai jōkyō no hōkoku" [Report about Economic Conditions], in *Gendai Chūgoku*, 246.

In reality, however, matters progressed beyond those bounds. Hu Yaobang, who was openly keen to go ahead with full-fledged reforms, exhibited a tolerant attitude toward China's democratization including a certain degree of liberalization. He also devised a daring proposal to recommend the retirement of elderly cadres, as well as equally daring policies aimed at rejuvenating the leadership. Moreover, he reportedly advocated the need to tackle head-on the issue of corruption among the children of high-level cadres. The conservative party elders, who were already skeptical about rushing ahead with reforms in general, reacted strongly against Hu's drastic proposals and repeatedly invoked the Four Cardinal Principles and anti-bourgeois-liberalization. From around September 1986 Deng, perhaps to sound a warning against Hu's extreme ideas, likewise came to stress that political reform would steer clear of Western-style liberalization in order to ensure stability and unity—in short, that the Four Cardinal Principles should be adhered to—and that these reforms must not be rushed but must be promoted with prudence.

The renewed advocacy of political reform inspired political scientists and other intellectuals to actively debate the subject. As early as the end of April 1986, the publisher of the journal *Zhongguo shehui kexue* (Social Sciences in China) sponsored an academic roundtable discussion about political reform. Here, bold arguments were made to the effect that the purpose of political reform was the process of political development—in other words, of democratization—and, more specifically, to aim for greater participation in politics and the introduction of a system of checks and balances.[12] At the Symposium on the Theory of Political Reform sponsored by the Party School of the Central Committee of the Communist Party of China in July of that

---

12 "Woguo de zhengzhi tizhi gaige yu zhengzhixue de fazhan: Zhongguo Shehui Kexue Zazhi zhaokai de 'Zhengzhi tizhi gaige' xueshu zuotanhui zongshu" [China's Political Structure Reforms and the Development of Chinese Political Science: Overview of the Academic Roundtable Discussion on "Political Structure Reforms" Convened by the China Social Science Journal Company], *Zhongguo shehui kexue* [Social Sciences in China] 4 (1986).

year, it was noted that political reform was just as important as economic reform and that its objective was to realize "a new structure of advanced socialist democracy."[13] As these examples illustrate, Chinese academic circles generally advocated the importance of political reform in its own right, rather than as a corollary of economic reform, and called for democratization as its goal.

These lively debates eventually generated audacious assertions that went beyond reforms of just the "political structure" and directly called for changes in the "political system" itself. Around this time Su Shaozhi, director of the Institute for Marxism-Leninism and Mao Zedong Thought of the Chinese Academy of Social Sciences, set forth a number of items as primary objectives of political reform, including doing away with feudal despotism as manifested by uxorial nepotism, abuse of privileges, and bureaucratism; reexamining democratic centralism; and making legislative and judicial organs independent from the party. "What we are seeking is not 'democracy' as a benefit bestowed by those above on those below, but rather socialist democracy—a real people's democracy," Su stated by way of conclusion. "Reform means nothing less than liberating the talents, creativity, and enterprising spirit of each individual."[14] Su was among those who were forced to leave China after the Tiananmen Square Incident and spent the remainder of his life overseas.

One of the representative figures who made the boldest arguments in this period was Fang Lizhi, a physicist who held the post of vice-president of the University of Science and Technology of China (USTC) in Hefei, Anhui Province. In his lectures at Shanghai Jiao Tong University and Shanghai Tongji University in November 1986, Fang asserted that democracy was something to be won by struggle rather than a

---

13 "Zhongyang Dangxiao zhaokai 'Zhengzhi tizhi gaige lilun yantaohui'" [The "Discussion Meeting on the Theory of Political System Reforms" Convened by the Party School of the CCP Central Committee], *Guangming Daily*, July 19, 1986.

14 Su Shaozhi, "Seiji taisei kaikaku sūgi" [Of Political System Reforms], in *Chūgoku no peresutoroika: Minshu kaikaku no kishu tachi* [China's Perestroika: Supporters of Democratic Reform], ed. Yabuki Susumu (Tokyo: Sōsōsha, 1988), 154.

gift bestowed from above, that a pluralistic political system should be created by dispersing power, and that the socialist movement had failed from Marx down to Mao Zedong.[15] These remarks are said to have directly triggered the student pro-democracy movement that began soon thereafter at USTC and spread from there, first to Shanghai and then to the rest of the country. Indeed, the bases of the student movement in Shanghai were the two universities at which Fang had lectured. The student demonstrations at USTC in Hefei were held to express dissatisfaction about the method for selecting representatives to the regional People's Congress and demand improved living conditions. But as the movement spread to universities nationwide and took on greater depth, the focus gradually narrowed to calls for democratization, including freedom of speech, although it generally did not take a head-on attitude against socialism or the leadership of the CCP.

A student demonstration in excess of 10,000 participants took place in Shanghai on December 19, 1986, followed by another protest with 4,000 to 5,000 students in Beijing on December 23. Although these numbers were small in light of the overall population, it is worthy of note that a spontaneous movement had spread and that the torchbearers of democracy had gained a broader social base than at the time of the Beijing Spring. The authorities began to harden their attitude in response. On December 25, an article titled "The Reform of the Political Structure Can Only Proceed Under the Leadership of the Party" appeared in *People's Daily*, and on December 30 Deng Xiaoping himself issued a statement titled "Take a Clear-Cut Stand against Bourgeois Liberalization."[16]

A crackdown on the student movement commenced in early January the following year. From there the situation further developed in an unexpected direction: at an enlarged meeting of the Politburo

---

15 Fang Lizhi, *Chūgoku yo kaware* [Change, China], trans. Sueyoshi Tsukuru (Tokyo: Gakuseisha, 1989), 208–74.
16 Deng, "Kishi senmei ni burujoa jiyūka ni hantai shiyō" [Take a Clear-Cut Stand against Bourgeois Liberalization], in *Gendai Chūgoku*, 271–78.

on January 16, Hu Yaobang resigned from his post of party general secretary, and in his place Zhao Ziyang assumed office as acting general secretary. This change was chiefly attributed to Hu's leniency toward the students' pro-democracy demonstrations. But the move was foreshadowed by his discord with the party elders including Deng Xiaoping and with conservatives about political reform and, going back further, his feud with the conservative faction over "liberalization" in the early 1980s. Around this time, three individuals—Fang Lizhi and writers Wang Ruowang and Liu Binyan, all of whom publicly voiced their views—were stripped of their CCP membership in retribution for their actions. Su Shaozhi was also expelled from the party rolls and lost all his positions in August 1987.

As seen above, political reform was a major factor behind the political drama that played out from the student demonstrations starting in late 1986 to Hu Yaobang's resignation in January 1987. The issue of political reform took on a life of its own, far outgrowing the bounds intended by the authorities, and set off student protests calling for democracy. Consequently, Fang Lizhi and other opinion leaders of the student movement were expelled from the CCP, while Hu, who had been sympathetic to the movement, was driven from his post as party general secretary. The key here is the change within the CCP itself, such that not only Fang and other intellectuals in the party but even General Secretary Hu showed understanding for the students' demands, which went beyond mere structural reform and extended to freedom of speech and other democratic rights.

3. Proposals for Political Reform at the Thirteenth National Congress of the CCP

After the events of late 1986 and early 1987 that began with the student demonstrations and culminated in Hu Yaobang's resignation, it appeared as though the moves toward political reform in China would stall for some time. Discussion of the issue quickly resumed, however, as evidenced by the republication of Deng Xiaoping's 1980 speech "On the Reform of the System of Party and State Leadership" in newspapers on July 1, 1987. Then at the Thirteenth National Congress of the CCP, held from late October to the start of November, a comprehensive blueprint for political reform was laid down in the political report by General Secretary Zhao Ziyang. Zhao had elaborated this plan at the request of Deng Xiaoping with a number of other individuals, including his strategist Bao Tong, who later became director of the CCP Central Committee's new Office of Political Reform in February 1988, and Yan Jiaqi, director of the Institute of Political Science of the Chinese Academy of Social Sciences.

Political reform reemerged as an agenda item because it had been judged that there was no way to break the deadlock over economic reform unless reforms were implemented to the political structure; problems of inefficiency in administrative management were standing in the way of economic reform. These problems included the confusion of party and state affairs, bureaucratism, bloating of the government apparatus, and personnel appointments dominated by "the rule of individuals." In short, the reforms to the political regime proposed at the Thirteenth National Congress of the CCP were expressly aimed at promoting reform of the economic structure, and the issues of democratization and liberalization were bypassed on the premise that the basic political system was correct.

But Chinese society was already exhibiting structural changes brought about by the advancement of modernization and opening up to the world based on economic reform. Quality of life had vastly improved, even though it was still low by global standards. The expansion of available information, including about moves toward democratization in Asia and Eastern Europe, and the significant increase in exchanges and contact with the outside world enabled Chinese people—particularly those living in urban areas—to see China in perspective with the rest of the world. As a result, a certain gulf already existed between the official plan announced at the Thirteenth National Congress of the CCP and societal needs from below, even in regard to political reform. Setting aside the pros and cons of socialism itself, a fairly broad stratum of Chinese society, primarily the urban intelligentsia, felt the need to reform more fundamental aspects of the "political system," such as the one-party dictatorship and the people's democratic dictatorship. Given the existence of forces within the Communist Party that opposed any reform, though, the political reform proposals of the Thirteenth National Congress of the CCP may have been the best that Zhao Ziyang and other leaders could manage. There was no denying that the blueprint, if implemented effectively, would still likely achieve some progress in the reforms overall, and the Chinese masses, for their part, must have harbored a small amount of hope despite their dissatisfaction. The envisaged structural reforms comprised the following seven items: (1) separation of party and government; (2) devolution of power; (3) reform of government organs; (4) reform of the cadre personnel system; (5) establishment of a system of social consultation and dialogue; (6) partial development of a socialist democratic political system; and (7) strengthening of the socialist legal system.[17] In the following paragraphs, I will briefly examine the specifics of each item and their subsequent progress.

Separation of party and government had consistently come up as the single most important issue in political reform since Deng Xiaoping's 1980 speech. The basic idea was to reduce excessive interference by the

---

17 Zhao Ziyang, "Chūgoku no tokushoku o motsu shakaishugi no michi ni sotte zenshin shiyō" [Advance along the Road of Socialism with Chinese Characteristics], in *Chūgoku Kyōsantō dai 13 kai zenkoku daihyō taikai bunkenshū* [Documents of the Thirteenth National Congress of the Communist Party of China] (Beijing: Foreign Languages Press, 1988).

CCP in policy decisions by separating party and state affairs in all work units and organs. Following the Thirteenth National Congress of the CCP, it was decided that the party organizations in economy-related ministries and commissions within the State Council would be dissolved in stages. In reality, though, this move met with resistance from party cadres at every level who were determined to hold on to their vested interests. Moreover, the rampancy of corruption among official brokers in the party and government, known as "official profiteering" (*guandao*), exposed different problems from that of the merging of party and state functions.

Devolution of power was proposed because advancements in economic reform gave rise to the need to delegate administrative authority to lower levels. In this particular instance, the intent was to guarantee the management rights of enterprises. But devolving authority also carried the risk of preserving official profiteering and similar practices, and in the course of its implementation the authorities were caught in a dilemma between the need to delegate and the need to retain macro control by the central government.

Reform of government organs was aimed at streamlining the organization and reducing personnel. In accordance with this, a portion of the ministries and commissions in the State Council were reorganized in the spring of 1988, and a reduction of 10,000 persons, or roughly 20 percent of all personnel working under the State Council, was decided. But this brought up a number of major practical issues, such as the question of management capacity after reorganization and how to reassign personnel, particularly cadres, after downsizing.

The centerpiece of reform of the cadre personnel system was the introduction of a national civil service system. This involved creating a more practical bureaucratic mechanism by replacing the traditional system of state cadres, which was dominated by interpersonal dynamics, with an exam system. This reform was one of the highest-profile, most-discussed plans after the Thirteenth National Congress of the CCP, but it eventually hit a snag, possibly due to opposition from state cadres, and took considerable time to officially get off the ground.

The consultation and dialogue system consisted of the cadres at each level actively mingling with the masses and listening directly to their unfiltered opinions—in the tradition of the CCP's popular line, as it were. Opportunities for "dialogue" (*duihua*) were evidently provided in some regions by bringing together the representatives of work units, but in reality, these appear to have ended up serving as forums for the CCP to propagandize its policies rather than for the attendees to voice their interests.

As for the partial development of a socialist democratic political system, one of the challenges was rejuvenating the membership of the NPC Standing Committee as a means of bringing new energy to the NPC. When the NPC selected the chairman and vice chairpersons of its Standing Committee in the spring of 1988, though, practically all of them were elderly. Also, part of this "partial development" was the introduction of a system of competitive elections (*chae xuanju*), whereby there were more candidates than posts. For a time, it appeared as though competitive elections might be taking root. But this did not happen, evidently due to unresolved problems in the individual localities, such as lack of information about candidates and excessive party interference in candidate selection.

The aim of strengthening the socialist legal system was to achieve the rule of law instead of the rule of individuals, primarily through administrative legislation relating to economic reform. But as to whether judicial authority and government by rule of law could really be established given the principle of guidance by the Communist Party, the question went unanswered.

The political reforms proposed at the Thirteenth National Congress of the CCP thus encountered various difficulties in the policy process and eventually came to a standstill. While technical problems may have been a factor, the outcome ultimately signified the limits of political reform itself; these difficulties arose largely because the reform measures skirted fundamental problems in the political system, such as the single-party dictatorship and basic human rights. By this time reform in the economic structure had likewise reached the stage of whether or not to amend the system of ownership, a fundamental problem of socialism, suggesting that the whole of China's structural reforms had reached the end of the road. To put it differently, the reforms in China had begun to challenge the socialist system itself on both the economic and political fronts.

4. The 1989 Democracy Movement and Political Reform

At the Third Plenum of the Thirteenth Central Committee of the Communist Party of China, convened in the autumn of 1988, inflationary pressures led to a decision to temporarily shelve economic reform and embark instead on economic adjustment. Since political reform had also encountered obstacles, as described above, and was originally intended to "serve" economic reforms, it mostly ceased to be discussed by the authorities after hitting a standstill.

What emerged in their place were calls to rectify the "party working style" (*dangfeng*) and strengthen discipline on cadres, perhaps inspired by the issue of official profiteering (*guandao*). This can be regarded as an offensive attempt by conservative forces, amid the growing momentum for a full revision of the reforms, to promote thorough political and ideological education by strengthening the leadership of the Central Committee of the Communist Party. As ever, though, only lesser evils were purged, while the greatest evils remained unscathed; as a case in point, in October 1988 an investigation was launched into corruption surrounding the Kanghua Company, an enterprise run by Deng Xiaoping's son, but the probe did not extend to the highest levels of the state.

From around the end of 1988, as the central party organization strengthened macro control in this manner, Zhao Ziyang's brain trust began hammering out the concept of neo-authoritarianism as the ideal style of governance for China. The most vocal proponent of this idea was Wu Jiaxiang of the Investigation and Research Department of the CCP Central Committee's General Office. His position was supported by Chen Yizi, director of the Research Institute for Reform of the Economic Structure, and other theorists—all of whom were regarded as close aides to Zhao Ziyang.

This concept was what might be described as a Chinese-style developmental dictatorship modeled on the experience of newly industrializing economies (NIEs), based on the assumption that China, whose social conditions were not yet ripe for democratization, needed an enlightened strong man to govern it for the time being. Wu Jiaxiang, for instance, saw neo-authoritarianism as a transitional system from traditional autocracy to a free and democratic society and argued that it was "new" in that authority would not deprive individuals of their freedom but rather curb infringements on the freedom of individuals. What Wu meant by individual freedom under neo-authoritarianism, though, was chiefly economic freedom.[18] The aforementioned Yu Haocheng rebutted Wu's argument. "Advocates of neo-authoritarianism confuse democracy and freedom with anarchism and worry that putting democracy into practice may adversely affect stability and unity," Yu wrote, "but in reality, it is precisely by implementing democracy that stability and unity will be created." He further reasoned, "We must establish democratic authority and legal authority, and it must not be the authority of any individual or of despotism."[19]

Others including Wang Yizhou, an associate professor at the Research Institute for Marxism-Leninism and Mao Zedong Thought

---

18 Wu Jiaxiang, "Xin quanwei zhuyi shuping" [Commentary on the New Authoritarianism], *Shijie jingji daobao* [World Economic Herald], January 16, 1989, reprinted in *Zhongguo zhengzhi* [Politics of China] (Information Center of Social Sciences, Renmin University of China) 1 (1989): 18–19.

19 "Fandui 'Xin quanwei zhuyi' Huhuan zhengzhi tizhi gaige: Guanyu 'Xin quanwei zhuyi' de xilie fangwenlu" [Oppose the "New Authoritarianism" and Call for Reforms of the Political Structure: A Record of the Series of Visits about the "New Authoritarianism"] (unfinished manuscript, May 1–19, 1989), reprinted in *Zhongguo zhengzhi 5* [Politics of China, vol. 5] (1989): 41.

of the Chinese Academy of Social Sciences, also resolutely opposed neo-authoritarianism on the grounds that it entrusted the outcome of reform in China to the authority of an individual and that it stressed only economic values while neglecting political values.[20] Even Yan Jiaqi, who was a member of Zhao's brain trust, was critical of the concept. In the course of a dialogue in December 1988 with Wen Yuankai, a professor at the University of Science and Technology of China, Yan implicitly criticized neo-authoritarianism by stating, "The first thing that China should do is to establish the supreme authority of the constitution, not to establish anything constituting a new authority other than this."[21]

In January 1989, as if to react against the emergence of plans for shelving political democracy like that seen in neo-authoritarianism, Fang Lizhi sent a letter to Deng Xiaoping calling for the release of Wei Jingsheng and other political prisoners on the fortieth anniversary of the founding of the PRC, the seventieth anniversary of the May Fourth Movement, and the two-hundredth anniversary of the French Revolution. Thirty-three intellectuals in Beijing's cultural circles including Su Shaozhi responded to this in mid-February by jointly sending a letter in support of Fang Lizhi to the Central Committee of Communist Party and the NPC. At the end of that month, 42 mainly scientific intellectuals in Beijing, among whom was Yu Haocheng, sent a jointly signed letter to each organ and leaders of the party center calling on them to follow through with "political restructuring" in the form of "democratization

---

20 Wang Yizhou, "Weishenme buneng zantong xin quanwei zhuyi" [Why I Cannot Support the New Authoritarianism], in *Xin quanwei zhuyi: Dui gaige lilun gangling de lunzheng* [The New Authoritarianism: A Debate about the Political Reform Guideline], eds. Liu Jun and Li Lin (Beijing: Beijing Economics Institute Press, 1989).

21 "Zhongguo gaige churu zai nali?: Yan Jiaqi yu Wen Yunkai de duihua" [Where Is the Direction for Chinese Reforms?: A Dialogue between Yan Jiaqi and Wen Yuankai], *Hainan kaifa bao* [Hainan Development Report], February 3, 1989, reprinted in *Zhongguo zhengzhi 2* [Politics of China, vol. 2] (1989), 10, quoted in *Chaina kuraishisu jūyō bunken 1* [Key Documents about the China Crisis, vol. 1], ed. and trans. Yabuki Susumu (Tokyo: Sōsōsha, 1989), 62.

of politics" and to recognize such basic rights as freedom of speech. In mid-March, moreover, a letter demanding the release of prisoners was sent to the soon-to-convene Second Session of the Seventh NPC with the signatures of 43 cultural figures in Beijing, including Yan Jiaqi.[22] Meanwhile, Deng Xiaoping urged Zhao Ziyang to resolutely reject the demands of cultural figures and scientists, instructing him on a number of points. Among other things, he directed that the problems of human rights and of Wei Jingsheng and other political prisoners are not to be addressed at this time for the sake of stability and unity, as well as that the Four Cardinal Principles should be observed. Deng also noted that political education had been inadequate in the preceding decade and that he agreed with the approach of neo-authoritarianism.[23]

In the midst of these political tensions, Hu Yaobang—whose tolerance of the students' calls for democracy had cost him the post of general secretary—suddenly passed away. The actions of students intent on commemorating Hu and restoring his reputation were what shortly precipitated a pro-democracy movement of unprecedented scale involving not just students but also citizens. A spate of events in the wake of Hu's death would soon lead to the Tiananmen Square Incident: Following a decision on April 26 to label the movement as a "distur-bance" (*dongluan*), a hunger strike was launched on May 13. May 16 saw a summit meeting between Soviet leader Mikhail Gorbachev and Chinese leaders. Demonstrations by about one million protesters in Tiananmen Square demanding the resignations of Deng Xiaoping and Li Peng arose from May 17 onward, and martial law was declared in Beijing on May 20. These tumultuous developments culminated in the armed suppression of the pro-democracy movement on June 4.

---

22 "Hō Reishi no Tō Shōhei ate shokan" [Fang Lizhi's Letter to Deng Xiaoping], "Pekin bunkakai 33 nin no kōkaijō" [An Open Letter by 33 Persons in Cultural Circles], "Pekin kagakukai 42 nin no kōkaijō" [An Open Letter by 42 Scientists and Educa-tors], and "Bunkakai 43 nin no kōkaijō" [An Open Letter by 43 Persons in Cultural Circles], in *Chaina kuraishisu* 1, 79–84.
23 "Tō Shōhei no Chō Shiyō e no shiji" [Deng Xiaoping's Orders to Zhao Ziyang], in *Chaina kuraishisu* 1, 85–86.

The student movement called for democratization and liberalization. While their claims were admittedly ambiguous and half-baked in some respects, the students were clearly fighting to ensure the right to challenge the powers that be. Their demands had to do with the lukewarm implementation of political restructuring; in the process of reform, the authorities had proven incapable of cutting deeply into the issue of official profiteering, which the students loudly criticized. The students' calls for freedom of the press and speech reflected the fact that corrupt cadres were not being adequately prosecuted, particularly if they were "big fish." Moreover, the CCP's one-party rule without any system of checks and balances provided a hotbed for illicit behavior by cadres, and this was partly why the students had called, albeit cautiously, for the right to object to the party's absolute leadership. Because the students believed that the structural reforms then in place were incapable of eliminating fundamental problems, they had resorted to direct action and demanded far-reaching "system reform" rather than just "structural reform."

The problems posed by neo-authoritarianism were likely also behind the students' decision to take direct action. Given that this concept was aimed at the practical shelving of moves toward political democracy and strengthening of the party's control, the students—who had come to harbor fervent hopes about democratization and liberalization, thanks to the expansion of information and knowledge—must have found it difficult to accept. What is ironic is that Zhao Ziyang himself, whose brain trust originally came up with the theory, came to support the pro-democracy forces as the movement unfolded, possibly reflecting the political logic within the Communist Party. It seems reasonable to assume that Zhao abandoned the idea of neo-authoritarianism at this point in time.

In Summary: Between "Political Structural (*Tizhi*) Reform" and "Political System (*Zhidu*) Reform"

Based on the above analysis, domestic Chinese positions regarding political reform in the 1980s can largely be grouped into three types. The first saw political reform as something that "serves" economic reform and believed in shelving political democratization until a later time in the interest of stability and unity. Reform in this case does not involve the political system—the basic architecture of the state, comprising the centralized leadership of the CCP and the people's democratic dictatorship, among other components; rather, it is limited to aspects of the political structure that supports the former, such as the administrative apparatus, personnel system, and legislation. This position was thus premised on the condition that reform would not undermine the party's leadership and took a favorable view of neo-authoritarianism. Deng Xiaoping and Zhao Ziyang, as well as intellectuals in Zhao's brain trust including Bao Tong, Chen Yizi, and Yan Jiaqi, appear to have belonged to this group. Yan, though, could arguably be included in the second group described below, having been the most progressive among these men. In the course of the 1989 pro-democracy movement, moreover, Deng shifted to the conservative third position, while Zhao switched to the second position, which favored democratization.

The second group took the progressive view that reform needed to reach beyond the political structure and address the more fundamental political system. Those in this position regarded political democratization and liberalization as urgent issues and embraced political pluralism, calling for basic human rights such as freedom of speech and, in the most progressive of cases, relativization of CCP leadership including the introduction of a multiparty system. No political development could be hoped for without permitting criticism of those in power, they claimed. According to this view, China needed to reform the political system from its very foundation. This group presumably included such intellectuals as Fang Lizhi, Yu Haocheng, and Su Shaozhi and, among the CCP leaders, Hu Yaobang and others.

The third group consisted of those relatively loyal to the centralist ideals of Marxism-Leninism, who harbored doubts not just about political reform but about reform in general. Their position was that strengthening the Communist Party's leadership should be the top priority, and as such, they advocated tightening discipline on cadres through political thought education both inside and outside the party while at the same time thoroughly enforcing the party's leadership. This appears to have been the position of such figures as Wang Zhen, Hu Qiaomu, and Deng Liqun, as well as Chen Yun, Li Xiannian, and Li Peng.

A look at the correlation between political reform after China's adoption of a modernization line and the pro-democracy movement reveals two contrasting aspects: the proposition of political reform gave rise to calls for democratization, on the one hand, while the insufficient implementation of those reforms—and the limitations of political reform itself—added fuel to the same demands, on the other. Chronologically speaking, the former gradually gave way to the latter over the course of the 1980s. To phrase this somewhat differently, in the context of China's modernization policy, social demands necessitated political reform, after which political reform expanded social demands, and finally, social demands outstripped political reform.

Chapter 2

The Impact of the Tiananmen Square Incident and
the Soviet Collapse: The Deng Xiaoping Era

When future historians look back on the twentieth century, how will they assess the year 1989? The first thing that will likely come to their minds is, of course, the end of the Cold War. Emblematic of this moment in history is a landmark summit meeting that took place between US President George H.W. Bush and General Secretary of the Communist Party of the Soviet Union (CPSU) Mikhail Gorbachev in Malta in December of that year, in which the two leaders confirmed that the Cold War had come to an end. The next year the Soviet Union would abolish the one-party dictatorship of the CPSU and introduce a presidential system, and Gorbachev would assume office as its first president. But after a failed coup d'état by conservative forces in August 1991 and the resulting breakup of the party, Gorbachev would resign from office that December, and the Soviet Union, too, would be forced to dissolve itself.

But there was more to the year 1989 than just the end of the Cold War: Countries in Eastern Europe helped tear down the rigid wall of the Cold War. People's democratic republics of the Eastern bloc, which until then had been nothing more than satellite countries of the Soviet Union, set out one after another on the road to democracy. These moves climaxed with the fall of the Berlin Wall, which had symbolized the division between West and East Germany, on November 9 and the reunification of the two Germanies on October 3 the following year.

In contrast with this spectacular struggle for democracy in the Soviet Union and Eastern Europe, a tragedy played itself out in China in that same year: the Tiananmen Square Incident of June 4, 1989. To this day, many aspects of the incident remain unclear due to the non-disclosure of documents. That said, one unmistakable fact is that China consequently failed to ride the wave of democratization that swept the world, and this in turn resulted in highlighting China's conservatism and feudalistic nature in the eyes of foreign observers.

Viewed from today's perspective, though, it is evident that China was in fact the first to experience the rising tide of democratization in 1989, ahead of Eastern Europe and the Soviet Union, but that the movement met a catastrophic end with the Tiananmen Square Incident. The democratization of Eastern Europe and the Soviet Union unfolded with the tragedy of Tiananmen Square in mind. This brings us to wonder whether the collapse of the Berlin Wall and the dissolution of the Soviet Union could have happened so swiftly had it not been for the tragedy in China; but this, admittedly, is only a speculation in hindsight.

In any event, 1989 was a year in which long-standing dysfunctions in the political systems of the Soviet Union, Eastern European states, and China—all of which upheld Marxism-Leninism as their national ideology—reached a tipping point. In short, this signified the limits of an authoritarian system based on one-party dictatorship. The Soviet Union and Eastern European states thus broke free of dictatorial systems in 1989, but they subsequently experienced the "Big Bang" of economic and political readjustment and suffered through many years of twists and turns. That said, their basic democratic foundations remain largely unchanged. China, on the other hand, turned the attention of its citizens to economic growth by only allowing marketization of the economy while moving to preserve and consolidate the conventional system on the political front. It went on to enjoy a sustained period of rapid economic growth, so much so that at times it was said that the twenty-first century was the era of China. In the face of this strong growth, meanwhile, the memory of the Tiananmen Square Incident began to fade. But the Chinese economy has come to show clear signs of a slowdown of growth in recent years, and with it, problems in China's politics and society that had been obscured by the rapid growth are coming to the fore and laying bare the country's institutional fatigue.

This chapter will consider the reality and limits of "Chinese socialism" premised on the Communist Party's dictatorship while discussing in depth—and in historical context—the circumstances and facts of the Tiananmen Square Incident, the significance of Eastern European democratization and the Soviet dissolution for China, and the essence and limits of the socialist market economy that China subsequently adopted.

1. Circumstances and Facts of the Tiananmen Square Incident

In the early hours of June 4, 1989, the eyes of the world were riveted on Beijing's Tiananmen Square. People across the globe witnessed the tragedy unfolding there through the medium of television. The world called the incident a "massacre," while the Chinese authorities labeled it a "counterrevolutionary rebellion." To this day there is no agreement regarding even the simple question of how many people died, with estimates ranging from a few hundred to a few thousand. Far too many details of the case remain unclear, including but not limited to the number of victims. If and when China is democratized someday, records that are currently sealed and confidential information that is kept under wraps will likely all be exposed to the light of day. But until that time comes, the "facts" cannot be established with any certainty. Hence, the description of the incident below is inevitably based on the limited material that is available at present.

Before discussing the Tiananmen Square Incident proper, we must first examine the pro-democracy movement that triggered it. As noted in the preceding chapter, the movement, led by students and intellectuals, began with the death of Hu Yaobang on April 15. Two years before that, in January 1987, Hu was suddenly dismissed from his post as general secretary of the CCP. This was the result of the severe backlash that he faced from conservative hardliners in the party for his leniency toward the pro-democracy student demonstrations that had been raging in major cities nationwide since the end of the previous year. Students at the University of Science and Technology of China in Hefei, Anhui Province, had responded to the calls for democratization by Fang Lizhi, the university's vice-president, and the momentum had then spread to universities across China. But the movement was ultimately put down, having been denounced as "Western bourgeois liberalization."

Hu's death disheartened the students. Students at universities in Beijing took to the streets demanding that his reputation be restored, but at his memorial ceremony on April 22, Hu's honor was not restored regarding his dismissal in 1987. This furthered aggravated the dissatisfaction of the students, who boycotted their classes and launched public protests centered on Tiananmen Square, with democratization as their foremost demand. The CCP party center responded by decreeing in the April 26 issue of *People's Daily* that the movement was a "disturbance" (*dongluan*) and calling for its immediate end. The students countered that theirs was a "patriotic movement" and sought to organize their efforts, such as by forming the Beijing Students' Autonomous Federation. In this process, Wu'erkaixi and Chai Ling of Beijing Normal University and Wang Dan of Peking University emerged as student leaders. When the "disturbance" editorial appeared in *People's Daily*, Zhao Ziyang, who had assumed the office of party general secretary after Hu Yaobang's dismissal, was on a visit to North Korea. As soon as he returned to China he made an effort to close the gap with the students, remarking that "no major rebellion will occur in China," among other things. As we know today, Zhao had become isolated within the party since 1988 as he struggled to deal with inflation in the Chinese economy and faced an impasse in the political reform plans that he himself had set forth as a key task.[1]

The student movement swelled to a scale of 100,000 participants on May 4, the seventieth anniversary of the May Fourth Movement, and on May 13 some 1,000 students launched a hunger strike calling for democracy, possibly eyeing the visit to China by CPSU General Secretary Gorbachev that was scheduled to begin on May 15. Owing to this, the welcoming ceremony for Gorbachev on May 15 was moved at the last minute from Tiananmen Square to Beijing Airport. At his meeting with Gorbachev, Zhao Ziyang revealed that all important matters were ultimately decided inside the CCP by deferring to the

---

1 Zhao Ziyang, *Chō Shiyō gokuhi kaisōroku* (see chap. 1, n. 7), in particular pt. 1.

orders of Deng Xiaoping[2]—a statement suggesting that Zhao Ziyang had completely become the odd one out in the party by this time.

At this stage, the scale of the demonstrations in Tiananmen Square jumped by an order of magnitude to one million participants, which is said to have been the result of Zhao Ziyang spreading word of his sympathy for the movement through his own channels. On May 18 Zhao and Premier Li Peng paid a visit to the students on hunger strike, and while Zhao shed tears and sympathized with the students, Li adopted a cool attitude. On May 20, martial law was declared in part of Beijing, and the area was placed under military control. Nonetheless, the students continued the demonstrations and hunger strike. The military, meanwhile, showed little sign of intimidating the students, and Beijing residents and soldiers were occasionally seen chatting and laughing together peacefully. It is said that the troops were unable to take strong action because the majority of them hailed from Beijing themselves and that they were later replaced by soldiers called in from outside the city. At one point, on May 27, the student protesters decided to withdraw from the square. But students who had traveled to Beijing from the provinces and joined the movement around this time disapproved of retreating so soon after their arrival, and the leaders ultimately decided to continue the movement. Nevertheless, the students, who were coming to sense both danger and exhaustion, gradually started leaving the square of their own volition, and the square began to lose its magnetism.

On the afternoon of June 3, an exasperated party center ordered the troops to suppress protesters in Beijing, and clashes erupted across the city between them and the citizens and students, who had erected barricades. After nightfall, the advance of the troops accelerated, and the students were ordered to withdraw from Tiananmen Square. But they did not move. Finally, from late evening to the early hours of June 4, the martial law forces stormed into the square. The crowds that were

---

2 Mikhail Gorbachev, *Gorubachofu kaisōroku* [Gorbachev's Memoirs], vol. 2, trans. Kudō Sei'ichirō and Suzuki Yasuo (Tokyo: Shinchōsha, 1996), 509.

out on Chang'an Boulevard (*Jie*) by Tiananmen at the time confronted the troops together with the students, but they quickly fled in the face of the troops' superior weapons, which included armored vehicles. As for the tragedy that ensued, we remember it vividly from the images that we saw on television.

Having brought the square under their control, the martial law troops began negotiations with the students. At this time Wu'erkaixi was carried away on a stretcher after suffering a heart attack, while the hardliner Chai Ling also left the square out of anger at the flexible policy of negotiating a withdrawal with the authorities; Wang Dan reportedly advocated leaving the square and found himself at odds with Chai over this. Among those who engaged in direct talks were Liu Xiaobo, a lecturer at Beijing Normal University, and Hou Dejian, a singer and songwriter from Taiwan. As a result of the negotiations between them and the armed forces, at around dawn on June 4 the students who remained in Tiananmen Square withdrew from the southeastern part of the square "in peace" and returned to their respective schools. In other words, the final withdrawal is said to have been a "bloodless surrender" of the square.[3]

At the Fourth Plenum of the Thirteenth Central Committee of the CCP on June 23, the dismissal of General Secretary Zhao Ziyang was formally decided, and Jiang Zemin, who had received a special promotion to the central government from the post of party secretary of Shanghai, was appointed to replace Zhao. A number of student leaders including Wu'erkaixi and Chai Ling escaped overseas through underground routes, while others, such as Wang Dan, Liu Xiaobo, and Hou Dejian, were arrested by the authorities. Fang Lizhi, who had sought shelter at the US Embassy in Beijing during the movement, continued to live there after the Tiananmen Square Incident, and in June 1990 he was permitted to leave China for "medical treatment" in the United

---

3 Yabuki Susumu discusses this point in detail in his work *Ten'anmon jiken no shinsō* [The Truth about the Tiananmen Square Incident], vols. 1 and 2 (Tokyo: Sōsōsha, 1990).

States. This was a concession to the West that Beijing made as a last resort so that a resolution condemning China would not be issued at the G7 summit slated for July 1990 in Houston, Texas.

In October 1989 the fourteenth Dalai Lama, the Tibetan leader living in exile in India, received the Nobel Peace Prize, and the pressure of world public opinion on China grew even stronger. As might be expected, China reacted strongly against this. At the Fifth Plenum of the Thirteenth Central Committee of the CCP held in November, Deng Xiaoping resigned from the chairmanship of the Central Military Commission and passed the baton to Jiang Zemin. According to Deng, this was to transfer power to the next generation of leaders as early as possible so as to give them sufficient time to consolidate the foundations of their regime. By ceding the post of chairman of the Central Military Commission, Deng Xiaoping retired more or less completely from political life. It goes without saying, though, that this was merely as a matter of form.

Why was the democratization movement suppressed? In other words, why did the Tiananmen Square Incident happen? Needless to say, the prime factor was the fear that the CCP leadership harbored for a collapse of the system. The situation was cause for much controversy within the party, it is said, but there is no doubt that Deng Xiaoping, as the all-powerful leader, had the final say. The students' demands were simply unacceptable to the party leadership. Although the students had not directly renounced the Communist Party or socialism, the party leadership nevertheless believed that demands for such things as freedom of the press and freedom of speech would inevitably come into conflict with the principle of CCP guidance and ultimately force a radical change in the existing system. Moreover, the presence of figures like Zhao Ziyang at the party's core who were sympathetic toward the student movement further amplified the leadership's sense of crisis.

2. The Soviet Collapse and China's Critique of "Peaceful Evolution"

The countries of Eastern Europe and the Soviet Union hastened the pace of democratization following the Tiananmen Square Incident, as if they were looking to it as a negative example. In Eastern Europe, Hungary—which was fast becoming a democracy—decided in September 1989 to allow the passage of East German refugees fleeing to West Germany. This current of events led to the resignation of Erich Honecker as chairman of the State Council of East Germany and, on November 9, to the fall of the Berlin Wall, which had symbolized the division of the two Germanies; German reunification followed in October 1990. Prime Minister Todor Zhivkov, who had ruled Bulgaria for 35 years, resigned shortly thereafter, and the country also joined the rising tide of democratization.

In Czechoslovakia, where democratization was gaining momentum, December 1989 saw the election of Alexander Dubček, who had fallen from power as first secretary of the Communist Party of Czechoslovakia in the wake of the Prague Spring, as chairman of the Federal Assembly, while Václav Havel, who had been imprisoned as an anti-regime writer, was elected president, marking an end to the one-party dictatorship. Anti-government demonstrations in Romania also climaxed around this time; President Nicolae Ceausescu and his wife Elena were executed by firing squad, and the country abandoned the name of "socialist republic." In Poland as well, the constitution was revised, and one-party rule was abolished along with the dissolution of the United Workers' Party, while the country's name was changed to the Republic of Poland. One year later, in December 1990, Lech Walesa—the leader of Solidarity, the labor union that had opposed the Jaruzelski regime since the early 1980s—took office as Poland's president.

It was against this backdrop of rapid democratization in Eastern Europe that US President Bush and Soviet General Secretary Gorbachev held their summit meeting in Malta on December 2, 1989, and confirmed the end of the Cold War. The Cold War had started in Yalta and ended in Malta. This wave of democratization, commonly known as the Eastern European revolutions, could not have happened without Gorbachev and his policies of perestroika and "new thinking" diplomacy. These countries had been regarded as Soviet satellite states until then, and their democratization became possible only after the Soviet Union abandoned the Brezhnev Doctrine, according to which even the national sovereignty of these countries had to be limited for the sake of the unity of the socialist bloc.

The Eastern European revolutions hastened the pace of democratization in the Soviet Union. In February 1990, Gorbachev decided on the abolition of one-party dictatorship and the introduction of a multi-party system at the CPSU Central Committee Plenum. At the Congress of People's Deputies held the following month, the constitution was revised and a presidential system introduced to transfer power from the party to the state and government institutions, and Gorbachev—who was chairman of the Supreme Soviet of the Soviet Union—was elected the first president. From that point forward, the president replaced the general secretary of the CPSU as the most powerful position in the system. The separation of party and state, which had failed in China, was thus achieved all at once in the Soviet Union.

Meanwhile, the rapid democratization of the Soviet Union began to tear at the seams of the "empire." In March 1990 Lithuania and Estonia, two of the three Baltic states, declared their independence from the Soviet Union, and the remaining Latvia also declared its independence the following May. The Soviet Union naturally did not accept this, and the situation with the Baltics grew tense, at times even volatile. The Baltic countries had been secretly slated for Soviet annexation under the nonaggression pact concluded between Nazi Germany and the Soviet Union in 1939, and these declarations of independence effectively invalidated the secret agreement.

On August 19, 1991, Soviet conservatives placed Gorbachev under house arrest and mounted a coup d'état aimed at forcing him to resign. But the attempt ended in failure on August 21 without having gained any support, and the ringleaders were arrested. In the aftermath, Gorbachev declared the disbanding of the CPSU and promptly set the country on the path toward a full-fledged democracy. Meanwhile Boris Yeltsin, who had been elected president of the Russian Federation and was at odds with Gorbachev, displayed leadership in handling the coup attempt and gained control of the political situation. Moreover, the Baltic countries once again declared their independence in the course of these events, and the Ukrainian Republic also declared its secession from the Soviet Union. Finally, in December 1991, the Union of Soviet Socialist Republics ended its history that had begun in 1917, and in its place the Commonwealth of Independent States (CIS) was founded by 11 of the republics that had comprised the Soviet Union, not including the three Baltic states and Georgia, under the Alma-Ata Protocol. Thus, Gorbachev retired from the limelight, having failed at in-system reform, and leadership of the Russian Federation—the successor state of the old Soviet Union—passed to Yeltsin.

How did China respond to these rapid moves toward democracy in Eastern Europe and the Soviet Union? The Chinese abbreviation for the Soviet Union and Eastern Europe, *Su Dong*, happens to be the first two characters of the name of a famed poet of the Northern Song dynasty, Su Dongpo. Making a pun on these characters, the Chinese dubbed the drastic changes in the Soviet Union and Eastern Europe the *Su Dong bo*, or the "Soviet and Eastern European wave." But there was no way that China would welcome the rapid democratization of the Soviet Union and Eastern Europe. When one-party dictatorship by the CPSU was abolished in February 1990, China ostensibly stood by the principle of noninterference in the internal affairs of other states. Internally, though, it is said to have sharply criticized Gorbachev, whom it deemed responsible for the whole situation. On the domestic front, it relaunched the "Learn from Comrade Lei Feng" campaign, which had been implemented prior to the Cultural Revolution to instill Mao Zedong Thought within the army, in the interest of thorough political-ideological education. Other efforts at extensive patriotic education were also undertaken, such as by incorporating military training in the curricula of colleges and universities.

As far as Sino-Soviet relations were concerned, though, in practical terms China strove to avoid conflicts with Gorbachev. As Gorbachev's recent visit to the country in May 1989 had finally put an end to three decades of Sino-Soviet tensions, China had judged it unwise to plunge back into a hostile relationship with the Soviet Union. During this period, the Chinese leadership lifted martial law in Beijing on January 10, 1990, and on January 18 it released 573 activists who had been detained. Martial law was also lifted in Lhasa, Tibet, on May 1. As noted above, China tacitly allowed the defection to the United States of Fang Lizhi, who had taken refuge in the US Embassy in Beijing, in a bid to avert a censure resolution against it at the Houston Summit in July. While tightening domestic controls after the Tiananmen Square Incident by beefing up political education, it frequently adopted compromise policies to avoid isolation in the international arena in between criticizing the United States' human rights diplomacy.

Needless to say, Chinese leaders welcomed the Soviet coup attempt by conservative forces in August 1991; but their elation was short-lived. "The salvoes of the October Revolution brought us Marxism-Leninism," Mao Zedong famously said in his 1949 speech "On the People's Democratic Dictatorship." As Mao himself clearly acknowledged, there would have been no Chinese revolution without the Russian revolution, and the collapse of the CPSU and the Soviet Union thus came as a massive blow to China. The internal instructions that Deng Xiaoping issued to the CCP at this time are known as the "24-character strategy." Although several versions exist with some variations depending on the source, the standard version in Hong Kong goes, "Observe calmly; secure our position; cope with affairs calmly; hide our capacities and bide our time; be good at maintaining a low profile; and never claim leadership."[4]

---

4 Kotake Kazuaki, "Chūgoku seiji no sakusō: Kako ichinenkan no dōkō" [Chinese Politics in Confusion: Trends in the Past Year], *Kokusai mondai* (January 1992): 37.

On the theoretical front, China countered the "Soviet and East-ern European wave" by drawing on a critique of "peaceful evolution" (*heping yanbian*): overturning a regime not by force of arms but through peaceful means such as pressure for democratization, human rights diplomacy, or market pressure. (*Heping yanbian* is also translated as "peaceful transition.") This involves a combination of interference in internal affairs and propaganda war. According to China, the United States devised peaceful evolution as a strategy against the socialist bloc in the early days of the Cold War, soon after World War II.[5]

In explaining, why the Soviet Union and Eastern Europe caved in so easily to the peaceful evolution, China invokes the dichotomy of the international macroclimate and the domestic microclimate. The international macroclimate refers to democratization pressure and mar-ket pressure and suggests that trends in the international community will be strongly inclined in this direction. The domestic microclimate operates in tandem with the former and points to hidden supporters within China plotting a peaceful evolution by capitalizing on opportu-nities like an economic crisis. Combined, these two climates present a regime crisis. According to this interpretation, domestic microclimatic elements in the Soviet Union, such as Gorbachev and Yeltsin or the economic crisis, succumbed to the democracy offensive led by the United States. With regard to the Tiananmen Square Incident as well, China's understanding is that a huge disturbance occurred because of the presence of microclimatic elements in the form of Zhao Ziyang and economic difficulties. This of course requires more objective analysis. One might even argue that domestic factors are what make up the macroclimate and that international factors are in fact nothing more than the microclimate. At least in the case of the Soviet Union and Eastern Europe, this interpretation holds fairly true; it seems implausible that a total collapse of the "empire" could have occurred otherwise.

---

5 See Liu Hongchao, ed., *Xifang heping yanbian shehuizhuyi guojia de zhanlue, celue, shoufa* [Strategy, Tactics, and Methods of the West and Peaceful Evolution Socialist Countries] (Wuhan: Hubei People's Publishing House, 1989).

What was China's strategy against the peaceful evolution? Deng Xiaoping's conclusion was clear: to continue with the policy of reform and opening up and enhance China's "comprehensive national power" (CNP). Of the various measures comprising CNP, such as political power, military force, economic strength, technology, and conceptual ability, the most important to Deng was economic strength. As noted above, Deng believed that, whether in the case of the Soviet dissolution or that of the Tiananmen Square Incident, one of the chief determinants of the domestic microclimate was the economy.

A key question remained unanswered, however. If China is to continue with reform and opening up and step up its economic power—the most important element of CNP—what should be made of the "osmotic pressure" that it would undergo over time, and the resultant social changes, as economic and cultural exchanges with the West including the United States inevitably cause an influx of foreign influences in Chinese society? Deng was vexed about whether or not this would amount to a peaceful evolution.

The answer to this dilemma was provided by Deng himself during his inspection tour of southern China in early 1992. It came in the Southern Tour Speeches (*Nanxun Jianghua*), a series of talks by Deng that provided the archetype for the socialist market economy model; this is widely regarded as Deng's declaration that China would forge ahead with reform and opening up.

3. The Southern Tour Speeches and the Socialist Market Economy

The Southern Tour Speeches summarize the key points discussed by Deng Xiaoping in the remarks that he made at various points during his inspection tour of Wuchang, Shenzhen, Zhuhai, Shanghai, and other cities. "The reason some people hesitate to carry out the reform and the open policy and dare not break new ground is, in essence, that they're afraid it would mean introducing too many elements of capitalism and, indeed, taking the capitalist road," Deng says. "The crux of the matter is whether the road is capitalist or socialist. The chief criterion for making that judgment should be whether it promotes the growth of the productive forces in a socialist society…"[6] In other words, he asserts that the core criterion in the reform and opening-up policy is whether or not something is conducive to improving productivity.

Deng then ventures: "The proportion of planning to market forces is not the essential difference between socialism and capitalism. A planned economy is not equivalent to socialism, because there is planning under capitalism too; a market economy is not capitalism, because there are markets under socialism too. Planning and market forces are both means of controlling economic activity."[7] The PRC's official view of the socialist economy until then had been that planning came first and the market was subordinate to it, but here Deng put them on an equal footing and even held that the two did not comprise the distinguishing criterion between socialism and capitalism. Deng continues, "Regarding reform and the open policy as means of introducing capitalism, and seeing the danger of peaceful evolution towards capitalism as coming chiefly from the economic sphere are 'Left' tendencies."[8] This statement suggests that it is not possible to eliminate those things that flow into and affect society as a result of reform and opening up, nor does such an influx constitute a peaceful evolution.

To recap, Deng's view was that anything that serves to develop productive forces was welcome and would not lead to a peaceful evolution. It is a well-known story that, when the Chinese economy hit rock bottom in the early 1960s, Deng introduced capitalist policies to

---

6 Deng Xiaoping, *Tō Shōhei bunsen 1982–1992* [Selected Works of Deng Xiaoping, 1982–92] (Tokyo: Ten Books, 1995), 374. English translation quoted from "Excerpts from talks given in Wuchang, Shenzhen, Zhuhai and Shanghai," *China Daily* (online), updated October 26, 2010, http://www.chinadaily.com.cn/china/19thcpc-nationalcongress/2010-10/26/content_29714457.htm.

7 Deng, *Tō Shōhei bunsen 1982–1992*, 374–75.

8 Deng, *Tō Shōhei bunsen 1982–1992*, 376.

salvage the economy, remarking, "It doesn't matter whether a cat is black or white, as long as it catches mice." (Deng originally said "black or yellow.") Although he would later come under criticism during the Cultural Revolution for this and other remarks, it seems evident that Deng remained essentially consistent throughout. He explicitly cautioned in the Southern Tour Speeches, however, that bourgeois liberalization must be opposed for at least 20 more years.

Following the Southern Tour Speeches, critical mentions of the peaceful evolution faded from official documents, and in its place "socialist market economy" (*shehuizhuyi shichang jingji*) gained frequency as the term representing China's new orientation. This was officially formulated in October 1992 at the Fourteenth National Congress of the CCP. Needless to say, the "retired" Deng Xiaoping did not appear before the congress, and General Secretary Jiang Zemin presided over the proceedings. In his report, Jiang devoted considerable time to explaining the socialist market economy and made little mention of the political reforms that had been a major topic of the Thirteenth National Congress of the CCP, thus taking a large step backward in this regard.

The rationale for proposing a socialist market economy was that expanding the market economy was essential to improving China's comprehensive national power and that bold reforms and opening to the outside world were needed to that end. In a nutshell, the word *socialism* here referred economically to the preservation of public ownership and politically to the leadership of the Communist Party. Public ownership and CCP leadership were closely interrelated, as the former was what essentially supported the latter. In other words, a socialist market economy was a market economy premised on public ownership under the leadership of the Communist Party. What this implied was that, it being a market economy, things like a joint stock system and land leasing would be permitted, but the state (party) would hold a significant portion of the shares, and leasing land merely meant that the state (party) would grant usage rights, not that it would give up ownership.

The development of China that Deng Xiaoping envisioned at the time followed the state-led development model by which the newly industrializing economies (NIEs) of East Asia, such as South Korea, Singapore, and Taiwan, achieved economic growth. Specifically, his blueprint for China's development involved shelving democratization in the process of development and starting out with government-led efforts to increase imports, thereby acquiring advanced technologies, as well as nurturing superior industries based on the government's industrial policies to achieve further industrialization. Eventually, foreign currencies would be obtained by exporting the products made by these industries, allowing China to develop more new industries.

Drawing on the Southern Tour Speeches and the proclamation of China as a socialist market economy, China aggressively introduced preferential treatment for foreign companies to attract capital from overseas, while also setting out to prepare the domestic market by adopting a joint stock system, land leasing, and other new components. Thanks to these measures, foreign direct investment in China soared severalfold on a contract basis from 1992 onward, and the economic growth rate also jumped to 14.2 percent in 1992 and to 13.5 percent in 1993. Having observed this, the International Monetary Fund, the World Bank, and others came to issue reports predicting that if China continued to grow at this rate, it would surpass Japan and eventually even the United States at some point in the twenty-first century.

As we have seen above, witnessing the shocking dissolution of the Soviet Union drove Deng Xiaoping to his remarks in the Southern Tour Speeches and to the decision to build a socialist market economy. China's primary objective was to focus on building up its economic power by shelving political reform and democratization and, by so doing, reinforce its foundations so as to avoid repeating the Soviet experience. In short, China believed that economic growth was precisely what gave the regime its legitimacy and that it would lead to political stability.

In Summary

The developments from the Southern Tour Speeches to the start of the socialist market economy represented a momentous policy shift in the history of the PRC—a bold shift that leveraged the Tiananmen tragedy and the collapse of the socialist bloc in the Soviet Union and Eastern Europe. In retrospect, this all would have been impossible but for the presence of Deng Xiaoping, a man of rare intellectual flexibility. Deng began to fade from the limelight soon after this and passed away in 1997, but his socialist market economy continues to the present day.

From day one, the socialist market economy was inevitably plagued by the dilemma of where to place the emphasis: on "socialism" or on "market economy." In a market economy where the ultimate decision-making authority lies with the Communist Party, political intervention in the economy is in effect institutionally guaranteed, and such an economy is bound to become a hotbed of political corruption. This should have been obvious from the outset and has indeed become a reality. Foreign investors, for instance, would surely cease to be attracted to a market in a half-baked market economy that is frequently subjected to murky government intervention—all the more so if the myth of endless growth on which that economy is premised began to fray at the edges.

The slowdown in economic growth in China directly ties in with the question of the legitimacy of the CCP's authority. Deng Xiaoping, the father of the socialist market economy, has already passed away, and the task of overcoming the limits of that policy has been entrusted to the generations after him. Deng must have been aware of the dilemmas that awaited down the road of the socialist market economy. We can only wonder how he envisioned the future of China and the fate of the CCP.

If and when China's political system is democratized one day, records related to the Tiananmen Square Incident will likely become public. When that day comes, will Deng be held responsible as the paramount leader who pointed the gun at the students and citizens in the incident, or will he be lauded as a courageous leader who made the decision to set China on the bold path to a socialist market economy? We must await the judgment of history.

Chapter 3

Economic Growth as Legitimacy:
The Deng Xiaoping and Jiang Zemin Eras

Since its establishment in 1949, China has seen a succession of political shifts. In retrospect, researchers, too, have often been at the mercy of the constant oscillations in real-world Chinese politics. While this has partly to do with the fact that for many years researchers could not freely set foot in China, which limited the availability of data, they were also prone to viewing China through a conceptual or political filter and were wanting in analytical ability and perspective. After the start of the reform and opening-up policy, the Tiananmen Square Incident, and other pivotal moments, researchers have come to undertake solid empirical analysis with a more objective and sober attitude and through actual fieldwork.

Precisely because of these prior circumstances, though, China studies in recent years has tended to fan out into a myriad of micro research topics, with the consequence that analyses and perspectives at the macro level are often neglected. The most crucial point when analyzing the course of a massive country like China is to keep sight of the country's big picture. Empirically studying individual cases is basic, but in the course of that work, scholars must not lose sight of how their research relates to the overarching theme of examining the larger national picture.

Given the above, in this chapter I will present my own bird's-eye view of China since the reform and opening-up policy was implemented, though it will admittedly involve repetitions from earlier chapters. Here I would like to discuss the interrelationships between China's political, economic, and foreign policies in the global age, focusing on the period from the 1980s, when the outline of China's overall national policies leading up to the present took basic shape, through the Tiananmen Square Incident and on to the start of the 2000s—spanning the Deng Xiaoping and Jiang Zemin eras. The policies referred to here are those of the Communist Party of China or, more precisely, the Central Committee leadership. Thus, the "interrelationship between China's political, economic, and foreign policies" that will be reconstructed in this chapter include the CCP leadership's take on policy and the actual policy process.

To help clarify the flow of logic in this chapter, I will start out by presenting a hypothesis, which can be summarized as follows. The foundation for all else in China is politics, and the core interest is the maintenance of power by the CCP—or, phrased differently, the preservation of the PRC. But achieving that final objective requires ensuring the legitimacy of power, the key to which is sustained economic growth. What then are the prerequisites for ensuring economic growth? For China, which has deepened its interdependence on the world economy, they are a robust growth of trade and direct investment, a peaceful international environment to that end, and a generally cooperative and all-round foreign policy stance.

In summary, diplomatic efforts are a means to achieving economic growth, which in turn serves the ultimate aim: politics. But whether such a logic can continue to hold true in the actual deployment of policies rests on whether or not the decision-makers in China are rational actors in the general sense of the term; we cannot exclude the possibility that Chinese leaders will resort to irrational acts due to circumstances within the CCP and various situational factors. This is particularly because the extent of openness and institutionalization is low in a closed one-party political system like China's, and what constitutes "rationality" from our standpoint may not necessarily be "rational" from theirs.

1. Political Power as the Ultimate Goal

The Principle of Party Leadership
The ultimate political goal in China is maintaining the state and the political system; more precisely, it is maintaining the state and the political system of the PRC, for which the CCP effectively serves as the sole ruling party. The current constitution of the PRC stipulates the following in its preamble: "Under the leadership of the Communist Party of China . . . the Chinese people of all nationalities will continue . . . to turn China into a socialist country that is prosperous, powerful,

democratic and culturally advanced."[1] The principle of CCP leadership is thus the basic premise of the political system. It goes without saying that this has been a fundamental principle of the PRC from its inception down to the present day.

The PRC further cites as its political ideal the "people's democratic dictatorship," which is premised on the guidance of the Communist Party. This implies democracy for its people but dictatorship for its enemies. As for who the "people" and "enemies" are, respectively, the distinction was long fundamentally based on class divisions. The worker-peasant alliance between the proletariat—which was to take the leading role—and the peasantry was placed at the center of the "people," and the party's status was defined as their "vanguard" or "representative." At the time of the PRC's founding, national capitalists from the pre-1949 era and the eight "democratic parties" and intellectuals that collaborated with the CCP were superficially also included in the "people" in addition to the proletariat and peasantry. The "enemies" were feudal landlords and bureaucratic capitalists in terms of class, but the use of the label during the Mao Zedong era was extremely arbitrary and political in practice.

An important concept in this connection is the "coalition government," which was proposed by Mao Zedong himself as the vision for the new regime. The CCP received support from the above-mentioned eight democratic parties in the civil war with the Kuomintang. Thanks to this, even after the PRC's founding, these political parties survived in the Communist Party system as part of the "coalition government" or "united front" and were accorded certain posts in the government. To thoroughly implement its policies and leadership, the CCP set up party committees in work units across China and embedded the party's cell organizations into government and state organs. The decision to establish these "party groups" (*dangzu*), as the cell organizations

---

1 "Constitution of the People's Republic of China," State Council of the People's Republic of China (website), updated August 23, 2014, http://english.www.gov.cn/archive/laws_regulations/2014/08/23/content_281474982987458.htm.

were called, was made in November 1949, shortly after the founding
of the PRC.

The positions held by those of the democratic parties were thus deprived of real authority. When they frankly voiced their dissatisfaction
in response to the call to "Let a hundred flowers bloom and a hundred
schools of thought contend" (*shuangbai*) under the Rectification (*Zheng-
feng*) campaign, they faced a backlash in the form of the Anti-Rightist
(*Fanyou*) campaign in 1957. Thereafter, members of the democratic
parties kept their mouths shut, and everything was centralized under
CCP leadership. The coalition government had failed in the new China,
as had the creation of democracy. Meanwhile, this failure displays the
arbitrary nature of labeling "friends" or "enemies." The Communist
Party continues to uphold a "multiparty cooperation and consultation
system" with these parties. But this, apart from some trivial progress
here and there, is obviously little more than an empty slogan, given
the major principle of CCP leadership in all things. If this process is
interpreted as the loss of democracy outside the CCP (*dangwai*), then
the juncture at which democracy within the party (*dangnei*) failed
completely would be, on the one hand, the incident involving Minister
of National Defense Peng Dehuai in 1959 at the Lushan Plenum, where
Peng incurred the wrath of Mao Zedong by denouncing the failures of
the Great Leap Forward and suffered a downfall as a consequence. The
other was when Premier Liu Shaoqi was permanently expelled from the
party during the Cultural Revolution.

Limits of Political Reform: Lessons of the Tiananmen Square Incident and the Soviet Collapse

Talk about the need to political reform began after Deng Xiaoping
assumed control at the Third Plenum of the Eleventh Central Committee of the CCP in December 1978 following Mao Zedong's death two
years earlier, setting China on the path of reform and opening up. As
I detailed in Chapter 1, political reform only got into full swing in the
latter half of the 1980s, after economic reforms—which were imple-

mented in the rural areas and cities in the first half of the decade—had gotten off the ground.

Various developments related to political reform were already taking place around the time of the Third Plenum. For instance, during the Beijing Spring—the focus of which was the Democracy Wall Movement that arose on the eve of the plenum—Wei Jingsheng, a key democracy activist, added "politics" as the fifth component to the Four Modernizations (industry, agriculture, national defense, and science and technology) and called for full democratization. These developments were ultimately put out as "demands for Western bourgeois democracy," though, and in March 1979 Deng announced the Four Cardinal Principles, consisting of upholding the socialist road, upholding the dictatorship of the proletariat, upholding the leadership of the Communist Party, and upholding Marxism-Leninism and Mao Zedong Thought, as the political and ideological envelope. That said, the criteria for setting the bounds of this envelope were ambiguous and were ultimately left to the arbitrary and subjective discretion of the higher-ups.

I would like to expand here a bit for the sake of Deng's reputation. Reflecting on Mao Zedong's personal dictatorship and lifetime tenure during the Cultural Revolution era, Deng opened up a path for criticizing those excesses under the slogan of liberation of thought, and in August 1980 he made a proposal regarding a leadership system for the party and state. In the proposal, he pointed out such issues as excessive concentration of power, excessive concurrent holding of posts, the intermixing of party and state affairs, and the replacement and succession of leaders; he also advocated rejuvenating cadres and increasing their knowledge and specialization.[2] Deng relinquished his key positions in the party and state, save for his post on the Central Military Commission, clearing the way for his successors.

---

2 For statements by Deng Xiaoping around this time, including about the Four Cardinal Principles, see Deng, *Selected Works*, vol. 2 (see chap. 1, n. 2).

It was from 1986 on that political reform formally appeared on the agenda in the Deng Xiaoping era. This was at Deng's abrupt proposal. Shortly before that, the Ferdinand E. Marcos regime in the Philippines was overthrown by a pro-democracy movement, while the Kuomintang in Taiwan began to talk about democratization out of the blue, and the Soviet Union launched perestroika under Gorbachev. China's sudden interest in political reform could not have been unrelated to these global developments. Simply put, the crux of Deng's political reforms was "political reform for the sake of economic reform." It did include one fresh idea, though: the separation of party and state. This was daring in as much as it was likely to bring about a relative decline in the role of the CCP.

A student pro-democracy movement arose soon thereafter at the end of 1986, and Hu Yaobang was dismissed from the top CCP post in January 1987 after expressing sympathy for the students' demands. It was expected that political reforms would be significantly delayed as a consequence of these events. But amid the global wave of democratization, Zhao Ziyang, who had succeeded Hu as party general secretary, once again brought up political reform at the CCP's Thirteenth National Congress with the backing of Deng Xiaoping. While Zhao's proposals included the introduction of a state public servant system and a large-scale delegation of authority to lower levels of the bureaucracy, the key proposal was the separation of party and state. It was reported that some party groups within government institutions were slated for abolition under that mantra.

But the signs of a gradual move toward democracy, as exemplified by such a relativization of the CCP's role, were extinguished in no time in the face of subsequent political developments. China experienced a series of shocks, namely the pro-democracy movement that students initially launched to commemorate the death of Hu Yaobang in 1989, the subsequent declaration of martial law, the military suppression of the student movement at Tiananmen Square on June 4, and finally, Zhao Ziyang's fall from power in connection with these events. After the Tiananmen Square Incident, the separation of party and state came to be excluded from debate due to its strong likelihood of weakening the CCP's leadership abilities. This was further reinforced by the example of the Soviet Union: After transferring authority from the party to the government and state under perestroika, the Soviet Union eventually succumbed to demands from below for democratization and abolished its one-party system. In 1991, moreover, it dissolved the state itself.

"The salvoes of the October Revolution brought us Marxism-Leninism"—these were the words of Mao Zedong.[3] It is likely true that the Chinese revolution could never have succeeded without the experience of the Soviet Union, and its dissolution was all the more shocking for China. After agonizing about the matter, Deng Xiaoping concluded that China must enrich the economic life of its people and actively participate in the market economy to that end, learning by negative example from the Tiananmen Square Incident and the Soviet collapse. In the course of his tour of China's southern regions at the start of 1992, Deng repeatedly gave lectures (the Southern Tour Speeches) advocating the need to boldly reform and open up the country. These lectures led up to the socialist market economy line that was formally adopted at the Fourteenth National Congress of the CCP in the autumn of that year.

The socialist market economy fundamentally stands for a shift to market economics. What, then, does the word *socialist* signify in this context? It implies public ownership (nationalization) of land and capital on the one hand and the leadership of the Communist Party on the other. The former is, in essence, a political guarantee of the latter. In that respect, at the root of the socialist market economy lies the political goal of ensuring the leadership of the CCP. China's economy began growing at an annual rate exceeding 10 percent soon thereafter, driven by the sudden influx of direct investment by foreign companies, which was premised on China's transformation into a market economy.

3 Mao Zedong, "On the People's Democratic Dictatorship," in *Selected Works of Mao Tse-Tung,* vol. 4 (Beijing: Foreign Languages Press, 1961).

The new objective of marketization under a socialist market economy gave rise to a growing debate about the government's role in that process. A full-scale transition from planned economics to market economics meant moving toward a small government, which specifically entailed streamlining the machinery and reducing staff, as well as downsizing the public sector; it was inevitable that the debate should head in this direction. Yet in reality, the CCP's existence and guidance were only reaffirmed, and China began to move toward further expanding and strengthening the party's role. This was the lesson that it had derived from the Tiananmen Square Incident and the dissolution of the Soviet Union.

But a market economy premised on Communist Party leadership is a surefire formula for political corruption. Indeed, as the 1990s progressed, corruption in China worsened rather than being reduced—a trend that, far from abating, has become the norm in the years since. According to a report made at the National People's Congress (NPC) in 2003, of the various corruption cases being investigated in the previous five years, as many as 207,103 cases proceeded to prosecution, which translates to an average of about 40,000 cases a year; guilty verdicts were rendered in 99,306 of these cases to 83,308 persons.[4]

For all the talk about the need for political reform, however, there were no signs of the Chinese government setting about it in earnest. Although direct elections of local leaders had been introduced at the grassroots level in rural areas and at the lowest-level units in the urban areas, these had no effect on the higher reaches of the political system.

---

4 "Zuigao Renmin Fayuan yuanzhang Xiao Yang zai Shijie renda yici huiyi shang de baogao" [Report by Xiao Yang, President of the Supreme People's Court of China, at the First Session of the Tenth National People's Congress], and "Zuigao Renmin Jianchayuan jianchazhang Han Zhubin zai Shijie renda yici huiyi shang de baogao" [Report by Han Zhubin, Procurator-General of the Supreme People's Procuratorate, at the First Session of the Tenth National People's Congress], *People's Daily*, March 12, 2003.

The CCP's Transformation and the "Three Represents"

In the immediate aftermath of the Tiananmen Square Incident, political power was entrusted to the Shanghai-based Jiang Zemin. Before long, Jiang had inherited from Deng Xiaoping not only the post of party general secretary but also that of chairman of the Central Military Commission, thus gaining a grip on China's military power. Deng likely continued to exercise his political influence in the shadows up until his death in 1997, but as the 1990s progressed, Jiang gradually took on a greater amount of substantive political power. During that time, Jiang devoted his efforts to maintaining economic growth as ordained by Deng. When it came to the party, meanwhile, he would only permit the augmentation of its presence and authority and shelved any political reforms that might tackle problems in the party head-on.

That said, the change in the party's character was remarkable. The CCP had sallied forth as a class-based political party rooted in a "worker-peasant alliance," but faced with the denationalization and privatization that accompanied the rapid switchover to market economics, it had no choice but to recharacterize itself. The "Three Represents" (*Sange Daibiao*), which Jiang Zemin began talking about in 2000, was originally a policy that sensitively reflected this change in conditions. Jiang announced the policy during an inspection tour of Guangdong Province in February 2000, as if to emulate Deng Xiaoping's Southern Tour Speeches. The Communist Party, he said, should represent three things: "China's advanced productive forces, the orientation of China's advanced culture, and the fundamental interests of the overwhelming majority of the Chinese people."[5]

The emphasis lay on the final point—that the party represents the "fundamental interests of the overwhelming majority of the Chinese people." This was because the worker-peasant alliance, which the CCP as a class party was supposed to represent, had been replaced by the

---

5 "Three Represents," *China Daily* (online), updated July 10, 2007, http://www.chinadaily.com.cn/china/2007-07/10/content_6142053.htm.

broader and vaguer concept of "the people." Viewed in a different light, this suggested an effective departure from the proletarian dictatorship and implied a possible change in the CCP's nature. The Three Represents then went dormant for a time, until Jiang began trumpeting the theory again following the eightieth anniversary of the CCP in July 2001. The next year's Sixteenth National Congress of the CCP, which served as Jiang's retirement ceremony as general secretary, was full of talk about the Three Represents.

One highlight of the CCP's eightieth anniversary was a major change in the criteria for joining the party, which Jiang set forth in his speech. Jiang expanded the scope of "the people" to include the new social strata that had emerged in the private sector, which in the course of marketization was fast replacing the public sector as the core of economic activity—in particular, the social elites comprising private entrepreneurs, businessmen and engineers working at foreign-owned enterprises, and the like. By doing so, he effectively steered the CCP toward allowing these strata to join the party. This policy was then given an extended interpretation in the new party constitution adopted at the Sixteenth National Congress of the CCP, which described the party as the "vanguard both of the working class and of the Chinese people and the Chinese nation."[6] The recent tendency in China to make heavy use of the concept of "strata" (*jieceng*) in place of "classes" (*jieji*) is rooted in these developments.

And so the Communist Party set forth on a path of changing from a class-based political party to a people's political party, signaling a relative decline in its attention to workers and peasants, on whose behalf it should have been working. A close examination is needed as to whether the CCP was a class-based party to begin with, but there is no doubt that today it is well on its way to becoming an elite political party. It is highly questionable whether deepening the collusive ties

6 "Constitution of the Communist Party of China," 16th National Congress of the Communist Party of China, China Internet Information Center, November 18, 2002, http://www.china.org.cn/english/features/49109.htm.

between politics and businesses will actually strengthen the party's leadership. "If we do not crack-down on corruption, the flesh-and-blood ties between the Party and the people will suffer a lot and the Party will be in danger of losing its ruling position, or possibly heading for self-destruction."[7] These were the words of Jiang Zemin, the very man who promoted the policy.

I will explore the problems of this policy of the Three Represents in greater detail by delving into it again in the next chapter.

2. Economic Growth for the Sake of Legitimacy

The "Plan versus Market" Debate

China embarked on its policy of reform and opening up after the Third Plenum of the Eleventh Central Committee of the CCP. For some time after that, though, the Chinese economy remained mainly a planned economy based on socialist principles, and the market was regarded as playing only an auxiliary role. While special economic zones and the like were introduced between 1979 and 1980, these were initially aimed at "contact" with foreign capital and its "utilization" and were not necessarily intended as preparatory measures for extending the market economy nationwide. When large quantities of material goods and information nonetheless flowed into China from the West in the early 1980s, wary conservatives in the party aggressively launched an "anti-spiritual-pollution campaign" in the hope of eliminating "bourgeois thought."

According to prior studies, it was in the vicinity of 1984 that China acknowledged in actual words and deeds that the global economy was

---

7 "Full text of Jiang Zemin's Report at 16th Party Congress on Nov 8, 2002," Ministry of Foreign Affairs of the People's Republic of China (website), November 18, 2002, https://www.fmprc.gov.cn/mfa_eng/topics_665678/3698_665962/t18872.shtml.

largely built around capitalism.[8] This was the year in which China shifted the locus of its economic reforms from the countryside to the cities
and set about reforms of the state enterprises with the aim of granting
a large measure of autonomy. At the same time, China began to actively
introduce preferential measures for promoting foreign trade and direct
investment by declaring 14 coastal cities, including Tianjin, Shanghai,
Dalian, and Guangzhou, open to foreign capital. The retrocession of
Hong Kong to China was also decided in 1984. A domestic boom in
durable consumer goods ensued, and foreign imports of television sets,
refrigerators, washing machines, and other electrical appliances began
to surge, especially from Japan.

China thus increased its external dependence while accelerating
its opening-up policy. On the domestic front, meanwhile, it decreased
the relative weight of planning and increased that of the market. In the
latter half of the 1980s, China hammered out a Coastal Development
Strategy under General Secretary Zhao Ziyang. This aimed to establish
an export-oriented economic system by integrating the coastal economy into the world economy and gradually expanding the system to
inland areas—a flying geese model of development. Although these
developments were a retreat in socialistic terms, the CCP leadership
justified them by positioning the current stage as the "preliminary stage
of socialism" at its Thirteenth National Congress of the CCP in the
autumn of 1987.

Before long, however, a crisis erupted in China: The Tiananmen
Square Incident of 1989. The democratization of Eastern European
countries and the disbanding of the Soviet Union added further impetus to that crisis. The impact of these events on China is as I have

---

8 Mōri Kazuko, "Chūgoku to ASEAN: Saigi kara kyōryoku e" [China and ASEAN:
From Suspicion to Cooperation], in *ASEAN no 20 nen: Sono jizoku to hatten* [ASE-
AN's 20 Years: Continuity and Development], ed. Okabe Tatsumi (Tokyo: Japan
Institute of International Affairs, 1987), 149; Kobayashi Kōji, ed., *Chūgoku no sekai
ninshiki to kaihatsu senryaku: Kankei shiryōshū* [China's Perception of the World and
Development Strategy: Collection of Related Materials] (Chiba: Institute of Devel-
oping Economies, 1989), 22.

already described in the preceding pages. Western countries applied economic sanctions against China following the incident, and political unrest forced foreign enterprises to temporarily pull out of the China market. Through this series of crises, China sensed a grave challenge to maintaining the regime of the Communist Party and state. What could be done to avoid such a threat to the party and state? China's answer to this question was to earnestly learn the lessons found in the Eastern European and Soviet collapses. The conclusion that it thus drew was that the domestic microclimate, created by the influx of Western culture accompanying the advance of reform and opening up, would work in concert with the international macroclimate, comprising loud calls for democratization, to engender a crisis of the system. (This is the "peaceful evolution" discussed in the preceding chapter.) This produced vigilance in certain circles toward conventional economic management with its single-minded focus on marketization and even led some to point out the importance of planning. But the economic system that had taken shape in real life took no heed. As a result of the economic reforms of the 1980s, China's economic structure had already become heavily dependent on the international economy.

Economic Growth and Its Driving Forces

What should be done to stabilize the state and party regime? China's decision was quick: It would pursue economic growth. In other words, it chose to strive for political stability by means of economic stability. Under Deng Xiaoping's leadership, China fully expanded its marketization policy by committing itself to a socialist market economy from the time of the Southern Tour Speeches onward. In the process, Deng came to assert that planning and the market were not what distinguished between socialist and capitalist economies, but rather that any means were consistent with the cause of socialism so long as they increased the productive forces. His thinking at the time was premised on the idea of "allowing some people to become rich first" (*Xian fuqilai*)—that those capable of doing so should get wealthy first, after which the advanced regions would raise up the backward regions. The idea was presumably modeled on the flying-geese theory of development, which invokes the image of wild geese flying in a V formation.

In his Southern Tour Speeches, Deng rebuked the conservatives[9]: "Some people argue that the more foreign investment flows in and the more ventures of the three kinds [Sino-foreign equity joint ventures, Sino-foreign cooperative joint ventures, and wholly foreign-owned enterprises] are established, the more elements of capitalism will be introduced and the more capitalism will expand in China. These people lack basic knowledge." The most important condition, he concluded, was that political power lay in "our hands." The theory of the socialist market economy was born out of this thinking and was recognized as the CCP's official line at its Fourteenth National Congress in 1992. Although crowned with the stock epithet "socialism," the line was novel in that it ultimately aimed at marketization even while being premised on the leadership of the Communist Party. Having quickly sensed these changes, foreign corporations scrambled to start investing directly in China.

The foreign direct investment that China received in 1990 was roughly US$6.6 billion on a contractual basis and $3.5 billion on an actual basis. These figures rose to $58.1 billion and $11.0 billion in 1992, $111.4 billion and $27.5 billion in 1993, $82.7 billion and $33.8 billion in 1994, and $91.3 billion and $37.5 billion in 1995, thus increasing by a factor of more than 10 within a few short years. Contracted direct investment from Japanese corporations alone showed extraordinary growth, from roughly $0.46 billion in 1990 to $2.17 billion in 1992, $2.96 billion in 1993, $4.44 billion in 1994, and $7.59 billion in 1995. China's economy also grew rapidly in proportion to this. The economic (gross domestic product) growth rate rose from 3.8% in 1990 to 9.2%

---

9 Deng Xiaoping, "Bushō, Shinsen, Shukai, Shanhai nado de no danwa" [Talks at Wuchang, Shenzhen, Zhuhai, Shanghai, and Elsewhere], in *Tō Shōhei bunsen 1982–1992* (see chap. 2, n. 6), 374.

in 1991, after which China proceeded to post figures in excess of 10%: 14.2% in 1992, 13.5% in 1993, 12.6% in 1994, and 10.5% in 1995.[10]

But the latter half of the 1990s saw a deceleration of the Chinese economy. The annualized growth rate kept plunging by roughly 1% every year, from 9.6% in 1996 to 8.8% in 1997, 7.8% in 1998, and 7.1% in 1999. Behind this trend was a gradual decline in foreign direct investment. From 1996, when contracted direct investment was roughly $73.3 billion and actual direct investment was $41.7 billion, these figures steadily decreased to $51.0 billion and $45.3 billion in 1997, $52.1 billion and $45.5 billion in 1998, and $41.2 billion and $40.3 billion in 1999.[11] This decline can be attributed to a number of presumed causes, such as frequent changes in the preferential measures for foreign corporations and the negative effects of the "China threat" theory that spread globally owing to the missile exercises conducted by the Chinese military ahead of the 1996 presidential election in Taiwan. Also, not to be forgotten are the economic stagnation in neighboring regions including Hong Kong due to the 1997 Asian financial crisis and the body blow dealt by this crisis. In the case of Japan, the decrease in direct investment to China had largely to do with the widespread negative image of the China market caused by the failure of the Guangdong International Trust and Investment Corp. (GITIC), which resulted in many Japanese corporations taking on large amounts of bad loans.

While various interpretations have been made as to what drove China's economic growth in this period, the most persuasive argument is that foreign trade and foreign direct investment were the prime factors.[12] It goes without saying that reforms of the domestic economic system in areas including enterprise management, administrative

---

10 Mitsubishi Research Institute, ed., *Chūgoku jōhō handobukku* [Handbook of Information on China], 2002 edition (Tokyo: Sōsōsha, 2002), 275, 444, and 488.

11 Ibid.

12 See, for example, Yasheng Huang, *Selling China: Foreign Direct Investment during the Reform Era* (Cambridge: Cambridge University Press, 2003), and Ōhashi Hideo, *Gendai Chūgoku keizai dai 5 kan: Keizai no kokusaika* [The Contemporary Chinese Economy, vol. 5: Globalization of the Economy] (Nagoya: Nagoya University Press, 2002).

authority, and financial authority were essential preconditions. But in more pragmatic terms, the key drivers of this growth were trade with other countries, particularly exports, and direct investment by foreign capital in various forms.

Looking at trade, China's trade dependence—the proportion accounted for by foreign trade in the gross national product—surged from 12.6% in 1980 to 29.9% in 1990, 40.9% in 1995, 44.5% in 2000, and 44.7% in 2001.[13] Exports were particularly important for China's economic growth, although a closer examination of the breakdown reveals that exports by foreign-based corporations accounted for a large share; from just 16.7% in 1991, by 2002 that figure had jumped to 52.2%. The domestic taxes paid by foreign corporations were also immense, exceeding 17% of China's overall tax revenue by 2000.[14] In sum, the growth of China's economy during this period was essentially mediated by direct investment from foreign corporations, making it a typical foreign-capital-dependent economy. In that sense, it can be argued that China's development was more a case of "opening up and reform" than one of "reform and opening up." This state of affairs is precisely what spurred China to join the World Trade Organization (WTO), the epitome of the rules and conventions of the capitalist world, and is behind the emergence of "globalization" as the biggest concern of the Chinese people. Unable to substantively reform the economic system on its own, China had no choice but to pursue marketization by relying on the external pressure created by its policy of opening up.

The prospect of China's accession to the WTO stimulated foreign capital investment. Foreign direct investment, which in 2000 was roughly $62.4 billion and $40.7 billion on a contractual and actual

---

13 *Chūgoku jōhō handobukku,* 2002 edition, 424.
14 See, for example, China unit, Asia Research Department, Mizuho Research Institute, "Yushutsu, seisan, zeishū, kotei shisan tōshi, koyō ni shimeru gaishi hiritsu no suii" [Trends in the Ratios of Foreign Capital in Exports, Production, Tax Revenue, Fixed Asset Investment, and Employment] (2003), and Chi Hung Kwan, ed., *Chūgoku bijinesu to shōsha* [Chinese Business and Trading Companies] (Tokyo: Tōyō Keizai Shinpōsha, 2003), 136.

basis, respectively, rose to $69.2 billion and $46.9 billion in 2001 and to $82.8 billion and $52.7 billion in 2002. In step with these increases, China registered economic growth rates of 8.0% in 2000, 7.3% in 2001, and 8.0% in 2002, thus curbing the gradual decline in growth.[15]

The Dilemma of Balanced Development and Growth

While the world watched China's economic growth with astonishment, one issue loomed steadily larger within China: the problem of economic disparity. The country is broadly divided into Eastern China, consisting of coastal areas such as the cities of Beijing, Tianjin, Shanghai, and Guangzhou and the provinces of Liaoning, Jiangsu, and Zhejiang; Central China, including Heilongjiang, Shanxi, Anhui, and Hubei provinces; and Western China, covering interior areas such as Inner Mongolia, Sichuan and Guizhou provinces, and the autonomous regions of Tibet and Xinjiang. The eastern areas are the obvious drivers of economic growth, whereas growth in the central and western areas has been slow. While Shanghai had a per capita GDP of around 5,000 US dollars in 2003, Guizhou lagged far behind at less than 400 dollars. As this example shows, the disparity between the coastal regions of the east and the interior areas of the center and west was more than tenfold; and, far from narrowing, it was only growing wider. The idea of "allowing some people to become rich first" and the flying geese model of development that Deng Xiaoping envisioned could only take China so far.

Economic disparity was an issue that absolutely had to be overcome to achieve the ultimate political objective of preserving the unity of the People's Republic of China. China's prescription for this was the Great Western Development (*Xibu Dakaifa*) Strategy, which it formulated around 2000.[16] But the challenge lay in executing the strategy.

---

15 *Chūgoku jōhō handobukku 2002*, 275, 444, etc.
16 See, for example, Du Ping et al., *Xibu dakaifa zhanlue juece ruogan wenti* [Some Problems with the Strategy and Tactics of the Great Western Development Project] (Beijing: Central Party Literature Press, 2000), and Katō Hiroyuki, *Gendai Chūgoku keizai dai 6 kan: Chiiki no hatten* [The Contemporary Chinese Economy, vol. 6: Development of the Regions] (Nagoya: Nagoya University Press, 2003).

As financing from the National Treasury was difficult in view of the deficit-ridden state finances, there was no choice but to capitalize on market principles. And so, having joined the WTO, China began to actively attract foreign capital to its western regions. In reality, though, it was inconceivable that foreign capital would readily express interest in the west, lacking as it did the basic infrastructure for economic growth. While the Great Western Development Strategy would continue to be touted as a slogan, it had little substantive content. The Jiang Zemin government exclusively focused its concern on rapid growth centered on Shanghai, through which it hoped to ensure the growth of China as a whole. As a result, the strategy was mentioned less and less, and its priority remained low. It only reemerged as a topic of interest in Premier Zhu Rongji's "Report on the Work of the Government" at the First Session of the Tenth NPC in March 2003, his final such report during his term in office. This was in line with the intentions of the new leadership headed by Hu Jintao and Wen Jiabao, which was formed at this congress.

In his press conference on assuming office as premier, Wen Jiabao cited five items as the immediate tasks of the new government: (1) remedying the stagnation of agriculture and expanding internal demand; (2) improving the management of certain enterprises; (3) establishing unemployment countermeasures and social security; (4) rectifying imbalances and disparities; and (5) disposing of nonperforming loans. Wen further touched on the necessity of reforming the political system to eliminate corruption.[17] These remarks were a clear departure from the Jiang Zemin leadership, which had prioritized economic growth above all else. Wen's emphasis was on coordinating economic growth with balanced development by introducing social justice policies.

The question was how to go about this. As the state's bankroll was limited, it would be dangerous to mobilize any further financial resources

---

17 "Wen Jiabao zongli da zhongwai jizhe wen" [Prime Minister Wen Jiabao's Responses to Foreign Journalists], *People's Daily*, March 19, 2003.

to such ends, and the only alternative was to promote marketization. The fundamental issue was expanding internal demand. To rectify matters on the social justice front, meanwhile, there was the key issue of how to reach out to the socially vulnerable and reflect their needs in policy. It was unlikely that this could be achieved by the conventional approach of top-down measures by the party. This was why the political system had to be reformed.

These were the issues faced by the newly installed Hu Jintao administration. But they all touched on the foundations of the system, and the reforms could not be undertaken immediately. As growth depended on foreign capital, for the time being China had little choice but to continue relying on an expansion of foreign direct investment. There were of course things that China should achieve by self-help efforts, including the above-mentioned political reforms. But in that connection, and in order to win the trust of foreign corporations as well as to jump-start the domestic market, it needed above all to fundamentally transform its economic system—specifically, to establish a limited system of private property ownership. If China were to go down this path, it could even lead one day to a change in the Communist Party label. But to this day, China's private property system remains half-baked.

3. A Pragmatic Foreign Policy Line

Foreign Policy before the Tiananmen Square Incident and the End of the Cold War

China's foreign policy in the Maoist era consisted of militarization on the domestic front to prepare the country for war, based on its position that war was inevitable. Mao Zedong, perhaps owing to his views on antagonistic contradiction (*maodun*), focused on the concept of the "main enemy" and attempted to form a united front against it by setting one country or another as the chief target of opposition. The main enemy in the 1950s was the United States. In the 1960s the target shifted to the Soviet Union, and this served as the justification for Sino-American rapprochement early the next decade. From the 1970s onward, therefore, the United States and China would form a partnership around opposing the Soviet Union as their common enemy. It was essentially in the context of this US-China partnership that the normalization of Japan-China relations was achieved.

A wholesale change in this foreign policy stance took place only after Mao died in 1976 and, following a brief interregnum under Hua Guofeng, Deng Xiaoping firmly established his political hegemony at the Third Plenum of the Eleventh Central Committee of the CCP. The plenum identified the Four Modernizations as China's basic strategy, and China fully shifted its focus from revolution to the productive forces. Now keenly feeling the importance of a peaceful international environment, it softened its stance that war was inevitable and came to hold that war could be put off or even avoided. Subsequently in 1985, Deng would position peace and development as China's two largest issues.[18]

In its relations with the Soviet Union as well, China shifted direction to reconciliation from the Twelfth National Congress of the CCP in 1982. The two countries entered formal negotiations, and along with it, China came to uphold a principle of independence and autonomy in its foreign policy, wherein it would not form an alliance with any country. (Sino-Soviet reconciliation was achieved during Mikhail Gorbachev's visit to China in 1989.) China's strategy may have been to fish in troubled waters by taking an intermediate position between the United States and the Soviet Union, but in reality, China consistently took more of a pro-US stance amid the deepening conflict between these superpowers. Thanks to this, while a variety of disputes arose in US-China ties in the 1980s, relations basically remained friendly. Japan-China relations also saw a number of issues, such as those pertaining to conflicting views of history, including the content of Japanese

---

18 On the theory that war is avoidable, see Deng Xiaoping, "The Present Situation and the Tasks before Us," in *Selected Works,* vol. 2 (see chap. 1, n. 2), 315–16. On peace and development, see Deng, *Gendai Chūgoku* (see chap. 1, n. 8), 173–79.

history textbooks, and the Kōkaryō case, a dispute over ownership of a dormitory for Chinese students studying in Japan. Nonetheless, all in all, yen loans to China rose dramatically, and China's policy toward Japan was fairly moderate.

The opening-up policy advanced rapidly in tandem with progress in reforms of the domestic economic system, as exemplified by the aforementioned opening of 14 coastal cities in 1984 and the Coastal Development Strategy set forth by the Zhao Ziyang government in the late 1980s. While there was disagreement among the Chinese leadership on various matters, the truth was that pressing forward with opening up to the world was pretty much the only means of promoting economic development. Crisis befell this relatively stable foreign policy climate with the occurrence of the Tiananmen Square Incident and the end of the Cold War in 1989, followed soon after by the disbanding of the Soviet Union and other socialist regimes. As discussed earlier in this chapter, China understood this state of affairs to be the result of an interplay between the international macroclimate of democratization pressure and the domestic microclimate consisting of internal forces linked to the former. As a way of interpreting foreign pressure for democratization, moreover, it adopted a stance of opposing peaceful evolution. Peaceful evolution refers to undermining another regime by peaceful means without resorting to war or the use of arms, and this, in China's eyes, was what the United States and other Western countries were plotting against it.

Following Deng Xiaoping's Southern Tour Speeches, though, China would come to refrain from officially using the concept of peaceful evolution. Presumably behind this change was the pragmatic judgment that it could no longer resist the influx of Western cultural products and mindset brought about by marketization and exchanges with Western countries. China was now prepared to willingly accommodate peaceful evolution as long as it served to boost the productive forces. A boom in foreign investment in the China market ensued, as I have already described. In foreign affairs, China came to behave pragmatically while remaining wary at heart, and it likewise dealt in a pragmatic manner with the new democratic Russia that arose from the ashes of the Soviet Union, withholding direct criticism. These decisions were underpinned by the spirit of "concealing one's strength and biding one's time" (*taoguang yanghui*)—meaning that one who is weak should keep a low profile and build strength for the future—a mantra reportedly uttered by Deng Xiaoping upon the collapse of the Soviet Union.[19] China's newfound modesty was influenced in part by the overwhelming victory of the US-led multinational coalition forces using high-tech weaponry in the Gulf War, which was set off by the Iraqi invasion of Kuwait in August 1990.

The "China Threat" and Partnership Diplomacy

As already noted, China's economic growth following the Southern Tour Speeches was spectacular. This evoked a variety of responses regarding what China will be like in the future. In Japan as well as around the world, there was growing discussion on the topic, including arguments that effusively praised the potential of the Chinese economy and speculations about the future of the Chinese economic area centered on such regions as Hong Kong and Guangdong. Theories of China as a superpower and as a threat began to appear as well. The "China threat" soon came to be discussed as being not only economic but also military in nature, particularly after China carried out missile tests near Taiwan in the wake of Taiwanese President Lee Teng-hui's US visit to attend a reunion at Cornell University, his alma mater, in 1995 and again conducted large-scale military exercises, including missile launches, to intimidate Taiwan immediately before its March 1996 presidential election.

---

19 Zhong Xiao, "Jiang Zemin Yang Shangkun tong pi *Renmin Ribao*: Deng tichu shisi-da renshi biandong yixiang" [Jiang Zemin and Yang Shangkun Criticize *People's Daily*; Deng Presents His Intentions about Personnel Changes at the Fourteenth National Congress of the CCP], *Jingbao* (October 1991): 33–36.

When the US administration of President Bill Clinton was in-augurated, it initially tried to take a tough stance toward China on such issues as human rights. But perhaps faced with China's economic growth, in 1994 Clinton decided to sever the US renewal of China's most-favored-nation (MFN) trade status from the issue of improving Chinese human rights practices, which until then had been a condition for the former. Given the rise of the China threat theory from around that time, however, the United States was hard-pressed to devise new guidelines vis-à-vis China. While it set a new direction in its relations with Japan between 1995 and 1996 with an eye to strengthening the bilateral security treaty—the new Guidelines for Japan-US Defense Cooperation—it also began working to improve relations with China, which harbored misgivings about the scope of these guidelines. The central question was whether the United States would adopt a policy of containment or of engagement toward China; at the end of the day, the United States settled on the latter.[20]

Based on such a premise, first Jiang Zemin visited the United States in October 1997, and Clinton reciprocated the next year by visiting China from late June to early July. Despite the lengthy nine-day itinerary of his China visit, Clinton did not stop over in Japan, a key ally of the United States, prompting a number of pessimistic views among the Japanese, including that this was "Japan passing." During this visit, moreover, Clinton showed consideration for China regarding the question of Taiwan by expressly stating the "three noes": The United States does not support independence for Taiwan; does not support either "one China, one Taiwan" or "two Chinas"; and does not support Taiwan's membership in any international body comprising sovereign states as its members.

In the course of these top-level exchanges with the United States, China came to frequently use the word *partnership* (*huoban*) to char-

---

20 A useful resource about this debate is James Shinn, ed., *Weaving the Net: Conditional Engagement with China* (New York: Council on Foreign Relations Press, 1996).

acterize its diplomacy. In US-China relations, a "constructive strategic partnership" was extolled from the time of Jiang Zemin's US visit. China had already established a "strategic cooperative partnership" with Russia during President Boris Yeltsin's visit in April 1996, and it also formed a "comprehensive partnership" with France in 1997. With Japan as well, it built a "partnership of friendship and cooperation for peace and development" during Jiang's visit to Japan in November 1998, although it must be noted that the word "strategic" did not make the cut.

While the establishment of partnership relations was part of the "omnidirectional diplomacy" that China professed as a general principle, it was also a manifestation of China's view of international politics, namely "one superpower and several great powers." China assumed that the world was steadily heading toward multipolarization, even as it accepted the premise of the United States' overwhelming power. The idea, therefore, was to maintain the basic stance of "concealing one's strength and biding one's time" with respect to the United States—which China would nonetheless criticize for its "high-handed politics" without mentioning it by name—while establishing partnership relations with the remaining advanced countries that constituted the multipolar world. It goes without saying that China included itself among the multipolar powers. As we have seen above, Chinese diplomacy in this period was grounded in a pragmatic mindset premised on the existing international order. We must keep in mind, moreover, that behind it was the rapid internationalization of the Chinese economy.

In May 1999, the NATO forces "accidentally" bombed the Chinese Embassy in the Yugoslav capital of Belgrade during the Kosovo conflict, causing casualties, and this set off protests in Beijing in which students hurled rocks at the US Embassy. Friction arose in Sino-American relations, but in several months' time, a settlement had been reached on compensation for the incident. A summit meeting was held between the two countries in September 1999 on the occasion of the Asia-Pacific Economic Cooperation (APEC) Economic Leaders' Meeting in New Zealand, and bilateral negotiations over China's accession to the WTO culminated in a final agreement in November. In connection with China's WTO entry, moreover, in 2000 the US House of Representatives and Senate passed a bill to change China's MFN status, which the Congress had approved each year until then, to that of permanent normal trade relations (PNTR), leading to major strides in bilateral trade relations. Although a variety of problems existed between the United States and China at the time, all in all China remained faithful to its policy of "concealing one's strength and biding one's time."

Chinese Diplomacy after 9/11

George W. Bush assumed office as president of the United States in January 2001. In contrast to his father, George H.W. Bush, who had sought a cooperative relationship with China during his own presidency, the junior Bush adopted a tough attitude toward the country. The "strategic partnership" of the Clinton years was abandoned, and the new administration labeled China a "strategic competitor." China grew secretly alarmed as Bush came to use such expressions as "rogue nations" and "axis of evil," even though he had not publicly named China as such. It was in this context that the Hainan Island incident, involving a collision between US and Chinese aircraft, occurred in April 2001. The death of the Chinese pilot in the incident temporarily strained bilateral relations, but China, having accepted the US statement that it was "very sorry," released the entire crew of the US plane that had crash-landed on Hainan Island. In July, moreover, it returned the aircraft in dismantled form. The same month in Moscow, Beijing was chosen to host the 2008 Olympic and Paralympic Games, a decision that the United States effectively condoned by maintaining a neutral stance throughout the process.

The terrorist attacks of September 11, 2001, had the effect of instantly quelling the discord that had plagued US-China relations since the start of the Bush administration. Jiang Zemin sent a telegram of condolence to Bush in the immediate aftermath of the attacks, making explicit his anti-terrorist stance. Bush, meanwhile, attended the APEC summit held in Shanghai in October 2001, perhaps with an eye to obtaining China's cooperation—which he succeeded in doing, particularly on the anti-terrorism front. In February 2002, he visited China after making stops in Japan and South Korea and, following a series of meetings with China's top leaders, reached consensus on developing a "constructive cooperative relationship."

The landscape of international politics changed dramatically in the wake of the 9/11 terrorist attacks. About a month after the attacks, the Bush administration launched military action aimed at overthrowing the Taliban regime in Afghanistan, which had close ties with the terrorist group al-Qaeda, and within another month it had occupied the capital city of Kabul by supporting the anti-Taliban Northern Alliance. The next year saw an expanding circle of anti-terrorist solidarity centered on the United States; many central Asian countries began approaching the United States, India strengthened its military ties with the same, and even Russia became a quasi-member of NATO. In China, the government continued to do its utmost to solidify its relations with the United States on the basis of anti-terrorism, even though many regarded these US actions as a form of preemptive containment against a future China. In view of the nagging issue of Taiwan, it had to avoid turning the United States against it by any means.

In March 2003, the United States launched the Iraq War. While France, Germany, Russia, and other countries opposed the war and denounced the United States, China refrained from criticizing the country by name even as it remained cautious about the issue. After the Iraq War ended, the international focus began to shift to North Korea. Here again, instead of taking North Korea's side as it previously had, China opted for a pro-US line and came to outspokenly oppose North Korea's development of nuclear weapons. By doing so, it was further abiding by the policy of "concealing one's strength and biding one's time." Perhaps owing to this, discussions about "one superpower and several great powers" and multipolarization became infrequent in the Chinese discourse on international issues.

A similar attitude was evident in China's Japan policy. China avoided being the one to bring up the issue of discordant perceptions of history that has often plagued bilateral relations. It also did not lodge any complaints about the set of bills on contingency legislation when they passed the Japanese Diet, nor did it make any mention of the reduction in official development assistance (ODA) from the Japanese government. In response to Japan's help in dealing with the SARS (severe acute respiratory syndrome) outbreak, moreover, China's leaders spoke words of appreciation.

Around this time, China was intent on strengthening its ties with neighboring countries. It was particularly keen to conclude a free trade agreement with ASEAN, the Association of Southeast Asian Nations, and it also signed on to the Treaty of Amity and Cooperation in Southeast Asia, the basic treaty of ASEAN. Given the increasing openness of its economy, China could not hope for further growth without coordination with the international economy. As such, it was presumably seeking a way forward by building trust with Southeast Asia and thereby advancing economic integration with the region.

The linchpin of China's foreign policy is its relationship with the United States. While keeping that in mind, China has sought to strengthen its ties with its neighbors—in particular, Japan and ASEAN. This traces back to economic demands and ultimately to political demands. What informs Chinese diplomacy as described above is pragmatism based on national interests with a view to becoming a major power.

In Summary

In the fifty-plus years of absolute leadership of the CCP since the People's Republic of China was founded on October 1, 1949, three paramount leaders reigned over the party: Mao Zedong, Deng Xiaoping, and Jiang Zemin. Through the Sixteenth National Congress of the CCP in the autumn of 2002 and the First Session of the Tenth National People's Congress in the spring of 2003, the party selected Hu Jintao as its new leader. The fact that just a handful of leaders account for the PRC's history of more than half a century is astonishing in light of the number of Japanese prime ministers who have come and gone over that same period. On account of this comparison alone, it is evident that the political circumstances of China and Japan are polar opposites.

Chinese politics may appear to be stable in that respect, but the seeming stability betrays the lack of democracy. In reality, the insular political system repeatedly gave rise to political upheavals. Chinese politics has been a long chain of massive oscillations, including the anti-rightist struggle, the Great Leap Forward, people's communes, the Cultural Revolution, the coup d'état by the Gang of Four, the reform and opening-up policy, the Tiananmen Square Incident, and the declaration of the socialist market economy. Such swings have been rare in Japanese politics, which has seen a dizzying succession of top leaders. This dichotomy likely stems from differences between the two countries in how institutionalized their political systems are overall and in the ways in which these systems function.

Meanwhile, the oscillations in Chinese politics seem to be becoming smaller since the advent of reform and opening up. This partly owes to significant progress in forging consensus on basic policy directions and in establishing the systems and organizations needed for that end, whereas things were previously set in motion at the discretion of the supreme leader alone. Another major reason is that with China's internationalization in the age of globalization, international factors have come to figure greatly in domestic politics. This is evident from the extent of China's foreign dependence in its economic growth.

That said, the CCP faced increasing difficulty in managing its policies even after Hu took over its leadership. In the past, policy directives were typically implemented in a top-down manner under the unitary leadership of the Communist Party. But the pluralization of Chinese society accompanying globalization, as well as the growing magnitude and complexity of social contradictions arising from widening disparities and the like, have necessitated a finer-grained approach to policy operation. And yet no fundamental change has come to the basic structure of a political system premised on top-down party leadership since the regime's establishment, and this has allowed a flood tide of political corruption to spew forth from between the cracks. The realities of the economy and society no longer conformed with real politics. The Chinese leadership recognized the pressing need to reform the political system, including by relativizing the Communist Party, but it put such decisions off the table on account of the likelihood that they would lead the country to repeat the Soviet Union's mistake.

This left China with little alternative but to focus on economic growth for the time being, and the only means then at the disposal of China as a developing country was to attract foreign capital predicated on a policy of cooperating with other countries, particularly the United States. The defining characteristic of China's foreign policy in this period could be summed up as "concealing one's strength and biding one's time" (*taoguang yanghui*). Conversely, these words could be taken to mean that China would rear its head and reveal its strength when the time was ripe—and this indeed has gradually come to pass as the twenty-first century moves forward.

Chapter 4

The Authoritarianism of the Party-State System:
The Jiang Zemin and Hu Jintao Eras

1. Authoritarianism and Corporatism

How should we understand the Chinese political system? In the Deng Xiaoping era that began in 1978 with the introduction of the reform and opening-up policy, and in particular the 1980s, China scholars often classified the Chinese political system of the time as authoritarianism, defined as an intermediate state between the totalitarianism of the Maoist era and eventual democracy.[1] This view was grounded in the thinking of Juan J. Linz, a pioneer in the debate on totalitarian and authoritarian regimes.[2] In China as well, the concept of new authoritarianism emerged under the leadership of Zhao Ziyang in the late 1980s, giving rise to arguments holding that, while a certain degree of pluralism was permissible in such areas as the economy and culture, China should not dispense with the centralized political power, particularly in the interest of concentrating on economic growth.[3]

As the "third wave" of democratization took global hold from the end of the 1980s onward, however, a student-led movement for democracy emerged in China. Its scale far exceeded all expectations, and the eyes of the world were glued to live coverage of its denouement. This was the Tiananmen Square Incident. Insofar as the heightening of direct calls for democracy was concerned, the student movement in China preceded perestroika in the Soviet Union. When that movement ultimately ended in tragedy with military suppression from above on

---

1 See, for example, Michel Oksenberg and Richard Bush, "China's Political Evolution: 1972–1982," *Problems of Communism* (September–October 1982); Elizabeth J. Perry, "China in 1992: An Experiment in Neo-Authoritarianism," *Asian Survey* 33, no. 1 (January 1993); and Jie Chen and Peng Deng, *China since the Cultural Revolution: From Totalitarianism to Authoritarianism* (Westport, CN: Praeger, 1995). When viewed as a one-party dictatorship whose goal is economic growth, such a political system can also be called a "developmental dictatorship."

2 Juan J. Linz, "Totalitarian and Authoritarian Regimes," in *Handbook of Political Science*, vol. 3: *Macropolitical Theory*, eds. Fred I. Greenstein and Nelson W. Polsby (Reading, MA: Addison-Wesley, 1975), 175–411.

3 Liu Jun and Li Lin, eds., *Xin quanwei zhuyi: Dui gaige lilun gangling de lunzheng* [The New Authoritarianism: A Debate about the Political Reform Guideline] (Beijing: Beijing Economics Institute Press, 1989).

June 4, 1989, the world denounced the Beijing government en masse, and China quickly found itself isolated. The psychological effect that the vivid images of these events in China had on the rising tide of pro-democracy demonstrations in the Soviet Union and Eastern Europe and on the political leaders faced with these movements is a question that merits further close examination. In other words, how did the memory of the Tiananmen Square Incident affect Soviet and Eastern European powers in the lead-up to the fall of the Berlin Wall and the end of the Cold War?

After the Tiananmen Square Incident, the discourse surrounding the Chinese political system underwent great change. One exemplar of this was an argument grounded in the framework of state-society theory predicting the flowering of civil society and the potential for protest in China; the idea had begun to draw the attention of American China scholars from the early 1980s.[4] Inspired by the achievement of democracy in the Soviet Union and Eastern Europe and by the theory of civil society that underlay it, this approach emerged from the wishful thinking that China's communist regime, too, would meet the same fate in due course. It was an extrapolation—and a hope—based on the facts that China had a communist regime founded on essentially the same Leninism as that of the Soviet Union and Eastern Europe and that a large-scale pro-democracy movement had actually arisen in China. But it was a subjective desire, not necessarily one in line with the reality of China.

The changes anticipated by the theory of civil society did not come to the Chinese political system in the 1990s. To the contrary, China officially endorsed as its paramount goal a market economy

---

4 See, for example, Laurence Sullivan, "The Emergence of Civil Society in China: Spring 1989," in *The Chinese People's Movement: Perspectives on Spring 1989*, ed. Tony Saich (Armonk, NY and London: M.E. Sharpe, 1990); David Strand, "Protest in Beijing: Civil Society and Public Sphere in China," *Problems of Communism* (May–June 1990); Thomas Gold, "Resurgence of Civil Society in China," *Journal of Democracy* (Winter 1990); and Martin K. Whyte, "Urban China: A Civil Society in the Making?," in *State and Society in China: The Consequences of Reform*, ed. Arthur Lewis Rosenbaum (Boulder, CO: Westview Press, 1992).

118

based on a bold policy of reform and opening up. It thus plunged headlong into a period of economic growth, and issues regarding the political system all but ceased to be discussed. That turning point came with Deng Xiaoping's 1992 Southern Tour Speeches and the declaration of a socialist market economy based on them. According to Deng, planning and the market were not what separated socialism from capitalism; rather, any policy to expand the market was acceptable as long as it served to enhance productivity. The minimum criteria for a system to be socialist were twofold: the preservation of a public ownership system in basic property rights, on the one hand, and the leadership of the Chinese Communist Party, on the other. This implied a market economy under CCP leadership and a strengthening of the party's role. These measures were motivated by the lessons that China drew from the collapse of the Soviet Union, which had stemmed from the failure of the economic policies and weakening of party leadership there.

The CCP's calculations were right on target—or at least they were until the mid-1990s, when China was achieving exponential economic growth. Moreover, market economics and the Communist Party, two elements that had been regarded as being in fundamental conflict, appeared on the surface to mesh with one another. Given this reality, the Chinese political system remained stubbornly unchanged, and academic discourse shifted away from the theory of civil society toward a new theory: corporatism. No hard-and-fast definition has been offered for the term *corporatism*, even from the leading figures in this debate. According to one such expert, Philippe C. Schmitter, a system built on corporatism comprises an established set of systemic characteristics, wherein the state recognizes the foundation and maintenance of interest associations, which gain representation in their respective occupational fields in exchange for tolerating a certain degree of state involvement in the selection of internal leadership and in their activities.[5]

---

5 Philippe C. Schmitter, "Still a Century of Corporatism," in *Trends toward Corporatist Intermediation*, eds. Philippe C. Schmitter and Gerhard Lehmbruch (London and Beverly Hills: Sage Publications, 1979).

This theory further classifies corporatism into two main types: state or authoritarian corporatism, which is proactively created from above by a fascist regime or a state, and societal corporatism or corporatism from below, in which interest representatives also play key roles. The latter is observed in the advanced countries of today and is commonly called neo-corporatism. While the Japanese political scientist Mōri Kazuko has argued for the possibility that the Chinese political system had advanced beyond the former to become a kind of neo-corporatism,[6] the mainstream view in China studies regards the Chinese system as an instance of state or authoritarian corporatism.[7] But China's case may be more accurately described as "party-state corporatism," being based on the principle of integration between the Communist Party and the state—the party-state system.

The corporatism debate first emerged as an extension of research in state-society theory. As scholars investigated and analyzed the society side of the equation, the question arose of why Chinese society would actively exhibit "deference" to the state. This question was a response to expectations being betrayed by such realities as the limits of local autonomy in central-local relations and the dominance of party-affiliated candidates in the direct elections of village chiefs in rural areas. Examples of this can be found in the works of Jean C. Oi, who introduced the concept of local state corporatism in examining rural governance[8]; Anita Chan, who analyzed labor unions in the Deng Xiaoping era[9];

---

6 Mōri Kazuko, "Chūgoku no seiji taisei no hen'yō: Tō Shōhei jidai no imi" [Transformation of the Chinese Political System: The Meaning of the Deng Xiaoping Era], in *Gendai Chūgoku ron 2: Kaikaku, kaihō jidai no Chūgoku* [Theory of Contemporary China, vol. 2: China in the Era of Reform and Opening Up], eds. Okabe Tatsumi and Mōri Kazuko (Tokyo: Japan Institute of International Affairs, 1987), 26–32.

7 On the Chinese political system and corporatism theory, see Kojima Kazuko, "Kokka to shakai no aida" [Between State and Society], in *Chūgoku seiji to Higashi Ajia* [Chinese Politics and East Asia], ed. Kokubun Ryosei (Tokyo: Keio University Press, 2004), 129–47.

8 Jean Oi, "Fiscal Reform and the Economic Foundations of Local State Corporatism in China," *World Politics* 45, no.1 (October 1992), and Oi, *Rural China Takes Off: Institutional Foundations of Economic Reform* (Berkeley: University of California Press, 1999).

9 Anita Chan, "Revolution or Corporatism? Workers and Trade Unions in Post-Mao China," *The Australian Journal of Chinese Affairs*, no. 29 (January 1993).

Jonathan Unger and Anita Chan, who focused on the Chinese People's Political Consultative Conference, a united front organization[10]; Kristen Parris, who studied private entrepreneurs[11]; and Edward X. Gu, who took a comprehensive look at various mass organizations.[12]

Wakabayashi Masahiro and Bruce J. Dickson each analyzed the course of democratization in Taiwan.[13] According to them, from the start of the 1970s the strongman Chiang Ching-kuo, who was the leader of the ruling Kuomintang party, aimed at the party's Taiwanization by aggressively promoting the appointment of Taiwanese individuals to ameliorate the problem of minority rule by the so-called *waishengren* (mainlanders who fled to the island following the Kuomintang's defeat in the Chinese Civil War of the late 1940s and their descendants). This, they argue, paved the way for Taiwan's departure from a Leninist political system and its subsequent democratization. Although the case of Taiwan differs from that of China in terms of history and ethnicity, a parallel can nonetheless be drawn with the path that China is now beginning to follow.

It is doubtful, though, whether corporatism alone can explain everything about the Chinese political system at the start of the twenty-first century. The concept came to the fore in the academic world at a time when China entered a phase of economic growth under the socialist market economy and the political regime palpably stabilized. That said, changes in Chinese reality are far more rapid than those in theory. A wave of globalization (*quanqiuhua*) swept over China, and

---

10 Jonathan Unger and Anita Chan, "Corporatism in China: A Developmental State in an East Asian Context," in *China after Socialism: In the Footsteps of Eastern Europe or East Asia?*, eds. Barrett McCormick and Jonathan Unger (Armonk, NY: M.E. Sharpe, 1995).

11 Kristen Parris, "Private Entrepreneurs as Citizens: From Leninism to Corporatism," *China Information*, no. 10 (Winter 1995–Spring 1996).

12 Edward X. Gu, "State Corporatism and Civil Society," in *Reform, Legitimacy and Dilemmas: China's Politics and Society*, eds. Wang Gungwu and Zheng Yongnian (Singapore: Singapore University Press, 2000).

13 Wakabayashi Masahiro, *Taiwan: Bunretsu kokka to minshuka* [Taiwan: A Divided Nation and Democratization] (Tokyo: Tokyo University Press, 1992), introduction, chaps. 5–6; and Bruce J. Dickson, *Democratization in China and Taiwan: The Adaptability of Leninist Parties* (New York: Oxford University Press, 1997).

the theory of the socialist market economy is fast becoming insufficient to account for the speed of marketization that has accompanied it.

What implications has this trend toward globalization had for the overall system in China, and for its political system in particular? And what has its impact been on theorization in the academic sphere? In this chapter, I would like to address these questions in the context of China's response to globalization, as exemplified by its accession to the World Trade Organization (WTO) and the "Three Represents" (*Sange Daibiao*), a theory proposed under the Jiang Zemin regime at around the same time.

2. Globalization and Systemic Transformation

Globalization was the most discussed theme in various fields in China as the twenty-first century arrived. This was particularly the case after China began seriously eyeing WTO membership and hastily embarked on the preparations needed for accession. Chinese people at every level and in every occupation—from senior party cadres to junior ones, from peasants to workers, from intellectuals to students—all expressed strong interest in the phenomenon of globalization and the international organization known as the WTO. This was because both offered the prospect of altering China from its very foundations.

The forerunner of the WTO was GATT, or the General Agreement on Tariffs and Trade. GATT laid down the fundamental rules for trade based on mutual recognition of the principles of free trade in the post-World War II capitalist world. The WTO was born in 1995 by evolving GATT into a more systematized form. It is distinct from other international organizations in one major respect: once a country becomes a member, it has no choice but to change its domestic economic system in accordance with WTO rules. In other words, the country must recast its economic system in conformity with market mechanisms as prescribed by the WTO. And fully setting up a market economy requires that the murky aspects of the existing system—including the economy, taxation, commercial practices, basic property rights, and intellectual property rights—be rendered more transparent. Herein is why questions about globalization in China were debated in direct connection with the issue of WTO accession. For China, as a country that adhered to socialism as its national policy, participating in an international regime founded on capitalism would necessitate modifications to a significant portion of its system.

In December 2001, China achieved its long-sought goal of joining the WTO. Taking its trade relations with the United States as an example, the two countries subsequently agreed to lower the average tariff rate on mining and industrial products from 24.6% to 9.4% by 2005; the average tariff rate on major agricultural products from 31.5% to 14.5%; and the tariffs on automobiles, which were between 80% and 100% at the time, to 25% by 2006. It was also decided that foreign banks and securities firms would be allowed to conduct domestic currency business with Chinese corporations starting two years after accession and with Chinese individuals in five years. In the telecommunications business, meanwhile, the cap on foreign ownership was set at 49% at the time of accession and raised to 50% two years later, and foreign firms were allowed to have shares in Chinese Internet service providers. China decided to permit foreign stakes of up to 50% in life insurance—a cap that would be further relaxed by 2005—as well as to immediately allow 100% foreign ownership of non-life insurance companies.[14] These were large concessions for China at the time, and they came with major implications in that the country could be forced to transform its regime.

As a WTO member state, China would be increasingly subject to the direct effects of the international economic system as it opened its economy to overseas trade and investment. On the other hand, this

14 Mitsubishi Research Institute, ed., *Chūgoku jōhō handobukku* [Handbook of Information on China], 2000 edition (Tokyo: Sōsōsha, 2000), chaps. 7–8.

implied better access to overseas markets for China's inexpensive but decent quality products. This would give an added boost to products that already enjoyed global success, such as textiles, while enhancing China's export capabilities in regard to machinery and home appliances—an area in which China was fast catching up technologically—as well as other basic industrial goods. The upshot of all this would be interdependence between the Chinese economy and the world economy, which would in turn foster economic cooperation but also increase the likelihood of economic conflict.

Why, then, was China in such a rush to join the WTO? The answer to that question lay in the state of its economic development. The Chinese economy saw pronounced growth in the first half of the 1990s (14.2% in 1992 and 10.5% in 1995), particularly after China officially set out to become a de facto market economy following Deng Xiaoping's Southern Tour Speeches of 1992 and the ensuing declaration of a socialist market economy. This growth was driven above all else by the dramatic increases in trade and foreign direct investment. In the latter half of the decade, by contrast, the economy slowed down (9.6% growth in 1996 and 7.1% in 1999). While this was due in part to the Asian financial crisis that began in 1997, the chief cause was a related plunge in foreign direct investment. The contractual value of foreign direct investment in China increased from approximately US$6.6 billion for 7,273 projects in 1990 to $111.4 billion for 83,437 projects in 1993, then slipped to $41.2 billion for 16,918 projects in 1999.[15]

China's trade dependence as a proportion of GDP, which was 29.8% in 1990, had risen to 43.9% by 2000. In other words, roughly half of China's economic growth relied on trade, on top of which foreign-owned enterprises were responsible for more than 50% of Chinese exports. Moreover, close to 20% of overall state tax revenues came from

---

15 *Chūgoku jōhō handobukku*, 2001 edition, 343 (on economic growth) and 506 (on direct investment).

taxes paid by foreign firms.[16] The initial stage of economic growth in China was thus heavily dependent on foreign capital, chiefly in the form of direct investment. It was precisely for this reason that China's central leadership wanted to leverage the external pressure wrought by WTO accession to add momentum to its opening-up policy, thereby bringing about further marketization of the economy and, with it, economic vitalization. In short, as I noted in Chapter 3, the reality was more of "opening up and reform" than of "reform and opening up." Although Jiang Zemin was in power at the time, Premier Zhu Rongji was the one at the forefront of promoting this policy. Zhu reportedly bore the brunt of criticism from state-owned enterprises, which would be threatened by the changes, and old-guard conservatives in the CCP, who were behind the former and were averse to the sudden reform.

Looking back over the centuries, China has long had a strong fondness and bent for Sinocentrism; it has been extremely wary of the infiltration of foreign influences and strongly inclined to eliminate them. The reforms by the reformists of the late Qing dynasty were an attempt to introduce Western science and technology purely as a means of modernizing the state while adhering to the spirit and values of Chinese tradition, as is summed up in the slogan, "Chinese learning as substance, Western learning for application" (*Zhongti Xiyong*). In essence, they amounted to reform within the system. But before long, the science and technology that were brought in as a means to an end would arouse people's interest in the Western values and spirit underlying them, and an alarmed Qing government eventually scrapped the reformist policies themselves.

Similarly, while today's socialist China has been following a modernization line under the slogan of "reform and opening up" since 1978, it is evident that Western science and technology were largely viewed as a means of complementing the all-important socialist system. In the

16 Hosokawa Mihoko, "WTO ni kamei shita Chūgoku keizai no genjō" [Current State of the Chinese Economy at China's Accession to the WTO], *International Finance*, no. 1078 (January 1, 2002): 68–69.

1980s, based on the policy of putting planning first and making the market subordinate to it, the Chinese government was clearly thinking of reform within the system premised on the continuation of a socialist system. In the wake of the Tiananmen Square Incident and Soviet dissolution of 1989, though, it began to recognize the limits of sticking to a planning-centered approach, and in 1992 it adopted a socialist market economy and launched a set of economic policies that unambiguously focused on a market economy—albeit one that was premised on the socialist system. Socialism in this case referred to two principles: the maintenance of public ownership and the guidance of the Communist Party. But the series of decisions and actions seen in the course of China's accession to the WTO contained the seeds of conflict even with these principles. Moreover, there was a high likelihood that the very act of reforming the domestic system by virtue of external pressure would erode the values and spirit that defined China.

Karl Marx advanced the proposition that the economic base, or substructure, effects change in the superstructure, politics included. In China, too, it was at first believed that converting the economy into a socialist form based on collectivism would inevitably result in the socialist transformation of the sociopolitical superstructure. Mao Zedong rejected this view and insisted that influences flow from the ideopolitical superstructure to the base. Accordingly, he devoted his efforts to political and ideological struggle, as seen in the Cultural Revolution based on the theory of uninterrupted revolution (*buduan geming*). But ultimately, the superstructure failed to change the base, and Mao's fight proved fruitless. In the subsequent Deng Xiaoping era, the effects of the rapid spate of economic reforms soon trickled down into politics and society, and the changes in the economic system—the base—began to exert an effect on the superstructure. On this score, Marx's understanding was correct.

This gave rise to the issue of state power and the political system supporting it. What would be a political system that is consistent with a transition to market economics? The market mechanism requires a small government. Theoretically speaking, to promote competition in the economy and ensure the transparency of economic information, the same principles of competition and information transparency are essentially expected in the political system as well. But the CCP could not simplistically accept this; in the interest of preserving the PRC regime, it could not allow the current one-party rule to give way to a multiparty system. Due to this dilemma, the principles of corporatism appealed to CCP leaders as an attractive model. The idea was for the Communist Party to maintain its power by co-opting the increasingly diverse interests, thus making itself the supreme interest-coordinating organ. This is much the same course as the one taken by Taiwan in the past.

The root theme here was the Communist Party. China had no choice but to push forward with marketization through WTO accession. Serious intervention in the market by the party would generate friction on various fronts, and administrative departments—if not the party itself—would most certainly be downsized, leading China toward a "small government." The CCP was able to skirt downsizing in this process thanks to the lessons derived from the Soviet collapse. But if the party were to become bloated and repeatedly engage in political intervention, the road to full-fledged marketization would be endangered. Given China's dependence on foreign capital for its growth, creating a stable market economy was a must. The question ultimately came down to where to locate the raison d'être of the CCP, giving rise to the urgent need for debates about the orientation of the Communist Party, which are central to thinking about the Chinese political system.[17] It was against this backdrop that Jiang Zemin proposed the theory of the Three Represents. In doing so, he was preparing the theoretical ground for party-state corporatism.

---

17 Bruce J. Dickson, "Cooptation and Corporatism in China: The Logic of Party Adaptation," *Political Science Quarterly* 115, no. 4 (Winter 2000–2001).

3. The Three Represents

Since China adopted the policy of reform and opening up, the composition of China's social strata has changed to some extent. There are, among others, entrepreneurs and technical personnel employed by scientific and technical enterprises of the non-public sector, managerial and technical staff employed by foreign-funded enterprises, the self-employed, private entrepreneurs, employees in intermediaries and free-lance professionals. Moreover, many people frequently move from one ownership, sector or place to another, changing their jobs or capacity from time to time. This trend of developments will continue. Under the guidance of the Party's line, principles and policies, most of these people in the new social strata have contributed to the development of productive forces and other undertakings in the socialist society through honest labor and work or lawful business operations. They join workers, farmers, intellectuals, cadres and PLA officers and men in an effort to build socialism with Chinese characteristics.[18]

The above comes from a speech given by General Secretary Jiang Zemin at a meeting held on July 1, 2001, to celebrate the eightieth anniversary of the CCP's founding. Jiang publicly acknowledged that even private entrepreneurs could join the party, reflecting the rapid expansion of the private sector accompanying the advance of marketization in inverse proportion to the shrinking role of the public sector in economic management. This signified that the CCP had effectively started to move away from its previous standing as a class-based political party. Owing to the number of individuals who embarked on entrepreneurial careers while retaining their party membership, the CCP had long had many members who were in essence private entrepreneurs. But the decision

---

18 Jiang Zemin, "Speech at the Meeting Celebrating the 80th Anniversary of the Founding of the Communist Party of China," China Internet Information Center, http://www.china.org.cn/e-speech/a.htm.

here was new insofar as Jiang approved the admission of emerging private entrepreneurs.

Given that private ownership has yet to be fully recognized, these individuals are "private entrepreneurs" who are only responsible for management, rather than "capitalists" who own private property. But partial acceptance of private ownership including that of land may be a matter of time, and this question is the focus of great interest. Should that happen, the CCP would cease to be a communist party as described by Marx, potentially necessitating a change in the party's name. These changes, then, can be viewed as a portent of the CCP's metamorphosis into a bourgeois party. This development can indeed be regarded as a process of establishing "state corporatism" or "authoritarian corporatism," wherein the CCP attempts to stabilize the political system by co-opting the burgeoning social elites into the power structure in response to the spread of a trend toward pluralism, as observed in the emergence of new social classes such as private entrepreneurs. But another problem lurked in the shadows. Private entrepreneurs actually joining the party were few and did not pose much of a problem in terms of their number; the bigger problem was that, of the many party cadres retiring into positions in state-owned enterprises or going back and forth between the party and business, some were using their power to reap huge profits and become wealthy. These individuals were enjoying a "bourgeois" lifestyle even while remaining Communist Party members, and the problem remained of how to classify this "new class," a concept which was presented by a Yugoslav communist politician Milovan Djilas in the 1950s, that had arisen inside the party.[19]

How did the CCP account theoretically for these real-life changes? From the early days of 2000, its leader Jiang Zemin came to propose the Three Represents. It started with a speech during an inspection visit that Jiang made to Guangdong Province, in a manner reminiscent of Deng Xiaoping's 1992 Southern Tour Speeches.

---

19 Milovan Djilas, *The New Class: An Analysis of the Communist System* (New York: Harcourt Brace Jovanovich, 1957).

An important conclusion can be reached from reviewing our Party's history over the past 70-odd years; that is, the reason our Party enjoys the people's support is that throughout the historical periods of revolution, construction and reform, it has always represented the development trend of China's advanced productive forces, the orientation of China's advanced culture, and the fundamental interests of the overwhelming majority of the Chinese people. With the formulation of the correct line, principles and policies, the Party has untiringly worked for the fundamental interests of the country and the people.[20]

In essence, the CCP represented three things: the forces of production, the culture, and the people. Although this formulation may not seem remarkable, there was a hidden intent behind it. Of the three elements, the most important was the people; while traditional Marxist-Leninist doctrine would assert that the communist party represents a specific class, namely the workers (the proletariat), in Jiang's speech this was subtly replaced by the broader and more ambiguous concept of the "people." Underlying this is the intent to theoretically shed the party's identity as a class party. By including under the capacious rubric of the "people" the party cadres who were building up immense wealth in the guise of private entrepreneurs, the CCP's mainstream faction led by Jiang Zemin aimed to ensure the cadres' standing as party members.[21]

This can be interpreted as part of China's theoretical preparations for its fundamental transition to market economics ahead of the globalization of its market, including WTO accession. But the move received considerable criticism from old-guard conservatives, given that it could also be seen as a stepping-stone to the capitalist transformation of the system. As numerous cases of political corruption within the party

---

20 "Three Represents," *China Daily* (online) (see chap. 3, n. 5).
21 Nishimura Shigeo and Kokubun Ryosei, *Sōsho Chūgoku-teki mondaigun 1: Tō to kokka—Seiji taisei no kiseki* [Collected Essays on Issues in China 1: Party and State—The Trajectory of the Political System] (Tokyo: Iwanami Shoten, 2009), 198–99.

were exposed around this time, moreover, the conservatives are said to have been simmering with fierce criticism toward the CCP's wording that it represented the "people." Examples of their criticisms include the assertion in the journal *Zhenli de zhuiqiu* (Pursuing the Truth), published by the Chinese Academy of Social Sciences, that allowing private entrepreneurs to join the CCP based on the Three Represents would eventually turn the CCP into a bourgeois party; and the lead essay that appeared in the July 2001 issue of *Zhongliu* (Middle Class), a journal affiliated with the *Guangming Daily*, arguing that private entrepreneurs are not the class basis of the party. But both publications were shut down in the summer of 2001 prior to the Sixth Plenum of the Fifteenth Central Committee of the CCP, and the series of moves from the Three Represents allowing private entrepreneurs to join the party began to yield the intended results.[22]

"The steadfast implementation of the Three Represents constitutes the foundation of our Party, the cornerstone for its governance and the source of its strength," Jiang Zemin said in a speech at the Party School of the Central Committee of the Communist Party of China on May 31, 2002. "The Three Represents is a powerful theoretical tool for strengthening and improving Party building and promoting the self-improvement and development of China's socialist system."[23] The Three Represents was thereby officially established as China's guiding theory, laying the theoretical groundwork for a Chinese version of state corporatism. This was officially articulated at the Sixteenth National Congress of the CCP, held from November 8 to 14, 2002. In his final report as party general secretary, Jiang stated that the theory of the Three

---

22 For more about these circumstances, see Ōe Shinobu, "Kō Takumin Sōshoki, saigo no tōsō: "Mittsu no daihyō" ron to Chūgoku Kyōsantō taikai" [The Final Struggle of General Secretary Jiang Zemin: The Theory of the "Three Represents" and the National Congress of the Communist Party of China], *Chōken Quarterly*, no. 3 (March 2002): 16.

23 "Jiang Zemin zai Zhongyang dangxiao shengbuji ganbu jinxiuban biye dianli shang de jianghua" [Jiang Zemin's Speech at the Graduation Ceremony of the Party School of the Communist Party of China Central Committee], *People's Daily*, June 1, 2002. English translation quoted from "Three Represents," *China Daily* (online).

Represents was a "continuation and development of Marxism-Leninism, Mao Zedong Thought and Deng Xiaoping Theory" and that it was the "crystallization of the Party's collective wisdom and a guiding ideology the Party must follow for a long time to come."[24] Although he stopped short of crowning the Three Represents with his own name, Jiang was in effect substantiating his authority by according such a high status to the theory.

In the amended Constitution of the CCP that was adopted at its Sixteenth National Congress, the Three Represents was positioned alongside Marxism-Leninism, Mao Zedong Thought, and Deng Xiaoping Theory as the party's "guide to action."[25] Accordingly, the Constitution stated at the start of its General Program that "the Communist Party of China is the vanguard both of the Chinese working class and of the Chinese people and the Chinese nation" and further stipulated that "any Chinese worker, farmer, member of the armed forces, intellectual or any advanced element of other social strata who has reached the age of eighteen" was qualified for party membership. Needless to say, these changes to the provisions were based on the CCP's stance of permitting the admittance into the party of the new social elite, including private entrepreneurs, and the self-enrichment of current party cadres.

4. Problems of the Political System

Having experienced the Tiananmen Square Incident in 1989 and witnessed the subsequent dissolution of the Soviet Union, China was extremely circumspect about straightforward political reforms. All in all, almost no noteworthy political reforms were undertaken from that

---

24 "Jiang Zemin's Report," Ministry of Foreign Affairs of China (website) (see chap. 3, n. 7).
25 "Full Text of Constitution of the Communist Party of China," China Internet Information Center, November 18, 2002, http://www.china.org.cn/archive/2002-11/19/content_1049193.htm.

time forward, other than the progress evidenced by, for example, direct elections of rural village chiefs. Even the election of village chiefs, which initially attracted considerable attention, has since ceased to inspire much hope as something that might lead directly to democracy. The CCP has instead focused on validating the legitimacy of its political rule by promoting economic growth and has essentially shelved reform of the political system proper. From the latter half of the 1980s, China set out to separate party and government functions. But when this ended up undermining the party organization and the Tiananmen Square Incident and Soviet collapse took place, the CCP eliminated all political reforms that presented any risk of enfeebling the party's leadership, particularly any idea or endeavor oriented toward separation of party and government. The upshot was the implementation of a market economy premised on Communist Party leadership—that is, under the party-state system.

Why are political reforms necessary in China? One reason is the problem of deep political corruption. The tens of thousands of corruption cases that are exposed in China every year are in a sense an unwelcome consequence of the socialist market economy—a market economy based on CCP leadership, and one where the party institutionally intervenes in economic management as the supreme authority holding the ultimate power to grant permissions. In short, economic corruption is an unavoidable corollary of the CCP-led market economy. The issue at stake is the political mechanism for exposing such corruption. Under a political system that does not fully allow freedom of speech and expression, the only means ultimately available is to place one's hopes in purification from above. The CCP has set up Commissions for Discipline Inspection at each level, but the absence of external checks has kept self-purification from functioning effectively. Most notably, even if it is possible to extirpate small-scale corruption to a certain extent, mutual deterrence makes it difficult to expose the worst offenders at the top of the system. With official endorsement of the Three Represents, moreover, party cadres who have amassed enormous wealth outside the market system through state-owned enterprises and the like have been guaranteed their continued standing and membership in the party. This in effect provides even greater institutional protection to the mechanisms that generate corruption.

Another reason why political reform is needed has to do with the expansion of economic disparity in China. Under Chinese-style party-state corporatism, the private entrepreneurs and others who comprise the new elite stratum that has arisen in the course of marketization will likely make it their top priority to maintain the existing regime, having become an increasingly powerful bloc of vested interests as a result of their "co-optation" into a cozy alliance with the CCP. The traditional party cadres, meanwhile, will become more and more wealthy. But one question remains unanswered—and a truly ironic one at that for the Communist Party: Who will represent the interests of those on the margins who are coming to be written off in the face of globalization, particularly the workers and peasants, once the heroes of Chinese society?

The root principle of socialism is the fair distribution of wealth. Marxist theory seeks to prevent the emergence of classes by socializing the means of production, such as land and capital. In real Chinese society, however, inequality is steadily increasing. The wealthy coastal regions stand in stark contrast to the backward areas in China's interior, particularly the impoverished villages scattered across the countryside, and within the cities are virtual slums packed with the "floating population" that has poured in from rural areas. Disparities are on the rise that may be more accurately described as being between classes rather than between strata. "Winners" and "losers" exist side by side even among the urban population, and the differentiation between these groups is also progressing.

Rectifying this uneven distribution of wealth falls on the shoulders of government. In the days when the CCP devoted its efforts to even distribution, it strove to balance things out by redistributing the surplus of the richer parts of China to the poorer ones. But today the wealthy regions are only concerned with their own development, while the poor regions seek aid from the central government. Individual regions, being exposed to the principles of competition under the slogan of globalization, cannot much afford to be considerate of others. Meanwhile the Communist Party, which should be providing political leadership, lacks adequate financial resources itself and is only enriching the coffers of individual cadres. It simply pins its hopes on economic revitalization via growth that relies on the injection of foreign capital and on fixed asset investments that are made without regard to the asset bubble. If this growth model goes unrealized, the marginalized masses will face further marginalization in the future. In fact, disputes and protests by marginalized peasants and workers have become incessant in China, and residents crying out in resistance against the threat of eviction are also on the rise.

Perhaps in the light of this state of affairs, calls for greater attention to the plight of peasants and rural areas soon began to be heard. The report on government activities by Premier Zhu Rongji at the Fifth Session of the Ninth NPC in the spring of 2002 focused significantly on discussing agricultural problems. Agricultural problems had been brought up frequently in China prior to that, but they had never been resolved. The reason for this also relates to problems regarding the political system. Back in the revolutionary era, the majority of the CCP leadership were individuals of rural origin whose families remained in the countryside; they thus had direct ties to rural society and maintained clear interests there. But the situation has since changed, so that today almost all the main leaders reside in large cities, and their families are based in the cities as well. While these leaders may have seen or heard about the poverty of rural areas, they have no direct stake in the matter. Despite the existence of grassroots-level elections, the lack of elections at a level where the peasantry's voice can directly reach the central government largely precludes the emergence of rural-based politicians who represent the interests of peasants on the national level.

In the final analysis, the crux of political reform in China is reform of the CCP itself. But that is no simple task, given the huge vested interests of party members that come into play. The inflation of the CCP's role in a market economy system undergoing globalization is a political deformation. What is needed is an ongoing effort to relativize the party's role as the economic reforms advance. To that end, it is important first and foremost to realize democracy within the party. The procedure for electing leaders in the party needs to be institutionalized so that they can be elected based on clear-cut rules, thus bringing transparency to the process. Also, important in the light of the party's ability to keep its house in order is the question of how to uncover corruption based on institutionalized rules and monitoring from outside the party. For a time, some young researchers in China were vocal about this point, but this has failed to grow into a widespread chorus.[26]

It is true that, in Taiwan and elsewhere, state or authoritarian corporatism served in some respects as a transitional stage on the way to democracy. China may be seeking to move in just such a direction; as can be seen in the theory of the Three Represents, the CCP is aiming to stabilize its governance by co-optation into the party of private entrepreneurs, who are on the verge of forming an interest group as the new Chinese elite. But a major pitfall awaits here given the premise of homogenous development, which is vital to the integrity of the huge country that is China. That pitfall is the question of how to provide relief to the workers and peasants who make up the overwhelming majority of the population and incorporate them into the regime. No effective solution has yet been found.

A social survey later compiled by the Chinese Academy of Social Sciences attracted the attention of China scholars around the world. By investigating actual conditions, it revealed that Chinese society was coming to show clear signs of stratification into an upper stratum comprising party and state officials, business managers, private entrepreneurs, experts, and technocrats and a lower stratum composed of industrial workers, peasants, and the unemployed.[27] The facts presented

---

26 See, for example, Lin Shangli, *Dangnei minzhu: Zhongguo Gongchandang de lilun yu shijian* [Intraparty Democracy: The Theory and Practice of the Chinese Communist Party] (Shanghai: Shanghai Academy of Social Sciences Press, 2002), which discusses the need for intraparty democracy.

27 See Lu Xueyi, ed., *Dangdai Zhongguo shehui jieceng yanjiu baogao* [Research Report about Social Classes in Contemporary China] (Beijing: Social Sciences Academic Press, 2002).

above would appear to indicate that the path of Chinese-style party-state corporatism is not a smooth one.

In Summary

Jiang Zemin later retired from politics, and the CCP's leadership shifted to Hu Jintao's team. The growth-at-all-costs policy of the Jiang Zemin era needed to be revised, and the new leadership came to advocate the "Scientific Outlook on Development" (*Kexue fazhanguan*), which stressed the "construction of a harmonious society" (*hexie shehui jianshe*), with an eye on the problems of disparity and inequality. As if to suggest that the previous outlook on development had been unscientific, "harmony" (*hexie*)—a concept calling for balanced development—became the word of the hour. With the transfer of central power from Jiang to Hu, mentions of the Three Represents in CCP documents decreased, and in its stead "Scientific Outlook on Development" and "harmony" came to appear regularly. Nonetheless, the fact remains that the Three Represents had joined Marxism-Leninism, Mao Zedong Thought, and Deng Xiaoping Theory as one of the CCP's orthodox teachings in various official documents.

Chinese realities failed to change. Private entrepreneurs joined the Communist Party, and, more significantly, the existing party cadres became even wealthier than before through state-owned enterprises. As a consequence of these developments, the CCP strengthened its reign as an elite party sustaining this stratum of vested interests.[28] China revised its constitution in 2004, taking the first step toward a capitalist

---

28 Two outstanding studies have been published about the increasing corporatism of the CCP and the transformation of its nature: Bruce J. Dickson, *Wealth into Power: The Communist Party's Embrace of China's Private Sector* (Cambridge and New York: Cambridge University Press, 2008), and David Shambaugh, *China's Communist Party: Atrophy and Adaptation* (Washington, DC and Berkeley, CA: Woodrow Wilson Center Press and University of California Press, 2008). While employing different methodologies, both discuss the difficulties involved in shifting away from the CCP's one-party system.

system in theory as well as in practice by officially acknowledging the protection of private property rights. In 2007, it set out to flesh out its definition of private property rights by adopting the Property Law. In reality, though, there has been no end to the protests of peasants and workers whose various rights have been violated in the face of the government's top-down system, and neither have these protests diminished in size or number. This has led to the oft-heard quip, "What China needs is a real communist party."

When the Hu Jintao era began, the CCP seemed willing enough to reform itself, as evidenced by the "Decision about the Strengthening of Construction of the Party's Ruling Ability," adopted at the Fourth Plenum of its Sixteenth Central Committee held in September 2004. This decision was epochal in that the party essentially admitted that there were problems in its "ruling ability." At the root of these problems was a loosening of the CCP's organization and ideology. To be sure, corruption cases involving senior party cadres were often exposed and punished following adoption of the decision. But these were just the tip of the iceberg and, more often than not, no more than instances of political opponents outing one another in the tug-of-war for power.

Over time, the CCP further strengthened its presence as the bastion of vested interests and normalized political corruption. What served to institutionalize and legitimize this were the socialist market economy, the Three Represents, and the preservation of political power by way of half-baked marketization—in short, Chinese-style party-state corporatism. In that respect, the Hu Jintao leadership's argument for the "construction of a harmonious society" was logically sound as a political ideal. But as the disparity and rift between the vested interests and the general public intensified, so too did the former's tendency to set itself apart from the latter. Rectifying the unequal income distribution calls for the introduction and enforcement of a rigorous tax system for redistributing the wealth that is largely concentrated in the hands of the vested interests, including personal income taxes, progressive taxation, and inheritance taxes. This implies reform of the political system rather than just that of the economic system. The Chinese, including those in intellectual circles, were aware of the need for such reform. But there was no way that the stratum enjoying vested interests would relinquish access to the information and networks tied to those interests. Moreover, many Chinese intellectuals are themselves looking to benefit from the same interests. This status quo is guaranteed by the coercive power of the military and public security apparatus.

China should be moving toward a political system that benefits not just a narrow range of vested interests but a broad spectrum of people—the so-called *laobaixing*, or common people. In other words, it should be heading toward democracy. Even within China, everyone says as much, the leaders included. But the usual narrative is that this is something to be achieved not now but gradually as a future objective. The bottom line is that there are no signs of any major change in the Chinese political system.

Chapter 5

The Xi Jinping System and the Cultural Revolution:
Continuities and Discontinuities

1. History and Politics

In contemporary China, history is politics. In 2015, a major campaign to commemorate the seventieth anniversary of China's victory in the Anti-Japanese War (Second Sino-Japanese War) was held throughout the year. The ostentatious military parade on September 3 was particularly memorable; China seemed to be asserting its dignity and legitimacy as a state by demonstrating a clean break with the weak China of the past. It was in February 2014 that the date for commemorating victory in the war was decided out of the blue. In other words, only in the sixty-ninth year did China officially choose September 3 as a national day of commemoration. Why was this day suddenly established after all these years? The decision was made on February 27, 2014, by the Standing Committee of the NPC, the chairman of which was Zhang Dejiang, the third most powerful leader in the Chinese Communist Party. A graduate of Kim Il-sung University in North Korea, Zhang is known as a key figure in the Jiang Zemin faction. Although he rarely attracts much attention, he has played a pivotal role in many crucial decisions.

When it was decided that only candidates who reflected Beijing's intentions would be allowed to run for Hong Kong chief executive in the 2017 election, local students reacted by launching large-scale demonstrations from September to December 2014. This youthful rebellion in a city that had been thought to be politically apathetic has become known as the Umbrella Movement. The decision regarding the election process was made on August 31, 2014, about a month before the protests, by the NPC Standing Committee chaired by Zhang.

Xi Jinping did not attend either of these meetings, as he held no official position in the NPC. While the fact remains that Xi consequently approved both decisions by the committee ex post facto, the extent of his involvement in the actual decisions is uncertain. Xi's personal network and political approach differ from those of Zhang Dejiang. In terms of policy, a case in point is the concept of "governing the country according to the law" (*yifa zhiguo*), or law-based governance. Law-based governance is the job of the NPC, a legislative body. But as far as can be gleaned from official records, Zhang Dejiang has rarely mentioned this concept touted by Xi Jinping. A closer examination of Zhang's statements reveals that at times he ignores it, while at others he gives it a low priority.

When Xi speaks of law-based governance, it is in connection with the anti-corruption struggle, implying that even CCP cadres may be subject to investigation. This makes it possible to administer justice to the party by means of the law. Under this reasoning, Xi ousted Bo Xilai, the candidate backed by the Jiang Zemin faction, before becoming supreme leader. Similarly, after assuming the post, he proceeded to crush Zhou Yongkang, who controlled the public security and resources sectors, as well as Xu Caihou and Guo Boxiong, who held sway over the armed forces. Intense power struggles were thus waged during the transition of power from Hu Jintao to Xi Jinping.

Jiang Zemin and others intent on maintaining the regime and protecting their vested interests responded to these developments by stressing the leadership of the Communist Party and its advantages over the law. Zhang Dejiang was presumably among those who shared this thinking. The importance of party leadership translated to the importance of studying the CCP's historical legitimacy, which in turn meant studying the Anti-Japanese War. The party's vested interest groups have entrenched themselves broadly and deeply in the system by way of the state-owned enterprises. Although Xi Jinping and Wang Qishan, secretary of the Central Commission for Discipline Inspection of the Communist Party of China, have together waged war on corruption, they remain unable to lay a hand on the innermost core of the party leadership, including the retired party elders. Even if a handful of the retired party elders who remain at the apex of the military and public security organs were to be eliminated, the vested interests infesting the massive CCP apparatus would just quietly stand their ground and wait for the storm to pass. The Central Publicity Department of the Communist Party of China Central Committee under Liu Yunshan, a member of the Politburo Standing Committee of the Communist Party of China over whom the influence of the Jiang Zemin faction remains strong, has persistently publicized the importance of party leadership and the Anti-Japanese War.

In sum, the decision about the day for commemorating victory in the Anti-Japanese War was part of a larger power struggle. The legitimacy of political authority should ideally be a guarantee of affluent and peaceful lives for the people. But in China, where popular elections do not exist, legitimacy continues to be placed more on the past than on the present for reasons between rulers. Ultimately Xi Jinping, too, showed a positive attitude toward the day for commemorating the Anti-Japanese War and the military parade, making him not much different from the vested interests. These days, in fact Xi seems to be leaning toward stressing party leadership rather than law-based governance. Economic instability and other factors in recent years have rendered it impossible for the time being to ensure affluence and peace for the people as a hallmark of the legitimacy of government, and Xi evidently has had no choice but to reach a certain level of compromise with the vested interests. Its contemporary efficacy aside, the day for commemorating the Anti-Japanese War was about using nationalism as a force to create cohesion among the populace.

It was Jiang Zemin who originally advocated the Anti-Japanese War as the grounds for the legitimacy of the CCP's power. An attempt is evident therein to interpret and use history in a political or arbitrary manner. In May 1995 China was invited to ceremonies held in Russia commemorating the fiftieth anniversary of victory in the Anti-Fascist War, and Jiang attended as the then supreme leader. But the government that ruled over China in 1945 was actually that of the Republic of China led by Chiang Kai-shek, not the People's Republic of China under Mao Zedong which was established in 1949. Strictly speaking, the PRC is not among the victors of World War II. For that matter, it was the Soviet Union that won in the war and not Russia, which did not exist in 1945.

In the mid-1990s, even as China achieved economic growth, the large-scale introduction of a market economy had led to growing indifference to the CCP and socialism. After returning from Russia, therefore, Jiang set out to establish PRC's status as a World War II victor by claiming that the CCP had been the prime mover in the Anti-Japanese War and replacing the study of patriotism that had been started the year before with the study of the war. Restrictions were imposed on the broadcast of Japanese films and television series, which had been popular in China until then; and the Chinese media, be it television, newspapers, or magazines, was inundated with content related to the Anti-Japanese War. At the same time, memorial halls for commemorating the war were set up across the country. Needless to say, an accurate examination of the historical facts tells us that while CCP forces—primary among them the Eighth Route Army (*Balujun*)—did indeed fight the Japanese during the war, the Chinese military consisted mainly of forces of the Kuomintang and not the CCP. "History" in today's China basically refers to the Anti-Japanese War. Although I do not deny the fact of Japan's invasion of China before World War II, its treatment in contemporary China is unduly one-sided and political. The Anti-Japanese War is but a part of history, not all of it.

In contemporary China, one cannot speak freely about history, not even that of the PRC. This is because there are simply too many dark chapters in the history of the CCP since the PRC's founding that do not fit in with the narrative of the legitimacy of the party's power. Unsurprisingly, the period that is considered most off-limits in discussions of PRC history is the Cultural Revolution. The year 2016 marked the fiftieth anniversary of the start of this movement as well as the fortieth anniversary of its end. Chinese research on the Cultural Revolution appears to be faltering year by year, and almost nothing is taught about the subject in school education from the primary to higher levels. Because research is impossible, it has likewise been impossible to establish various facts about the Cultural Revolution; the establishment of the facts is being avoided in the interest of stability within and without the party. The principals may have all retired by now, given that a good half century has passed, but this avoidance of the subject may be understandable in the light of the fact that those who were both enemies and allies during the revolution were working in the same workplaces until just recently.

"Do not provoke any trouble" (*Buyao re yishensao*) is an oft-used phrase among the Chinese public today regarding the subject of the Cultural Revolution, the idea being to solve the problem by ignoring it. One must wonder what Xi Jinping truly thinks about the whole matter, given that his father, erstwhile vice premier Xi Zhongxun, was among the CCP cadres who suffered the most during the revolution, causing much tribulation on the part of the son. The official history of the CCP regarding the Cultural Revolution is the "Resolution on Certain Questions in the History of Our Party Since the Founding of the People's Republic of China," adopted in 1981. Although more than three decades have passed since its adoption, China remains unable to diverge even slightly from the assessment made in it, as if in a state of paralysis. The resolution describes the Cultural Revolution as an upheaval that was "initiated by a leader labouring under a misapprehension and capitalized on by counter-revolutionary cliques, led to domestic turmoil and brought catastrophe to the Party, the state and the whole people" and concludes that "chief responsibility for the grave 'Left' error of the 'cultural revolution,' an error comprehensive in magnitude and protracted in duration, does indeed lie with Comrade Mao Zedong."[1] The interpretation is that while the responsibility for launching the movement lies with Mao Zedong, things were worsened due to misuse of the same by Lin Biao and Jiang Qing. By positioning this as Mao's "mistakes in his later years," the resolution left a path to preserving his status as the founding father of the PRC. Completely renouncing Mao's legacy would have been tantamount to denying the PRC itself. In short, the Cultural Revolution has not been passed down

1 *Beijing Review* 24, no. 27 (July 6, 1981): 22, 23, and 35.

in the memory of young Chinese today. Although Chinese people in their fifties had a passing experience of the revolution and may remember something of it, only those 65 years and older can recall firsthand its most tumultuous period, which occurred in the first three years. Xi Jinping, who was born in 1953, no doubt witnessed in his youth the way in which his father, Xi Zhongxun, was viciously attacked.

Today, when even the Tiananmen Square Incident of 1989 has all but faded into oblivion, it seems as though the memory of the Cultural Revolution is barely hanging on by a thread. Most of those who recall it—whether they were the attackers or the attacked or, in some cases, both—have submerged their respective nightmares in the depths of their memories. The instant that this Pandora's box is opened, every conceivable resentment and fear might be let loose. Many commentators note that China has changed greatly due to reform and opening up, and it is true that many things have been transformed. But it is inconceivable that the Chinese mentality depicted in Lu Xun's "The True Story of Ah Q" will ever fully vanish into the mists of history.

Before turning to an analysis of the Xi Jinping regime, the main subject of this chapter, I would like to offer my own perspective on the Cultural Revolution. This is in order to make clear that while there certainly have been momentous changes in China's economy and society in the 40–50 years since, the essence of the political system has not changed by much.

2. The Essence of the Cultural Revolution: The Disquietude and Power of a Dictator

The Cultural Revolution was essentially a power struggle, at the root of which lay the impatience of the aging Mao Zedong. Nothing captures the essence of the revolution more accurately than the title of a 1967 book on the subject by the late Muramatsu Ei, a Japanese expert on Chinese literature: *Mō Takutō no shōryo to kodoku* (The Disquietude and

Solitude of Mao Zedong). Mao was 72 years old when he launched the Cultural Revolution. It was an expression of the impatience of a lonely dictator who feared what would become of China after his death—a manifestation of his concerns about the future of the PRC, a state that he had founded, and in particular that of the Chinese Communist Party and socialism, as well as about how his successors would evaluate him after his passing. These concerns stemmed from witnessing the free economic policies that were launched as adjustment policies following the Great Leap Forward by such successors as Liu Shaoqi and Deng Xiaoping, whom he himself had appointed. Mao was also disturbed by the trend toward breaking away from the collective economy, which emerged as a consequence of those policies, and the passive stance of Liu and Deng and the like toward the socialist education movement (*Siqing yundong*) that he had launched in an effort to rectify that trend. The heart of the CCP's power ultimately boiled down to the Organization Department of the Central Committee, responsible for the party's personnel affairs; the People's Liberation Army, which is in effect the party's military; the police and public security organs; and the Central Publicity Department, which oversees the media. This picture remains basically unchanged today.

Mao, who retired from the front lines in the early 1960s, had by then given control of the party organization to Liu Shaoqi and Deng Xiaoping. His subsequent efforts to seize power thus focused first on the army. After Peng Dehuai's 1959 dismissal Mao had appointed Lin Biao, his right-hand man, to succeed Peng as defense minister. Under Lin, the PLA extensively implemented such campaigns as learning Mao Zedong's political thought and learning from Lei Feng. This helped minimize the repercussions of the failure of the Great Leap Forward and the aforementioned Peng Dehuai incident, as well as fostering loyalty to Mao Zedong and his thought.

In December 1965, prior to the Cultural Revolution, Lin Biao and others successfully made a motion at an enlarged meeting of the Standing Committee of the Politburo, chaired by Mao Zedong, to dismiss Chief of General Staff of the Central Military Commission Luo Ruiqing from office on the grounds that he had disobeyed the party's politically oriented policy.[2] Luo had consistently held top posts in public or state security ever since the PRC's founding until he was appointed chief of general staff in 1959 on the heels of the Peng incident. As such, his dismissal additionally served as a bid for control of the political and legal affairs departments, where his influence was strong. The public security apparatus is key to seizing power, given the amount of personal information it holds about cadres. In this connection Yang Shangkun, who had been director of the CCP Central Committee's General Office since the PRC's founding, and who served concurrently as secretary-general of the Central Military Commission, was also removed from office for eavesdropping on Mao and other top party leaders.[3]

The final center of CCP power is the propaganda apparatus. The struggles in this department hold the key to answering the question of why the Great Proletarian Cultural Revolution was a "revolution" of "culture." At the start of the 1960s, satirical essays about the Great Leap Forward and Mao Zedong in forms drawn from classics and legends appeared on the Beijing literary scene. These included Deng Tuo's *Yanshan yehua* (Evening Talks at Yanshan), which was serialized in the newspaper *Beijing Wanbao*, and the *Sanjiacun zhaji* (Three Family Village Essays) series by Deng Tuo, Wu Han, and Liao Mosha, which was published in the journal *Qianxian* (Front Line). Given that these individuals were all officials in Beijing, it appeared, at least to Mao, that their literary activities were being protected by Lu Dingyi, the head of the Publicity Department of the CPC Central Committee, and Peng

---

2 Fan Tianshun and Zhao Bo, eds., *Zhongguo Gongchandang zuzhi gongzuo dashiji* [Chronicles of Events in the Organizational Work of the Chinese Communist Party] (Beijing: China Radio International Press, 1991), 182.

3 Party History and Party Building Research and Teaching Group, PLA National Defence University, "Guanyu Lu Dingyi tongzhi he Yang Shangkun tongzhi cuowu wenti shuoming" [Explanation about the Problems and Errors of Comrade Lu Dingyi and Comrade Yang Shangkun], in *"Wenhua Dageming" yanjiu ziliao* [Research Materials on the "Cultural Revolution"], vol. 1 (Beijing: National Defence University, 1998), 24–25.

Zhen, the mayor of Beijing. It was against this backdrop that Jiang Qing, Mao's wife, emerged on the political stage and began to loudly insist that art and literature should serve politics.

Soon there arose the problem of *Hai Rui baguan* (Hai Rui Dismissed from Office), a play written by Wu Han, the deputy mayor of Beijing. Wu, a dramatist of Beijing Opera, had originally written articles about Hai Rui, an incorruptible official of the Ming dynasty, partly at the suggestion of Mao Zedong. According to Seto Hiroshi, Wu himself had no particular political intentions in taking up Hai Rui, but Mao would eventually come to criticize him in the course of launching the Cultural Revolution. This was because Mao interpreted the story of Hai Rui, who had been fired for speaking frankly to the emperor, as ridicule over the incident involving his own dismissal of Peng Dehuai at the Lushan Conference.[4] This surfaced in the form of Yao Wenyuan's November 1965 essay titled "On the New Historical Beijing Opera *Hai Rui Dismissed from Office*." The essay is said to have fired the opening shots of the Cultural Revolution, as it attacked Peng Zhen by striking at Wu—and, by doing so, brought the higher-up Liu Shaoqi into target range. This was the moment when it became evident that the Cultural Revolution was in fact a political revolution.

The Cultural Revolution is generally thought to have begun at the Eleventh Plenum of the Eighth Central Committee of the CCP, held in August 1966. A decision comprising 16 articles regarding the revolution was issued at the meeting, thus clarifying its aim. This aim, as stipulated in the decision, was to "overthrow those persons in authority who are taking the capitalist road" and thereby institute a

---

4 Seto Hiroshi, "Go Kan to *Kai Zui hikan*: *Kai Zui hikan* no shippitsu ito" [Wu Han and *Hai Rui Dismissed from Office*: Intentions behind the Composition of *Hai Rui Dismissed from Office*], in *Gendai Chūgoku bunka no shinsō kōzō* [The Deep Structure of Contemporary Chinese Culture], ed. Ishikawa Yoshihiro (Kyoto: Institute for Research in Humanities, Kyoto University, 2015). "Mao Zedong sixiang wansui 4" [Long Live Mao Zedong Thought 4] (November 1967), an internal document in the author's possession, makes note of the direct orders of Mao Zedong, who interpreted Wu Han's *Hai Rui Dismissed from Office* as being a satire of the Peng Dehuai incident (252).

power mechanism based on a "system of general elections, like that of the Paris Commune."[5] The same Eleventh Plenum demoted Liu Shaoqi from number two to number eight in the party. Liu had already been deprived of actual power by this time, thanks to Mao's careful preparations for the power struggle, as described above. He would go on to be repeatedly denounced at mass meetings, be stripped of his party membership as a "traitor" at the Twelfth Plenum of the Eighth Central Committee of the CCP in October 1968, and meet an untimely death in Kaifeng, Henan Province, in November 1969. When viewed narrowly as a power struggle aimed at ousting Liu Shaoqi, the Cultural Revolution had achieved its aim as soon as it had started.

The Cultural Revolution could just as well have ended at the Eleventh Plenum with Liu's demotion. But instead it took off from this time forward, as a movement initiated by the Red Guards (*Hongweibing*), which mobilized young students, to destroy the organizations of the party and the state. There were two reasons for this development. The first is that when Mao Zedong imagined the future of China after his own death, the isolated dictator was increasingly concerned about the ideologies not only of the top leadership of the party but also of the central and local cadres who were running the party, state, and government, as well as of the young Chinese who would become the next generation of leaders. "Each person must be ready with successors," Mao said on June 16, 1964, regarding the cultivation of successors for cadres and the youth. "One must have three lines of successors. One must have one, two, and three pairs of hands, and one must not be fearful of heavy storms."[6] The second reason is that Mao dared to draw

---

5 Mōri Kazuko and Kokubun Ryosei, eds., *Genten Chūgoku gendaishi dai 1 kan: Seiji (jō)* [Contemporary Chinese History Based on Original Texts, vol. 1: Politics (Book 1)] (Tokyo: Iwanami Shoten, 1994), 256–57. English translation quoted from "Decision of the Central Committee of the Chinese Communist Party Concerning the Great Proletarian Cultural Revolution," *Peking Review* 9, no. 33 (August 12, 1966).
6 Mao Zedong, "Talk on Putting Military Affairs Work into Full Effect and Cultivating Successors to the Revolution (June 16, 1964)," in *Selected Works of Mao Tse-Tung*, vol. 9, available at https://www.marxists.org/reference/archive/mao/selected-works/volume-9/mswv9_21.htm.

on violent destruction by the students as a means of dealing a blow to the party and state institutions, which remained unscathed despite his seizing power in the army, public security, and propaganda organs. Seen in a different light, this goes to show that not even Mao held absolute power at the time of the revolution's launch.

The Cultural Revolution plunged into further turmoil from this point on. The policy decisions of the top leadership went astray, and the movement made its way into the venues of everyday life without clearly defined ideals and objectives. Although the youth-led Red Guards were initially caught up in the fervour of the Cultural Revolution, they soon lapsed into anarchy dominated by destruction, violence, and decadence. Worker organizations across China underwent internal confrontations and divisions, and the workers had little choice but to sacrifice others for their own preservation. The People's Liberation Army, which intervened to suppress the chaos, also experienced internal rifts in many parts of the country and frequently found itself pitted against worker organizations. Power within the party fell into a state of confusion as well. First Lin Biao, the military leader who had been appointed Mao's successor, fell from power in 1971. Premier Zhou Enlai, who worked hard to settle the chaos, and the recently rehabilitated Deng Xiaoping then became the targets of relentless attacks from the Gang of Four led by Jiang Qing. These attacks would only end with the death of Mao Zedong in 1976. All this was the consequence of a political system devoid of rules and institutions, dominated by personal rule.

3. The Xi Jinping Regime Examined

Today China has grown into an economic giant with the world's second largest GDP, and in the United Nations it enjoys great influence as a permanent member of the Security Council. China's new clout is based on the massive changes that have come over its economy and society since it introduced the reform and opening-up policy. Put another way, it is the fruit of the Deng Xiaoping line, which set out to marketize the Chinese economy while maintaining the premises of long-term economic growth and socialism. China still regards itself as a developing country, but who would agree with this, given that the country is now known as the workshop of the world and engages enthusiastically in foreign aid and foreign direct investment? To be sure, its per capita GDP remains low by global standards, and China still has aspects that justify classifying it among developing countries. If we supposed that just 10 percent of China's total population of roughly 1.4 billion enjoys a decent standard of living, though, that is enough for a nation with a population equal to Japan's to suddenly pop up in East Asia.

Despite this growth, the Chinese political system remains insular and outdated and has not changed at its foundations since the time of the Cultural Revolution. As I have noted in the preceding chapters, the political system may have actually been more open in the 1980s and 1990s than it is today. At present, China under the Xi Jinping regime is trying to strengthen the dictatorship of the Chinese Communist Party, elevating the importance of Marxism as a state doctrine and suppressing democratic activists. China is always justifying its conduct in its official explanations to the outside world, while it continues to pursue military expansion by building one beachhead after another in the South China Sea and to enlarge its sphere of influence by making a fait accompli of its presence in the East China Sea. It is doubtful that this mercantile attitude on China's part, whether on the domestic or international front, is a show of true strength.

In October 2016, the CCP held the Sixth Plenum of its Eighteenth Central Committee. A serious sense of crisis was expressed at this meeting regarding the corruption in the party. Xi Jinping's remarks are reported as follows:

> Xi noted the questionable faith and loyalty of some Party members, including senior ones. He cited a number of faults among such members, including: lax discipline, detachment from the

people, arbitrariness and inaction, acts of individualism, faction-alism, money worshipping and violations linked to formalism, bureaucracy, hedonism and extravagance. Nepotism and election fraud have endured while some Party officials sold positions of power and bartered positions, Xi said, adding that power abuse, corruption as well as legal and disciplinary violations have been spreading. In particular, a handful of senior Party officials, over-come by their political cravings and lust for power, have resorted to political conspiracies by working with ostensible obedience, while forming cliques to pursue selfish interests.[7]

While it is remarkable that Xi told the stark truth with such brutal hon-esty, the CCP that he describes hardly holds the semblance of a political party. Xi's assessment of the state of the Communist Party is shocking. If this were an era in which ongoing economic growth is guaranteed, problems like the above might be somehow manageable. But that is not the case, which means that the Deng Xiaoping line is no longer effec-tive. Economic growth was palpable from the Deng Xiaoping era up until the time of Jiang Zemin and Hu Jintao. Even while suppressing political democratization, the CCP was still able to convince the Chi-nese citizenry of the legitimacy of its rule. But if growth is sluggish and yet political democratization is also impermissible, how can the party possibly demonstrate its legitimacy in the absence of elections? There appears to be no means other than strengthening domestic controls and flaunting China's superpower status to the world.

The Sixth Plenum is said to have been significant in that it accord-ed Xi the status of "core" (*hexin*) of the CCP. The title of "core" was not to be conferred on Hu Jintao, who was instead referenced by the phrase "the party center with Comrade Hu Jintao as general secretary." This was an attempt by Jiang Zemin and his faction to dilute Hu's authority and thereby realize a collective leadership system as well as

---

7 "Xi Spells Out Party Codes on Stricter Governance," Xinhua, November 3, 2016, available at http://en.people.cn/n3/2016/1103/c90000-9136484.html.

preserving the faction's vested interests and influence. Being aware of this, Xi Jinping launched an intense power struggle from the outset aimed at smashing the Jiang Zemin faction. Specifically, he attacked Bo Xilai, who presumably had his sights set on controlling the propaganda apparatus, and his wife; overthrew Zhou Yongkang, the big boss in the public security departments and of state-owned enterprises in energy and other areas; and exposed corruption by Xu Caihou and Guo Boxiong, who held sway over the armed forces. These strikes on the organizational system stylistically echo the struggle launched by Mao Zedong at the start of the Cultural Revolution. This is not surprising, as these organs comprise the very locus of the Communist Party's power.

It is highly likely that these ferocious power struggles were undertaken in coordination with the Hu Jintao faction, given that the party's top leadership included some of the faction's members, namely Li Keqiang as premier, Li Yuanchao as vice president, and Wang Yang as vice premier. These leaders are known as part of the Youth League (*Gongqingtuan*) faction (*tuanpai*), which suggests that the Communist Youth League of China held some degree of control over the CCP organization. Accordingly, Xi Jinping appears to have gradually entered into a power struggle with the Communist Youth League in the course of dealing crippling blows to the Jiang Zemin faction, as was evident in recent efforts to marginalize Li Keqiang.

Mao Zedong gained control of the propaganda, public security, and military apparatuses during the Cultural Revolution but was ultimately unable to seize power in the party apparatus led by Liu Shaoqi and his allies. Mao therefore set out to destroy the party apparatus itself, which he attempted by means of the Red Guard Movement. How, then, might Xi Jinping be intending to take over the party organization? Mobilizing the Red Guards is of course no longer an option, as we are now living in a very different era. I cannot help but think that Xi has launched his fierce anti-corruption campaign as the means for winning control of the party organization. Everything is for the sake of gaining power.

Were that not the case, Xi would probably not be able to accomplish anything as the supreme leader. The questions are how he will go about continuing to exercise power and how that power will be transferred with an eye toward the post-Xi era. In China, where there is no such thing as election by the people and no rules or system for determining the supreme leader, that tug-of-war is fought in the dark.

4. The Present Day and the Cultural Revolution: The Tragedy of Succession without Rules

As to how many people were victimized during the Cultural Revolution, the Chinese government has given no official numbers. Many estimates have been offered to date. At an enlarged Politburo meeting that followed the First Plenum of the Twelfth Central Committee of the CCP in September 1982, Ye Jianying, then chairman of the Standing Committee of the NPC, gave an account citing specific figures. According to him, there were approximately 123,700 deaths due to large-scale violence; 2.5 million cadres were persecuted, of whom 115,500 persons died unnatural deaths; 4.8 million city dwellers from various quarters were attacked, of whom 683,000 died unnatural deaths; 2.5 million persons in rural areas, primarily those who had been landlords or rich peasants, died unnatural deaths; 113 million persons were subject to political attacks of varying severity; and the whereabouts of 557,000 persons is unknown.[8] While these numbers have not been verified, they come to a total of approximately 3.42 million dead and 557,000 missing. If we add those who suffered physical or psychological injury, the total number of victims is beyond imagining.

As I have repeatedly noted in this chapter, there are too many things about the Cultural Revolution that remain unknown, not least the number

---

8 Jin Zhong, "Zuixin ban, Wenge sizhe renshu" [The Latest Version of the Death Toll of the Cultural Revolution], *Kaifang* [Open Magazine], October 2012.

of victims. The PRC's secrecy in the name of party unity with regard to facts that touch on the finer points of its history, including the Cultural Revolution, will probably remain unchanged. Although many Chinese researchers of modern history have likely already collected a wealth of material—oral and otherwise—on the subject, it is impossible to publish these domestically under the present circumstances. If a major falsification were found of just a single fact in China's official account to date, that alone could radically alter the big picture of contemporary history. What future could there be for a political entity that is incapable of objectively reflecting on its own path?

Around 2009, 60 years since the establishment of the PRC, many attempts were made to comment on the significance of the first three decades from 1949 until the advent of reform and opening up and the second three decades from 1979 onward, as well as on the relationship between these two periods. The key figure in this was Zhu Jiamu, who was then vice president of the Chinese Academy of Social Sciences and director of the Institute of Contemporary China Studies. Zhu argued that these two eras were continuous and did not contradict each other.[9] According to him, although the first three decades saw some chaos from a certain point in the Cultural Revolution onward due to Mao Zedong's personal dictatorship and the leftist inclination of the Gang of Four, China was not off the mark in its overall construction of a socialist society. The policy of reform and opening up in the latter three decades was based on that foundation and experience, Zhu maintained, and thus the two periods were continuous. In addition to this argument, there were many others along the lines that it was only after the failure of the Cultural Revolution that the social basis for reform and opening up was created—or to phrase it differently, that there would have been no reform and opening-up policy if there had

---

9 Zhu Jiamu, "Xin Zhongguo liangge 30 nian yu Zhongguo tese shehuizhuyi daolu" [The Two 30-Year Periods and Socialism with Chinese Characteristics], *Zhongguo Gongchandang xinwen wang* [News Network of the Chinese Communist Party], October 23, 2009.

been no Cultural Revolution.[10]

Although this assertion may seem to have some truth in it, there is a serious pitfall: the questions remain of why the errors of the Cultural Revolution were not rectified at an early stage and whether systemic checks were firmly established after it so that similar mistakes might never be repeated. The answers to these questions are certainly not written in the aforementioned resolution on CCP history, nor are they to be found in the many discussions of these subjects including those by Chinese politicians and academics. Everything is explained away in the context of Mao Zedong's personal dictatorship and the machinations of Lin Biao and the Gang of Four, and no sincere efforts have been made to search within the Chinese political system for the root cause of these problems. It is as if to say that the CCP's history always progresses dialectically in a defect-free manner. And from there arises the obsessive preoccupation with a bygone legitimacy predicated on China's modern history, particularly the Anti-Japanese War, in which the CCP reversed a long history of Chinese humiliation. This rigid stance remains unchanged even today.

In a separate study, I examined the nature of the Cultural Revolution from five different angles: Mao Zedong Thought, power struggles, policy conflicts, social contradictions, and international factors.[11] As I have repeatedly pointed out, though, the Cultural Revolution was essentially one big power struggle. While social contradictions became evident as well, these were due to major disruptions triggered by the

---

10 Wang Haiguang, "Shilun 'Wenhua Dageming' de fasheng yu Zhongguo gaige de yuanqi" [An Essay on the Occurrence of the "Cultural Revolution" and Origins of the Chinese Revolution], in *Dangshi yanjiu yu jiaoxue 2* [Party History and Teaching] (1989), vol. 2, reprinted in *Fuying baokan ziliao: Zhongguo xiandai shi* [Reprints of Newspapers and Journals: Chinese Contemporary History] (Information Center of Social Sciences, Renmin University of China) 9 (1989).

11 Kokubun Ryosei, "Chūgoku no shakaishugi to bunka daikakumei" [Chinese Socialism and the Cultural Revolution], *Iwanami kōza Higashi Ajia kingendai tsūshi 8: Betonamu sensō no jidai—1960–1975 nen* [Iwanami Lectures on East Asian Modern and Contemporary History, vol. 8: The Era of the Vietnam War, 1960–75], eds. Wada Haruki et al. (Tokyo: Iwanami Shoten, 2011).

instability of authority. At the heart of the power struggles was the issue of who would succeed Mao Zedong. Mao had chosen Liu Shaoqi, Deng Xiaoping, and others as his successors in the 1950s and stepped back from the front lines since 1959. But upon seeing the policies and attitudes of those to whom he had supposedly entrusted power, he became deeply mistrustful and launched the Cultural Revolution. During the Cultural Revolution, Mao chose Lin Biao as the next successor and went so far as to stipulate this in the party constitution. No sooner had he done so, though, his suspicions about Lin began to grow. Seeing the odds stacked against him, Lin reportedly attempted a coup d'état with his family and confidants in the military but failed and died while fleeing China. The aged Mao, whose judgment was impaired by this time, then chose Hua Guofeng as his final successor and passed away shortly thereafter. But Hua suffered from a weak power base, and Deng Xiaoping's rehabilitation and rise in power soon forced him to withdraw from the political scene.

As noted above, the Cultural Revolution was a process of successor selection by Mao Zedong, which ultimately failed at every step of the way. And those whose lives were tossed around and victimized by it were ordinary Chinese people. After Mao's death, Deng Xiaoping took over the helm of Chinese politics. Deng did not seek many posts other than chairman of the Central Military Commission, the locus of political power. Reflecting on Mao's dictatorial tendencies, Deng abolished lifetime tenure and replaced it with fixed terms of office; the state chairman (*guojia zhuxi*: the official English translation of which was changed to "president" in 1982) could serve up to two five-year terms. Deng also repented Mao's tyrannical ways and abolished the post of chairman of the CCP, establishing the general secretary as the highest post in the party. He did not stipulate a term of office for this, though, instead making it a practice to have the general secretary double as state chairman and serve a maximum of two terms, the same as the latter post. While these measures were noteworthy new developments in the long history of China, the custom was continued whereby the authority to designate the next successor is entrusted to the most influential or powerful individual.

Deng Xiaoping first named Hu Yaobang as his successor. But Hu's liberalism and bold reform policies soon incurred the hostility of conservative party elders, and he fell from grace in January 1987, a move that Deng consented. Deng next selected Zhao Ziyang as his successor, but Zhao also became isolated due to his support for the 1989 student movement and lost power in the course of the Tiananmen Square Incident. In the wake of the incident, Deng endorsed and promoted a proposal to make Jiang Zemin as his successor. He even decided who the next leader after Jiang would be, as if to take a page from the imperial court politics of China's past; Deng's final choice was Hu Jintao.

Jiang Zemin was consistently fixated on power. As the transition to a market economy progressed, the party's authority to grant permits and approvals expanded, as did its economic benefits. Power was directly linked to profit. Jiang relinquished his position as general secretary to Hu Jintao in 2002, given that it was a predetermined policy. Even after he ceded the posts of general secretary and president, though, he extended his tenure as chairman of the Central Military Commission and clung to power. Hu's faction was a minority in the Politburo as well, and even though he promoted collective leadership, he ultimately yielded to the Jiang faction. During this time, Hu permitted the Jiang faction to have the monopoly on state-owned enterprises, from which it continually sapped private profits. The consequence was widespread political corruption.

The transfer of power from Hu Jintao to Xi Jinping was also opaque. In the absence of a figure of Deng's stature, the only means of deciding on a successor were power struggles and collusion in the wings of the political stage. As if to satirize the precedent set by Jiang Zemin, Hu also relinquished all of his posts when his term in office expired. Although the Jiang faction did all it could to maintain its grip on actual power, Xi, who had witnessed the failure of collective leadership in the Hu Jintao era, cornered the faction's leaders one after another on charges of corruption. And so it was that senior cadres wielding power in the party over key areas such as propaganda, public security, and the military—namely Bo Xilai, Zhou Yongkang, Xu Caihou, and Guo Boxiong—fell from grace. The efforts to contain and oppose the new leader, Xi Jinping, continue to this day.

There is no question that China has changed considerably since the Cultural Revolution. In particular, its economy and society have been greatly liberated and are undergoing major transformation. But there has been no fundamental change in the political system, which is still based on the one-party dictatorship of the CCP. While there obviously are some facets that have changed, there is still no system or rules for deciding on the next supreme leader. Political participation by the Chinese populace is not anticipated, whether direct or indirect. The supreme leader is determined in the course of intense factional struggles over power and interests, waged behind a blackout curtain. Despite the fact that China now enjoys a huge presence on the world stage, the political system seems hardly different from the days of the Cultural Revolution.

The age of mass mobilization, like that seen in the Cultural Revolution, may have ended in China. However, when the dissociation between the unchanging political system and actual society becomes too large, the Chinese masses may turn into a huge dragon and run amok. The key to avoiding such an outcome is not a chaotic "great democracy" (*Daminzhu*)—a kind of populist politics based on violence as seen in the Cultural Revolution—but rather the establishment of institutional mechanisms for hearing the voices of the people and ensuring their participation in politics. That is a far-off dream, though, as long as the domination of the CCP in its current form continues. Given that the political system has not changed, and given that the history of the PRC is not shared as the common memory of the Chinese citizenry, it would be no wonder if one day, for one reason or another, discipline is lost and China is once again consumed by massive confusion or chaos, even if not to the same extent as the Cultural Revolution.

Part II

China's Japan Policy as an Extension of Domestic Politics

Chapter 6

Establishment of the 1972 System and Its Limits:
From the Cold War to the Post-Cold War Era (1970s–1990s)

Almost all past studies of Japan-China relations addressed Japan's policies toward China. But the relations between the two countries have developed amid bilateral interactions, and a perspective on the relationship from one side only is inevitably lacking in balance. Accordingly, in Part II of this book, I build on my examination of the actual state of Chinese politics in Part I to reinterpret Sino-Japanese relations from the standpoint of China's domestic politics, something that has received little attention to date. In sum, it seems to me that the bilateral relationship is characterized to a considerable degree by the fact that Japan has been drawn into China's complicated domestic politics and factional struggles, whether Japan likes it or not.

Before I delve into the realities of China's policy toward Japan, I will first address the question of how to interpret Japan-China relations as a whole since normalization. I start in this chapter with a reorganization of the so-called 1972 System, observed from the standpoints of both Japan and China. My view is that the chill seen in their relations up to the present day can be traced to the fact that the 1972 System, which began to take shape at the time of normalization of bilateral ties that year, has yet to evolve into a form that can cope with the changes within the two countries and the international environment surrounding them.

The focus of the analysis here is the period from the 1970s, when Japan-China ties were normalized, to the late 1990s, when frictions became pronounced between the two sides. The limits of Sino-Japanese "friendship" were already becoming apparent at that time.

1. The Widening Gap between Japan and China

When relations were normalized between Japan and China in 1972, Japan was swept by a "China fever," and the slogan "Japan-China friendship" (*Nicchū yūkō=Zhongri youhao*) was on everyone's lips. It bears remembering that in those days, China—in the midst of the Cultural Revolution and engaged with constant power struggles far outstripping anything seen at present—was effectively cut off from the outside world. In spite of that, Japan and China plunged into a honeymoon period. There had already been some moves afoot within Japan to seek warmer ties with Beijing, but the primary trigger for this was Sino-American rapprochement due to President Richard Nixon's visit to China.

There was a palpable sensation in Japan that Sino-Japanese friendship had truly been established, thanks to publicity and commercial media reports on topics ranging from pandas to the historic Silk Road. A large number of goodwill groups for visiting China were organized up to the mid-1980s. These groups forged "direct ties" with the Chinese people through visits to model people's communes, state-owned enterprises, primary and secondary schools, and the like, and popular enthusiasm for "friendship" with China continued to grow. Slogans like "The eyes of the Chinese people are shining, and they are marching forward united toward modernization" were a constant presence in the media. But it was only in the latter half of the 1980s that ordinary travelers became able to move relatively freely around China and that large numbers of Chinese students began coming to Japan on study-abroad programs. Only at this stage, in other words, could the Japanese finally have unmediated contact with China and its people—and even then, with only a relatively small portion of the populace.

A public opinion survey conducted by the Japanese Cabinet Office shows that the percentage of Japanese expressing a "feeling of affinity" toward China in 1980 was 78.6%, while those who did not feel this constituted a mere 14.7%.[1] By way of comparison, the responses to the same question were 77.2% and 17.7%, respectively, for the United States, indicating that favorable sentiments for China had surpassed those for the United States at this point. This Japanese affinity for China would remain for some time in the upper 60% to low 70% range, a level that vied with the figures for the United States. This positive

---

1 Public Relations Office, Minister's Secretariat, Cabinet Office of Japan, *Gaikō ni kansuru yoron chōsa* [Survey of Public Opinion about Foreign Relations] (October 2001), 4–5, 13–14.

image of China collapsed in one fell swoop with the 1989 Tiananmen Square Incident. According to the same Cabinet Office opinion survey, Japanese people's positive feelings for China marked 68.5% in 1988 but fell to 51.6% after the incident; the percentage of respondents who did not feel affinity for China surged from 26.4% to 43.1% in that same period. There was no subsequent improvement in the image of China held by Japanese people. Since the latter half of the 1990s, due to further factors including the Taiwan Strait crises, the percentage of Japanese reporting negative views of China have for the most part outstripped the portion with positive views to exceed 50%.[2]

A similar process was unfolding in China. Although it is somewhat old, a survey of Chinese images of Japan that appeared in the *Zhongguo Qingnianbao* (China Youth Daily) on February 15, 1997, demonstrated the depths of the distrust of the Japanese among young people in China. Just 14.5% of respondents reported a positive impression of Japan in this survey, compared to 43.9% with ordinary and 41.5% with negative impressions. Tōjō Hideki was the most renowned Japanese figure who came to mind when young Chinese heard the word *Japan*, named by 28.7% of respondents. The most common "thing" that young Chinese thought of when they heard the word *Japan* was the Nanking Massacre (83.9%, based on multiple responses), followed by "Japanese demons," a Chinese term for the wartime invaders, and the "Anti-Japanese War" (both cited by 81.3% of respondents).

Leaving aside the discussion of popular imagery and focusing on actual Japan-China relations, it is evident that the bilateral relationship has not always been harmonious from the 1990s onward. At the beginning of that decade, though, there were signs of positive developments—primarily in the form of the visit by Emperor Akihito to China. For Japan, the emperor's visit to China in October 1992 was expected to put an end to the so-called history issues and serve as a turning point for establishing a new relationship. At the welcoming banquet during

2 *Gaikō ni kansuru yoron chōsa*, 13–14.

this visit, President Yang Shangkun touched only tangentially on the tragedy of the war, but the emperor's response was stated with conviction: "In the long history of the relations of our two countries, there was an unfortunate period during which our country inflicted severe suffering upon the Chinese people. This is a deep sorrow to me."[3] This brought about a considerable thaw in the atmosphere on the Chinese side, and it is believed that the visit ended as a great success overall.

In Japan, meanwhile, some opposed Emperor Akihito's China visit on the grounds that the Chinese could manipulate it for political ends. Qian Qichen, who was Chinese foreign minister at the time, would later state in his memoir that welcoming the Japanese emperor was a policy move aimed at raising China's international standing in the wake of its isolation due to the Tiananmen Square Incident.[4] This was a rather irresponsible comment, coming as it did from China's former top diplomat, and it must be pointed out that it was not entirely accurate. An imperial visit to China had been a matter of specific discussion well before the Tiananmen Square Incident. Furthermore, as I detailed above, China had embarked on its shift to a market economy based on Deng Xiaoping's Southern Tour Speeches at the start of 1992, and the boom in investment by foreign corporations had already begun. Exchanges between China and Western countries, particularly the United States, had already been revived; most significantly, China had normalized its diplomatic relations with South Korea in August 1992. As will be discussed below in Chapter 9, when Hu Jintao subsequently made a state visit to Japan, he gave a statement that essentially negated Qian's claim.

---

3 Kazankai, *Nicchū kankei kihon shiryōshū 1972 nen–2008 nen* [Collection of Basic Materials on Japan-China Relations, 1972–2008] (Tokyo: Kazankai, 2008), 377. English translation quoted from David Holley, "Emperor Voices 'Deep Sorrow' to Chinese," *Los Angeles Times*, October 24, 1992, https://www.latimes.com/archives/la-xpm-1992-10-24-mn-705-story.html.

4 Qian Qishen, *Waijiao shiji* [Ten Diplomatic Episodes] (Beijing: World Affairs Press, 2003). Published in English as *Ten Episodes in China's Diplomacy* (New York: Harper-Collins, 2005).

After that relative high point, Sino-Japanese relations soured. This turnaround was related to China's domestic politics. Starting from around 1995, a half-century after the end of World War II, the Chinese Communist Party launched a patriotism campaign under Jiang Zemin calling for vigilance against an increase of liberal tendencies accompanying the introduction of market economics from 1992. From the summer of 1995 in particular, the Chinese leadership began to stress the significance of the Anti-Japanese War (Second Sino-Japanese War) in the context of a fresh focus on historical study. Japanese television dramas and the like, which had frequently been broadcast up to that point, were banned, and in their place Chinese TV switched to dramas and documentaries related to the Anti-Japanese War. Jiang Zemin himself played a leading role in this, an issue I will touch on at several points in the following chapters. On top of this, there was the visit by Taiwanese President Lee Teng-hui to the United States in 1995, followed by Lee's re-election in the direct presidential elections in 1996. The Chinese response to these events was a series of military exercises, including missile launches, in the seas adjoining Taiwan, which provided fodder for those painting China as a threat.

Jiang Zemin's initial visit to Japan as president in November 1998 also ended in discord, as I will analyze in more detail in the following chapter. Originally the plan was to hammer out the direction of a new relationship under the slogan a "partnership of friendship and cooperation for peace and development." In the end, though, scant attention was paid to the accomplishments of Jiang's tour. Because the Japanese side did not incorporate the word "apology" (*owabi*) about the past in the joint declaration, an infuriated Jiang obstinately raised historical issues throughout his stay in Japan—even at the banquet at the Imperial Palace in Tokyo—and was sharply criticized by his hosts as a consequence. When Japanese Prime Minister Obuchi Keizō visited China in July 1999, talks did not touch on issues of history, and the trip ended without incident. In October 2000 Chinese Premier Zhu Rongji visited Japan, making various attempts to improve China's image in Japan. These included a skillful performance in a televised town hall forum with Japanese citizens, with the Chinese leader replying deftly to Japanese questioners. This was a successful effort to improve bilateral relations, which had cooled in the aftermath of Jiang's visit two years earlier.

Perhaps following reflection on the problems caused by Jiang's visit, from the start of the new century China refrained from mentioning historical issues and instead adopted a softer stance toward its neighbor. This may have been a manifestation of the hopes that China had for a boost from Japan's economy to the Chinese market. In addition, President George W. Bush took office in the United States around this time; as his administration adopted a tough posture toward China, China presumably also wanted to avoid stirring up trouble with the US ally Japan. In particular, after the terrorist attacks on September 11, 2001, China assumed an extremely low profile in dealings with the United States, matched by a similarly quiet posture toward Japan. But this was not evidence of any substantive improvement in Sino-Japanese ties. In reality, a range of other problems were arising, and the image that each side held of the other was also spiraling into ever more negative territory.

Why did the countries succumb to such a vicious cycle from the 1990s onward? Below, by means of a comparison of the structural changes in Japan-China relations from the Cold War era to the post-Cold War period, I will probe the background of this worsening of relations that has continued to the present day from a macro perspective. Specifically, these are changes to the structure of the relationship that was created after diplomatic normalization in 1972. This structure entered a process of transformation due to a variety of international and domestic factors as the Cold War came to an end, from the late 1980s through the 1990s. I interpret this as a shift impacting the 1972 System of bilateral relations and examine the course of this transformation from four angles: (1) Sino-Japanese relations in the Cold War era and the post-Cold War period; (2) a phase change in Sino-Japanese economic relations; (3) friendly ties between members of the war-era

generations and the changes they later underwent; and (4) the 1972
System and the transformation of Taiwan.

"The 1972 System" has become established as an expression of the
relationship structure in the age of Japan-China friendship up to the
present day, and it has often been the subject of debate. My memory
may not be entirely clear, but I believe that I was the first person to use
this expression, in the spring of 1997, at a Sino-Japanese Youth Forum
in Beijing sponsored by the Institute of Japanese Studies of the Chinese
Academy of Social Sciences.[5]

2. Japan-China-US Relations in the Cold War and the Post-Cold War Periods

The broad framework of the 1972 System in Japan-China relations
was prescribed by certain conditions of international relations. For
Japan, diplomatic normalization with China would not have been
possible without the consent of the United States. Moreover, it was
also impossible unless China accepted the Japan-US Security Treaty.
The Sino-American rapprochement that unfolded from 1971 to 1972
was the primary driver making these conditions a reality. The sudden
reconciliation between the United States and China was premised on
their opposition to a common enemy, the Soviet Union, and the Cold
War structure in Asia, previously rooted in US-China antagonism, was
completely transformed by the détente between the two countries.

After this, the United States agreed to Japan's normalization of
diplomatic relations with China, and China also accepted the existence
of the Japan-US Security Treaty. China was able to accept the presence of
this framework as an effective part of the anti-Soviet strategy. As recorded

---

5 Kokubun Ryosei, "'1972 nian tizhi' de bianhua yu fazhan xietiao guanxi zhi lu"
[Changes in the "1972 System" and the Road to Developing a Cooperative Rela-
tionship], *Riben xuekan* [Japanese Studies] (Institute of Japanese Studies, Chinese
Academy of Social Sciences) 5 (September 1997): 43–50.

in William Burr's *The Kissinger Transcripts: The Top-Secret Talks with Beijing and Moscow*, in February 1973, just after normalization of ties with Tokyo, Mao Zedong remarked to US presidential aide Henry Kissinger, "Rather than Japan having closer relations with the Soviet Union, we would rather that they would better their relations with [the United States]."[6] An additional point that has been frequently noted as a reason for Chinese acceptance of the Japan-US security relationship is China's view of it as an effective check on Japanese remilitarization (the so-called "cork in the bottle" theory). In this manner, the United States and China, and then Japan, came to essentially form a strategic partnership based on a common rival—the Soviet Union. This was the single most important reason for the stability of the relations between these three countries until the end of the Cold War and the Soviet dissolution. Further study will be required, though, to explore the extent to which Japan was strategically aware at this stage of the fact that it had essentially been incorporated into an anti-Soviet alliance by the United States and China.

Under the 1972 System, China's modernization had been envisaged as being in the mutual interest of the United States and Japan. China had long been under the leadership of Mao Zedong and had been consumed with political struggles as symbolized by the Cultural Revolution instead of prioritizing real economic development, the result being that it lay outside the global system of competitive market economies. From the early 1970s on, however, China gradually achieved a return to the international stage under the political leadership of Zhou Enlai. In the era from 1978 onward, under Deng Xiaoping and his policy of reform and opening up, it actively sought to make contact with and learn from the international community. Both Japan and the United States welcomed this new Chinese posture and actively supported its heightened international participation.

---

6 Suzuki Chikara and Asaoka Masako, trans., *Kisshinjā saikō kimitsu kaiwaroku* [Records of Kissinger's Top-Secret Talks] (Tokyo: Mainichi Shimbun, 1999), 124–25. Originally published in English as *The Kissinger Transcripts: The Top-Secret Talks with Beijing and Moscow*, ed. William Burr (New York: New Press, 1999).

But with the end of the Cold War, the Soviet Union—until then the common rival that had cemented the relationship between the United States, Japan, and China—disappeared. The three countries lost the glue that had kept them together. After the Tiananmen Square Incident, the United States and China frequently clashed over such issues as Taiwan, human rights, most favored nation trading status, China's accession to the World Trade Organization, and growing Chinese weapons exports. The outcome was greater currency in the United States for the "China threat theory." The Chinese in turn grew increasingly disenchanted with the United States in reaction to its constant diplomatic pressure on China. This reached a peak following the bombing of the Chinese Embassy building in Belgrade in May 1999 by NATO forces, which the United States described as an accident.

During the 1980s, the United States provided weapons to and engaged in military cooperation with China as part of the strategy of opposing the Soviets. Washington almost never made an issue of China's nuclear testing and defense expenditures during that period—a stance that was basically adopted by Japan as well. In the 1990s, though, the so-called redefinition of the Japan-US Security Treaty proceeded in the context of American hopes for expanded Japanese international contributions on the security front. To the extent that the treaty originally had the Soviet Union as its target, such a redefinition had to be undertaken based on the need for a new alliance purpose once the Soviet Union disappeared. This effort resulted in the Japan-US Joint Declaration on Security at the summit between Prime Minister Hashimoto Ryūtarō and President Bill Clinton in April 1996, as well as the law related to new defense guidelines that passed the Japanese Diet in May 1999. Moreover, Japan began to express interest in the joint development of TMD, or theater missile defense, with the United States to counter missile development by North Korea.[7]

---

7 See Kokubun Ryosei, "Higashi Ajia anzen hoshō to Nichi-Bei-Chū" [East Asian Security and Japan-US-China], *International Affairs*, no. 478 (January 2000): 28–30.

China reacted strongly against these moves, viewing this redefinition of the Japan-US security relationship as part of a strategy for containing China now that the Soviet Union no longer existed. Moreover, the timing was poor. While the security relationship redefinition had been undertaken over some years since the end of the Cold War, the Hashimoto-Clinton summit that drew the most attention in this long process took place in the immediate aftermath of the March 1996 Taiwanese presidential election and China's military exercises near Taiwan. For the Chinese, the redefinition appeared to be the opening moves of joint action by Japan and the United States in response to the Taiwan issue. Likewise, in the case of TMD, China harbored suspicions that North Korea was being used as a pretext and that the system would eventually be directed at China. But there was no change in Japanese and US views on China's modernization; both countries continued to welcome China's reform and opening-up policy and its increased integration in the global economy. After lengthy, complex discussions regarding China's accession to the WTO, Japan approved the move in July 1999, followed by the United States in November of the same year, and China entered the body in fall 2001. During this time, China made some major concessions aimed at hastening its membership in the WTO despite considerable domestic opposition.

The fact remains, though, that as China increased the scale of its socialist market economy, there were latent misgivings about the future in both Japan and the United States. Key among these concerns was the increased role of the Chinese military, as seen in the trend toward enhancing the capabilities of the armed forces—which were enjoying budget increases of more than 10 percent annually—and the provocative military exercises held in the Taiwan Strait in 1995 and 1996. China began publishing its Defense White Papers in response to repeated foreign demands for greater transparency in its national defense, but these publications fell far short of substantive transparency. And even the Defense White Papers put out in that period clearly set forth a policy of consolidating its national defense capabilities in the interest of "active defense," specifically by "taking the road of fewer but better troops with Chinese characteristics."[8]

Policymakers in Japan and the United States were naturally concerned, even startled, by the rises in the Chinese defense budget. As major Japanese dailies related in their evening editions on June 24, 2000, the US Department of Defense issued a report on China's military strength in June 2000 in which it concluded that China was seeking great-power status along with economic clout, that it would begin to outstrip Taiwan in military strength after 2005, and that it would likely strengthen its nuclear deterrence policy and compete with the United States before long. In Japan as well, *Defense of Japan 2000* touched on the issue of China's missile development in more depth than previous white papers when it stated as follows: "In terms of intermediate-range ballistic missiles, China possesses a total of 70 intermediate-range missiles whose range takes in the Asian region, including Japan, and is proceeding with the transformation from DF-3 (CSS-2) missiles to the improved new-type DF-21 ICBM (CSS-5) missiles. Additionally, it possesses short-range ballistic missiles, and is said to be building a new missile base on the shore across the strait from Taiwan."[9]

Thus, the disappearance of the Soviet factor, which had supported good relations among Japan, China, and the United States, together with the end of the Cold War engendered confusion in Japanese and American perspectives on China. As a result, cracks appeared in the fixed relations of the regional order that had supported the 1972 System until then.

---

8 State Council Information Office of China, "2000 nian Zhongguo de guofang" [China's National Defense in 2000] (October 16, 2000), *People's Daily*, October 17, 2000, available in English at http://en.people.cn/features/NDpaper/nd.html.

9 Japan Defense Agency, ed., *Heisei 12-nen-ban Nihon no bōei* [Defense of Japan 2000] (July 2000), 53.

3. A Phase Change in Japan-China Economic Relations

After the normalization of Sino-Japanese relations in 1972, various agreements were concluded between the two governments. Among these were the Japan-China Trade Agreement (January 1974), the Japan-China Aviation Agreement (April 1974), the Japan-China Marine Transport Agreement (November 1974), and the Japan-China Fisheries Agreement (August 1975). Once these practical agreements were established, Japan and China entered in earnest into negotiations toward the conclusion of a Treaty of Peace and Friendship. It is well known that this process included a dispute about the possibility of including an "anti-hegemony" clause in the treaty, a step that could have positioned the Soviet Union as an enemy. Following complex negotiations, the treaty was finally concluded in 1978.

Until that point, the two governments had been the leading actors in almost all facets of Japan-China relations. The role of the private sector increased starting slightly before the Peace and Friendship Treaty, when the broad outline for the trade policies between Japan and China was spelled out in the February 1978 Japan-China Long-Term Trade Agreement. In the immediate term this agreement, launched at the same time as the Peace and Friendship Treaty, was interlocked with China's overly ambitious ten-year economic plan, which aimed at large increases in petroleum production and subsequently met with serious setbacks. Over the longer term, though, it was tied more broadly to China's wholesale switchover to the economic modernization line that was symbolized by the Third Plenum of the Eleventh Central Committee of the CCP in December 1978.

As Ishikawa Shigeru has argued, the basic structure of subsequent Sino-Japanese economic relations was laid down in that first agreement.[10] China was to export raw materials like petroleum and coal to

---

10 Ishikawa Shigeru, "Sino-Japanese Economic Co-operation," *The China Quarterly*, no. 109 (March 1987): 1–21.

Japan, while Japan was to export advanced plants and technology to China. This framework ultimately collapsed owing to the stagnation of China's oil production, but what was envisaged here—bilateral trade based on the bartering of raw materials for advanced technology—was the typical pattern for economic relations between an advanced country and a developing country. In other words, the relationship was a vertical rather than a horizontal one.

While this agreement represented a private-sector move toward an ideal bilateral economic relationship, government bureaus naturally also supported it. Immediately thereafter the Japanese government decided to provide official development assistance (ODA) to China, a sign that Tokyo intended to support China's economic modernization. In this period in particular, the Japanese policy was to support China's engagement in the existing international system via its economic modernization policies so as to avoid reversion to a closed system like that seen during the Cultural Revolution. This did not conflict with the intentions of the United States, which had just normalized its diplomatic relations with China in January 1979.

A major subsequent change in Sino-Japanese economic relations occurred when Japanese corporations, seeking cheaper labor, started exploring expansion into mainland China during the time of the strong yen following the 1985 Plaza Accord. Yet Japanese businesses remained cautious about moving into China in the late 1980s, and their continental expansion only accelerated from the 1990s onward—in particular, after Deng Xiaoping issued his commands for reform and opening up and proposed the socialist market economy line in his Southern Tour Speeches.

According to Chinese statistics, on a contract basis, there were 27 cases of direct investment by Japanese corporations totaling US$950 million in the five years from 1979 to 1983, but this grew rapidly to 2,946 cases totaling $7.59 billion in 1995 alone; with respect to trade as well, China had an unfavorable balance of trade with Japan up to 1987, but this situation reversed in 1988, after which Japan suffered an increasing trade deficit.[11] This was because China had improved its industrial competitiveness by way of foreign direct investment and other resource inflows and was increasingly promoting its exporting industries. In sum, the structure of Japan-China economic ties changed in large part from the initial vertical relationship to a horizontal one in tandem with China's rapid economic growth in the 1990s. To phrase it differently, economic interdependence had further deepened.

Such increasing interdependence can be easily understood if we look at exchanges of people. In 1979, when China embarked on its program of modernization in the seventh year after normalizing its ties with Japan, approximately 54,000 Japanese visited China. A decade later, in 1989, this figure had risen to 395,000; it leaped again to 1,227,000 in 1999. In addition, the number of Chinese visiting Japan increased from some 12,000 in 1979 to 100,000 in 1989 and then continued to grow rapidly to 327,000 in 1999.[12] But negative exchanges also increased. There was a rapid rise in the number of illegal Chinese immigrants to Japan from the 1990s onward, a fact not reflected in official statistics. This illegal population became a hotbed of crime, wide media coverage of which further exacerbated the negative image that some Japanese held about China.

Thus, the deepening of interdependence had two aspects: a positive one of stronger bilateral ties and a negative one of increased frictions. Sino-Japanese relations had been resumed in the 1970s under the banner of "friendship," but these friendly ties ended up being forged between a limited number of people. Moreover, since interdependence was advanced on the premise of friendship, participants suppressed acknowledgment of latent incongruities or discomfort in their relationship even as mutual exchanges widened and deepened. Ordinarily, friendship is something that can only be realized in the context of exchanges while accounting and adjusting for differences in the process.

---

11 On the statistics, see Mitsubishi Research Institute, ed., *Chūgoku jōhō handobukku 2000* (see chap. 4, n. 10), 510–14.
12 *Chūgoku jōhō handobukku 2000*, 564.

But in the case of Sino-Japanese relations the direction was the reverse. Precisely because the relationship was premised from the beginning on the achievement of friendship, it was instead the incongruities or "sense of otherness"—things that should have been faced and overcome in a longer process of forging friendship over time—that spread.

Such feelings ultimately surfaced in Japanese views of the country's ODA to China. There had never been any objection to offering aid to China as a developing country under the 1972 System. But as China's military buildup became evident with the rapid rise in its economic clout, and given the lack of transparency involved, it was inevitable that Japan would reconsider the meaning of its aid to China. These misgivings came to the forefront starting in the late 1990s.

4. The Friendship between the War Generations and Later Developments

In the Joint Communique of the Government of Japan and the Government of the People's Republic of China in 1972, the Japanese side stated that it "is keenly conscious of the responsibility for the serious damage that Japan caused in the past to the Chinese people through war, and deeply reproaches itself," and by so doing it expressed clearly its position about its responsibility for the wars of the past.[13] In return, the Chinese side also declared that "in the interest of the friendship between the Chinese and the Japanese peoples, it renounces its demand for war reparation from Japan." Moreover, the two countries declared an end to the state of war between them and mutually confirmed that they would overcome the differences in their social systems and aim at the establishment of "good-neighborly and friendly relations." This represented the resolution of the two countries to never again repeat

---

13 "Joint Communique of the Government of Japan and the Government of the People's Republic of China," Ministry of Foreign Affairs of Japan (website), September 29, 1972, https://www.mofa.go.jp/region/asia-paci/china/joint72.html.

the tragedy of invasion and war, the symbol of which was the grand principle of "Japan-China friendship." To be sure, people may have had varying standpoints on the conflict that had taken place, but one thing that was shared by the generations who had experienced war was the determination to prevent it from happening again. The slogan of "Japan-China friendship" forged at this time was premised on the two sides setting aside minor differences in the pursuit of a greater harmony (*qiu datong, cun xiaoyi*).

Many years have passed since the deaths of the key actors in the process of diplomatic normalization between Japan and China, such as Tanaka Kakuei and Ōhira Masayoshi on the Japanese side and Mao Zedong and Zhou Enlai on the Chinese one. Liao Chengzhi, who undertook much of the hands-on work of negotiation on the Chinese end, has also passed away, and Takeiri Yoshikatsu of Japan has retired from any active role in political life. Other key figures like Fukuda Takeo and Sonoda Sunao, who subsequently played important roles at the time of the Sino-Japanese Peace and Friendship Treaty, are also no longer with us today. And Deng Xiaoping, who played an absolutely critical role as China's dominant leader from the end of the 1970s on, retired from the front stage in the 1990s and died in 1997.

China's renunciation of war reparations from Japan was one of the Japanese side's preconditions for the normalization of diplomatic relations. At the same time, China's agreement to do so left Japanese leaders in the political, business, and other fields at the time with a certain moral responsibility and consciousness of guilt. These factors would go on to play a hidden catalyst role when it came to Japan's economic cooperation with China in subsequent years. Given that renunciation of reparations was an official decision of the Chinese government, there was never any public discussion about how this was related to such things as yen loans and economic cooperation, and it is not mentioned in any official documents. We can only infer that the connection existed purely in the minds of the war generation. It bears observation that it was Prime Minister Ōhira Masayoshi who cleared the way for yen loans to China and that the Japanese foreign minister at the time was Ōkita Saburō, an economist. Both of them were representative figures of the generation that stressed friendship with China.

There were also many advocates of friendship with China in the business world. The Japan-China Treaty of Peace and Friendship was concluded in 1978, but when the Sino-Japanese Long-Term Trade Agreement was signed at the private level earlier that year, Japanese corporations flooded into the Chinese market. Hailed as a symbol of bilateral friendship at the time was the Baoshan Steel Works in Shanghai, a project launched with the full-scale technical support of Nippon Steel. Major figures in the Japanese business world devoted their energies to creating favorable public opinion about Japanese economic cooperation with China, including Inayama Yoshihiro, the former chairman of Nippon Steel, vice chairman of Keidanren, and chairman of the Japan-China Long-Term Trade Committee; Dokō Toshio, who had served as the chairman of Keidanren and chairman of the Japan-China Economic Association; Kawai Ryōichi, president of the Japan-China Economic Association; and Okazaki Kaheita, an advisor to the same association.

In a 1983 book he coauthored, Okazaki wrote: "Zhou Enlai stressed the following: 'Let's improve Asia through Sino-Japanese cooperation and make Asia stronger.' He said that he was willing to forget his enmity toward Japan to that end. It would be marvelous to achieve this. Given that, I think that Japan is going to have to change its ways of thinking and its actions when it comes to its attitudes about cooperation with China's 'Four Modernizations,' for instance, its stance on the Korean Peninsula situation."[14] This is an effective summary of the mindset that was shared by Okazaki's generation.

Beginning in the 1990s, however, the war generation that had supported the new bilateral relations gave way to a younger one. The year 1995 marked a full half-century since the end of the war, and at

14 Itō Takeo, Okazaki Kaheita, and Matsumoto Shigeharu, *Warera no shōgai no naka no Chūgoku* [China in Our Lives] (Tokyo: Misuzu Shobō, 1983), 280.

this point the human network that had sustained the new Japan-China relationship began undergoing serious structural change. Needless to say, the facts of history do not simply disappear with the changing of the guard. But no matter how much emphasis is given to historical awareness and education, a younger generation's lack of direct experience of war will inevitably generate definite differences in its reactions to and awareness about war, when compared with the preceding generation. This is true in China as well as in Japan.

We must qualify this statement somewhat, though. There is a considerable asymmetry in approaches to education between China, where students undergo extensive education during primary and secondary school in modern and contemporary history in a program strongly connected with the history of the CCP, and Japan, where historical studies are not singled out for this sort of special treatment. When the frictions symbolizing this difference in approaches first surfaced in the form of the history textbook controversy in 1982, the issue largely subsided as the two sides opted to "set aside minor differences in the pursuit of a greater harmony."[15] But starting in 1995, 50 years after the war's end, China strengthened academic study of the Anti-Japanese War in order to buttress the CCP's legitimacy. This took place under the guidance of Jiang Zemin, perhaps for the purpose of addressing the political indifference of Chinese youth and their declining faith in the party. This period also saw a string of incidents that further strained bilateral relations in connection with the issue of historical awareness, such as the visits to Yasukuni Shrine by the Japanese prime minister and cabinet officials and the "intemperate comments" of some Japanese cabinet members.

And then came Jiang Zemin's autumn 1998 visit to Japan. At this time, his excessive statements about history became an issue—a matter

---

15 For background on the textbook issue, the following study, which offers a detailed analysis based on the domestic situations of the two countries, is enlightening: Caroline Rose, *Interpreting History in Sino-Japanese Relations: A Case Study in Political Decision-Making* (London and New York: Routledge, 1998).

I treat at greater length in Chapter 8 below—and many people in Japan who had previously been willing to acknowledge their country's past actions in China succumbed to a certain "fatigue" about haranguing by the Chinese. China subsequently tended to refrain from mentioning historical issues, perhaps out of concern for a variety of other matters. But in 2001, the Japanese Society for History Textbook Reform—a group with a pronounced nationalistic hue—published its infamous junior high school history textbook, and Prime Minister Koizumi Jun'ichirō made an official visit to Yasukuni Shrine in August of that year. The tenor of Japan-China ties again reached a nadir in connection with historical issues.

As the generations changed, the slogan "Japan-China friendship" came to be used far less than before. This phrase had formerly been a panacea whenever frictions arose, but now the younger generation was inclined to view the other side more realistically and dispassionately. Compared to the period when the parties attempted to solve various problems with the simplistic balm of "friendship," Sino-Japanese ties now appeared to be headed in a more pragmatic direction. Precisely for that reason, though, there was a pressing need in the relationship for solid institutional channels and human networks for the resolution of disputes. The generational change in bilateral relations progressed without resolving that inherent weakness.

5. The 1972 System and the Transformation of Taiwan

To normalize relations with China, Japan severed diplomatic ties with Taiwan and recognized the People's Republic of China as the sole legitimate government representing China. From 1952 to 1972, Japan recognized the Republic of China as the sole legitimate government representing China, but normalization of Sino-Japanese ties took place in the context of Sino-American rapprochement and the groundswell of positive domestic public opinion on normalized ties with Beijing. The severing of Japan's ties with Taiwan and the end of the Japan-Republic of China (ROC: Taiwan) Peace Treaty were announced by Prime Minister Ōhira Masayoshi. At the private level, however, ties between Japan and Taiwan remained in place, particularly in the economy; and while their continuation was in doubt for a time, the aviation routes between Japan and Taiwan were maintained. Subsequently, with the notable exceptions of business and tourism, Taiwan receded from the consciousness of the average Japanese. Whether politicians or academics, in a certain sense most of the Japanese people with political ties to Taiwan sympathized with Chiang Kai-shek personally or with his anti-communist stance; some even harbored fierce antipathy toward China. But such people were by no means the majority in Japan. Taiwan at the time was being ruled by the one-party dictatorship of the Kuomintang, with Chiang at its helm, and was moreover under martial law. Its political system was a far cry from democracy.

After Chiang's death in 1975, it was believed that his son Chiang Ching-kuo, who assumed power a short while after his father's death, would continue his father's policies. However, as if triggered by the collapse of the Ferdinand Marcos regime and democratization in Taiwan's neighbor the Philippines, Chiang Ching-kuo moved to introduce democratization in Taiwan from 1986, eventually allowing a multiparty system to be realized with the formation of the Democratic Progressive Party (DPP). When the junior Chiang died suddenly in January 1988, Vice President Lee Teng-hui, who was a genuine Taiwanese—a *benshengren* born on the island, rather than a *waishengren* from the mainland—automatically assumed the office of president.

There is no need to dwell at length on Lee's introduction of a bold democratization policy after he took office or the rapid advance of the "Taiwanization of the Republic of China" due to this. In short, postwar Taiwan had been dominated by the *waishengren*—mainlanders who came to Taiwan after World War II, as well as their descendants—and its political party, the Kuomintang, which had taken over control of the island following the war and formed a rump regime as the ruling elite on Taiwan. The changes of the 1980s marked an end to the era where the *waishengren* and the Kuomintang ruled over the *benshengren*, despite the fact that the latter constituted the vast majority of Taiwan's population. The denouement was the overwhelming victory of Lee Teng-hui in the historic direct presidential elections in 1996, followed later by the 2000 victory of the Democratic Progressive Party's candidate Chen Shui-bian, who advocated Taiwanese independence. This all signified a final and utter defeat for the Kuomintang. These events also marked the end of the China-Taiwan relationship as one pitting the CCP and the Kuomintang against each other.

In the same period when Taiwan was gradually achieving democratization, China was in fact taking its own steps toward political reform, as if to follow Taiwan's lead. This first led to the fall from grace of General Secretary Hu Yaobang, who had been lenient toward the student movement, in January 1987. Political reforms were then pursued under General Secretary Zhao Ziyang, almost as if to vie with the developments on Taiwan, but these efforts at political reform ultimately ended with the tragedy that unfolded in Tiananmen Square on June 4, 1989. There was a clear asymmetry between Taiwan, which achieved a "soft landing" with democratization without any loss of life, and China, which failed at democratization despite the considerable sacrifices by those advocating it, including loss of life. It goes without saying that the CCP, which had supposedly "won" historically, had complicated feelings about the Kuomintang, which had "lost."

These developments attracted worldwide attention. As noted above, in Japan the Tiananmen Square Incident led to a precipitous decline in the feeling of goodwill toward China, while positive interest in Taiwan suddenly increased. This was thanks in significant part to Lee Teng-hui, who felt a special attachment to Japan, given that he had grown up under Japanese rule when Taiwan was a Japanese colony before 1945, and who dazzled high-level Japanese guests visiting Taiwan with his impeccable Japanese.[16] In the blink of an eye, those people in Japan who had felt respect for Chiang Kai-shek or whose anti-communist leanings had given them a sense of antipathy for China, or those who had drawn near to Taiwan due to their involvement with the interests of the Kuomintang—not to mention those who had been concerned only with China and had had almost no interest in Taiwan—all began parting company with the *waishengren* and the Kuomintang and came to sympathize with the democratic Lee Teng-hui and Taiwan.

Even today, both Japan and the United States recognize the PRC as the sole legitimate government representing China. It is highly improbable that they would ever recognize Taiwan's ROC again as the sole legitimate government representing the Chinese people, and it is equally unlikely that they would readily support Taiwanese independence, given the likelihood that this would lead to China's use of armed force to prevent such a move. In other words, there has been no change in the "one China" principle. On that score, there has been no change in the 1972 System when it comes to Taiwan. But there has been a huge change in how Japan and the United States, as well as other countries around the world, evaluate Taiwan's autonomous development on the economic and political fronts. Positive assessments about Taiwan after its democratization and a certain kind of sympathy for the island have spread far and wide throughout the world.

In Summary

In this chapter, I discussed the "friendly" relations between Japan and China that were formed from the normalization of bilateral diplomatic ties in 1972 the 1972 System, and then analyzed the contents thereof and their subsequent structural changes from four angles. Based on the

---

16 On the relationship between Lee Teng-hui and Japan, see Lee Teng-hui, *Taiwan no shuchō* [Taiwan's Assertions] (Kyoto: PHP Institute, 1999).

results of this analysis, I can underscore the following four features as the basic contents of the 1972 System: (1) the partnership of Japan, the United States, and China, which regarded the Soviet Union as the enemy in the Cold War system; (2) a shared agreement on aid for China's modernization and the creation of interdependence; (3) the common understanding of the war generations arising from their drive to overcome the tragedy of the war era and establish a firm friendship between Japan and China; and (4) agreement on the point that the People's Republic of China on the mainland, rather than the Republic of China on Taiwan, is the sole legitimate government representing China.

Over the course of the late 1980s and 1990s, however, (1) the Cold War ended and the Soviet threat evaporated. In addition, (2) various concerns about the rise of an increasingly nontransparent China grew; (3) divergences appeared in the awareness of history as the generations that had directly experienced the Sino-Japanese War passed away; and (4) even though there was no change in the "one China" principle, definite changes started to occur in the presence and standing of Taiwan on the world stage due to the rapid advance of democratization there. Along with these changes in the various factors that had sustained the 1972 System, the need for a new framework for Japan-China relations that addressed such changes grew more acute from the late 1990s. But no such new framework was constructed, and the result was that the 1972 System remained unchanged even as a variety of frictions were generated within it.

Chapter 7

The Shadows of "Japan-China Friendship":
The Kōkaryō Case and the Hu Yaobang Incident (1980s)

In the preceding chapter, I clarified the structural characteristics of Japan-China relations since normalization of diplomatic ties under the rubric of the 1972 System, describing the process whereby various frictions increased without the parties achieving a new framework for governing the relationship. This new framework failed to take form even though the bilateral relationship had undergone a qualitative transformation along with the changes in the era and circumstances from the 1990s through the beginning of the twenty-first century.

In this chapter, I will turn the clock back to the mid-1980s and focus on the Chinese stance toward one 1987 legal case, known as the "Kōkaryō dormitory court case" in Japan, which impacted Japan-China ties and influenced Chinese policies in turn.[1] In examining this case, I attempt to show that although friendship between the two countries appeared stable under the 1972 System, the trial's outcome offered an early preview of the manifestation of bilateral frictions from the 1990s onward and domestic Chinese politics cast a large shadow in the background of this case. At the same time, though, strong forces were still at work that aimed at returning the bilateral relationship to the friendship track.

1. The Kōkaryō Issue and Its Denouement

The Historical Background [2]
The Kōkaryō is a Kyoto University dormitory for Chinese students located in the Kitashirakawa Nishimachi district of Kyoto's Sakyō

---

1 An excellent recent study on the Kōkaryō dormitory court case is Kojima Kazuko, "Kōkaryō mondai: 1987–88 nen" [The Kōkaryō Dormitory Issue: 1987–88], in *Nicchū kankeishi 1972–2012, I: Seiji* [The History of Japan-China Relations 1972–2012, vol. 1: Politics], eds. Takahara Akio and Hattori Ryūji (Tokyo: University of Tokyo Press, 2012).

2 The particulars of the case are detailed in the texts of the four court rulings, all of which have been reprinted in *Chūgoku kenkyū geppō* (Institute of Chinese Affairs), no. 475 (September 1987), an issue focused on the Kōkaryō problem. Itō Kazuhiko's "Kōkaryō mondai: Sono keii to haikei" [The Kōkaryō Dormitory Issue: Its Development and Background], included in the same issue, also provides a detailed account of the facts.

Ward. The structure itself was built in 1931, but the dormitory's history began in April 1945, just before the end of World War II, when the university was commissioned by the Japanese government to lease property from the Rakutō Apartment corporation and provide this as housing for about 100 students, the purpose being the collective education of students visiting from China. After the war's end, however, Kyoto University was no longer able to pay the rent. The students, who had no money to spare either, named the property the Kōkaryō (Ch. *Guanghualiao*). They set up an autonomous committee in October 1945 and started self-management of the property, continuing to live in the dormitory without paying any rent. Fujii Shōjirō, the landowner and the representative partner of Rakutō Apartment, did not know how to address this situation. He considered selling the property and undertook negotiations with the National Tax Administration Agency and other parties, but owing to the complex nature of the situation, he was unable to sell the land and building.

In 1947, supplies that had been seized by the Japanese army in China during the war were discovered, and the students pressured the Allied Occupation authorities to convert these supplies into money that could be used to cover their living expenses. This request was accepted, and on May 27, 1950, the delegation of the Republic of China stationed in Japan at that time used the proceeds of the sale of the supplies to purchase the property from Fujii for 2.5 million yen. However, no steps were taken to register the transfer of ownership at this point. Further complicating matters, it was during this same period that the People's Republic of China was born in October 1949, and the defeated Chiang Kai-shek and his Kuomintang fled to Taiwan. The ROC delegation that purchased the Kōkaryō in May 1950 was, naturally, the government of Taiwan.

In 1952, the Peace Treaty between Japan and the ROC was concluded, and Japan recognized the ROC on Taiwan as the sole legitimate government representing China. The management of the Kōkaryō was accordingly transferred to the Embassy of the ROC—namely, the Taiwanese government. Fujii, the seller, reportedly made frequent demands after the property was sold for an increase in the price paid. This led to a reconclusion of the purchase and sale contract, this time with Taiwan as the counterparty, on December 8, 1952. But Fujii dragged his heels when it came time to register the transfer of ownership, and Taiwan filed a lawsuit seeking such registration. Taiwan finally won this case in 1960, at which point the ownership transfer based on the 1952 sale contract was acknowledged. The registration was transferred on June 8, 1961. During this entire time, the Kōkaryō was entrusted to the self-management of the students who lived there.

Soon afterward, though, the number of dormitory residents supporting the PRC on the mainland increased. These students organized an executive committee and strengthened their pro-mainland stance. They also began to express sympathetic views with the Cultural Revolution, which was underway by that point. In response to these developments, on September 6, 1967, the ROC Embassy demanded the expulsion of eight dormitory students with pro-PRC leanings and filed a lawsuit seeking their eviction in the Kyoto District Court. It was not until September 16, 1977—a full decade later—that the district court handed down its final decision, which rejected the claims of Taiwan, the plaintiff, based on the determination that when Japan established diplomatic relations with the PRC on September 29, 1972, simultaneously severing its diplomatic ties with the ROC, the ownership itself of the dormitory had been transferred to the PRC.

Taiwan, naturally dissatisfied with this decision, immediately filed an appeal with the Osaka High Court. Five years later, on April 14, 1982, the high court overturned the decision of the Kyoto District Court with a ruling that the transfer of ownership could not be recognized, given the outstanding civil lawsuit. The case was remanded to the Kyoto District Court. Four years later, on February 4, 1986, the Kyoto court acknowledged Taiwan's complaint in a decision more or less following that issued by the Osaka High Court and requested the eviction of the eight dormitory residents. At this point, the students filed an appeal with the Osaka High Court, but on February 26, 1987, that tribunal rejected their appeal. The students made a last-ditch effort by means of a final appeal to the Supreme Court, but no decision was handed down until March 2007—a full three decades since the first court decision was rendered—when the Supreme Court once again remanded the matter to the Kyoto District Court, concluding that retrial was appropriate given the fact that the authorities in Taipei had ceased to be the plaintiff in the lawsuit as of the moment of normalization of diplomatic relations in 1972 and Beijing had inherited the role of plaintiff in the suit. It goes without saying that Taiwan expressed its vehement displeasure about this outcome.

A Sudden Wave of Criticism

Up until the Osaka High Court issued its February 1987 ruling, the PRC government had offered almost no comments about the Kōkaryō court battle, but it suddenly ramped up its tone of condemnation in the immediate wake of that decision. On February 26, 1987, when the decision was issued, a spokesman at the Chinese Ministry of Foreign Affairs criticized it as erroneous, both politically and in terms of legal theory. Vice Minister of Foreign Affairs Liu Shuqing summoned Japanese Ambassador to China Nakae Yōsuke and delivered to him a note verbale seeking appropriate steps from the Japanese government. Tokyo responded by explaining that the Kōkaryō case was a civil lawsuit and the government could not intervene in judicial matters from the standpoint of the separation of powers; it also reiterated that Japan recognized the PRC as the sole legal government of China, among other points.[3]

On March 6, Professor Zhao Lihai of Peking University published a *People's Daily* article stating that the Kōkaryō decision was not a simple civil lawsuit and criticizing it as a "serious violation of international law." On the same day, Ambassador Nakae visited Vice Minister Liu and delivered to him a note verbale setting forth the position of the

---

3 *People's Daily*, *Yomiuri Shimbun*, and *Asahi Shimbun*, February 27, 1987.

Japanese government, as noted above.[4] This was followed by a lengthy interview in the March 16 *People's Daily* in which Professor Zhu Qiwu of the Chinese University of Political Science and Law stated that the Kōkaryō decision had essentially created "two Chinas," or "one China and one Taiwan," and there was no way for the Japanese government to evade responsibility behind the shield of the separation of powers.[5]

On March 27, Chinese Ambassador to Japan Zhang Shu met with Japanese Vice Minister for Foreign Affairs Yanagiya Kensuke, delivering a formal rebuttal of the Japanese government's position. Moreover, on April 3, Vice Minister of Foreign Affairs Qian Qichen stated in his press conference that the Kōkaryō was the state-owned property of China. On April 17, Vice Chairman of the Central Advisory Commission Wang Zhen, who was the honorary president of the China-Japan Friendship Association, visited Japan and stated at a meeting with Japanese Prime Minister Nakasone Yasuhiro his hope that the Japanese government would exercise its influence in the matter.

On May 5, 1987, Central Advisory Commission Chairman Deng Xiaoping met with Utsunomiya Tokuma, the chair of the Japan-China Friendship Association, expressing concern about the "possibility that a handful of people in Japan, some of whom probably have political influence, may revive militarism there."[6] Deng touched on the Kōkaryō situation and pointed out the similarity with the United States' Taiwan Relations Act, noting that this, too, appeared related to the revival of Japanese militarism. Also during this meeting, Deng expressed his hopes

---

4　Zhao Lihai, "Riben fayuan dui Guanghualiao an de shenpan yanzhong weifan guoji-fa" [The Decision of the Japanese Court about the Kōkaryo Dormitory Case Seriously Violates International Law], *People's Daily*, February 27, 1987; and *Asahi Shimbun*, March 7, 1987.

5　"Zhongguo Zhengfa Daxue guojifa jiaoshou Zhu Qiwu jiu Guanghualiao wenti da benbao jizhe wen" [Zhu Qiwu, Professor of International Law, China University of Political Science and Law, Answers Our Reporter's Questions about the Kōkaryō Dormitory Court Battle], *People's Daily*, March 16, 1987.

6　*Asahi Shimbun*, *Mainichi Shimbun*, and *Nihon Keizai Shimbun*, May 6, 1987, evening edition. The meeting between Deng and Utsunomiya is recorded in *Selected Works of Deng Xiaoping*, vol. 3 (Beijing: Renmin Press, 1993), 230–31, but remarks about the Kōkaryō situation have been excised.

that Prime Minister Nakasone would show leadership in resolving the Kōkaryō affair. This was followed by hints on May 6 from a spokesman at the Chinese Foreign Ministry that if the Japanese government continued to tacitly approve the Kōkaryō situation, China would respond forcefully. Soon afterward, on May 8, the Chinese Ministry of State Security ordered the expulsion from China of a Kyodo News special correspondent in connection with his coverage of the forced resignation of CCP General Secretary Hu Yaobang.

The "Man above the Clouds" Statement

On June 4 Deng Xiaoping met with Kōmeitō Secretary-General Yano Jun'ya, who was visiting China. Deng harshly criticized the response of the Japanese government to the Kōkaryō issue as follows: "There may be nothing we can do about the treatment of this problem by the government and judicial organs of Japan, but Japan will create a debt in the ledger book of history. That is the debt of not observing the Sino-Japanese Peace and Friendship Treaty concluded between our two countries."[7] Deng went on to raise China's waiver of compensation for the Second Sino-Japanese War as a "debt" owed by Japan: "Frankly speaking, I think that Japan owes more to China than any other country in the world. At the time of the reestablishment of diplomatic relations between China and Japan, we did not put forward any demands for compensation for the war.…Speaking as an Asian person, I highly value reasonableness, so I think that Japan should make a larger contribution in order to assist China's development."

The Japanese reaction to Deng's statement was fast and furious. A senior official in the Japanese Ministry of Foreign Affairs (identified as Vice Minister for Foreign Affairs Yanagiya Kensuke by Xinhua News Service on June 19, 1987) responded in the evening of the same day by commenting to the press corps: "[Deng] seems to have become a

---

7 Deng Xiaoping's remarks at this meeting are covered in detail in *Mainichi Shimbun*, June 5, 1987.

man above the clouds, hasn't he? Has a report been delivered from below? Anyone will become obstinate when he or she gets old....Japan should not waver between hope and fear in response to statements from Chinese leaders."[8] This remark in turn provoked a backlash from the Chinese side. On June 7, Chairman of the China-Japan Friendship Association Sun Pinghua criticized it as diplomatically discourteous, and Tang Jiaxuan, deputy director-general of the Department of Asian Affairs, summoned Yushita Hiroyuki, minister of the Embassy of Japan in China, to the Chinese Foreign Ministry to hand him a formal protest. In response to this, on June 8, Fujita Kimio—head of the Japanese Foreign Ministry's Asian Affairs Bureau—summoned Xu Dunxin, counselor of the Chinese Embassy in Japan, and stated to him that Deng's criticisms were sometimes at odds with Japan's actual situation and its take on the issues, furthermore emphasizing that the senior Foreign Ministry official bore China no ill will in his statement.

However, China once again reacted negatively to this. On June 10, a spokesman at the Chinese Foreign Ministry criticized the "man above the clouds" statement as "lacking any sense of diplomatic protocol." Fearing that the situation was getting out of control, on June 15 Foreign Vice Minister Yanagiya sought to defuse the situation by saying, "There was a disrespectful expression in the portion of my statement about Chairman Deng, and I regret that this has caused displeasure to the Chinese."[9] China appeared somewhat mollified by this, stating that it would "take note of" this statement of regret before moving to clear the whole situation off of its books. Days later, on June 18, Yanagiya declared his intention to resign from Japan's foreign service, although his departure was described as compulsory retirement due to his age.

8 *Nihon Keizai Shimbun*, June 5, 1987.
9 *Mainichi Shimbun*, June 16, 1987.

The Matter Is Settled

From June 26 to 28, 1987, the fifth Japan-China Ministerial Conference took place in Beijing. The Kōkaryō case became a central point of this meeting, but both sides only repeated their prior assertions and failed to reach any agreement. While their positions differed, though, Japan and China agreed that mutual understanding had been furthered by exchanging opinions. On June 28 seven of the Japanese cabinet ministers attending the conference, including Foreign Minister Kuranari Tadashi, met with Deng, who urged a swift resolution of the problem, stating that the Japanese government should deal with the Kōkaryō case just as it had addressed the problem of Japanese history textbooks.[10]

Since the fiftieth anniversary of the Marco Polo Bridge Incident fell on July 7, 1987, the number of reports about Japan's invasion of China during the Sino-Japanese War increased around that time. This was accompanied by a rise in reports about the Kōkaryō situation. On July 7, President Li Xiannian told the Japanese delegation of the Japan-China Friendly Exchange Conference that the handling of the Kōkaryō issue had been unacceptable; he added, moreover, that China did not need economic aid with strings attached. Perhaps in response to these repeated Chinese statements, Prime Minister Nakasone noted: "If the court requests it, I will present an opinion on behalf of the Japanese government."[11] He subsequently retracted this statement, however, instead noting that "This matter has reached a point where it is beyond the government's reach."[12]

Subsequently, in meetings between Chinese and Japanese leading figures, as well as at the meeting of the Japan-China Friendship Committee for the Twenty-First Century that was held in Beijing from November 30 to December 2, 1987, the Chinese side raised this issue with less frequency and in more formulaic terms. For example, Deng Xiaoping did not mention the Kōkaryō case to former Liberal Democratic Party

---

10 *Mainichi Shimbun* and *Yomiuri Shimbun*, June 29, 1987.
11 *Yomiuri Shimbun* and *Tokyo Shimbun*, July 8, 1987.
12 *Yomiuri Shimbun*, July 17, 1987.

Vice-President Nikaidō Susumu, who was visiting China in early September; he also stated that "I have said all that I have to say" about the case to Chairman Tsukamoto Saburō of the Democratic Socialist Party, who came to China in the middle of that month.[13] This trend intensified from the start of 1988. In May that year Premier Li Peng went so far as to state, "I understand the situation in Japan, which is such that considerable effort and time are needed for resolving the matter."[14] The Kōkaryō case thus disappeared from public view for the time being.

The Three Chinese Arguments

Broadly classified, the points raised by China surrounding the Kōkaryō case can be summarized as follows. First, since no diplomatic relations existed between Japan and Taiwan, the Taiwanese authorities did not have the capacity to serve as a party to a court case in Japan. Second, at the point when Japan diplomatically recognized the PRC, the latter should have inherited all property owned by Taiwan in Japan. And third, while the Japanese government sought to evade responsibility behind the shields of the separation of powers and the independence of the judiciary, it is government that bears responsibility for foreign relations, and it is unacceptable for a government to not perform its international obligations on the grounds of domestic law.[15]

With respect to the first point, the Chinese side argued that Taiwan could not file a lawsuit in a Japanese court in the name of a state or government, since a regime lacking diplomatic recognition in

---

13 Various newspapers, September 5, 1987, evening edition, and various newspapers, September 12, 1987.

14 *Asahi Shimbun*, May 5, 1988.

15 Works summarizing and organizing the points at dispute in the court battle include the following: Hirobe Kazuya, "Kōkaryō mondai no hōteki ronten" [The Legal Points in Dispute in the Kōkaryō Case], *Chūgoku kenkyū geppō*, no. 475 (September 1987); Hirobe, "Kōkaryō jiken no hōri to kadai" [The Legal Points and Issues in the Kōkaryō Incident], *Jurist*, no. 890 (July 15, 1987); Sekino Shōichi, "Kōkaryō mondai no sōten to kangaekata" [The Points at Issue and Viewpoints in the Kōkaryō Case], *Hōritsu jihō* 60, no. 2 (February 1988); and Honma Hiroshi, "Kōkaryō hanketsu o meguru hōteki mondaiten [Legal Issues Surrounding the Court Rulings on the Kōkaryō Case], *Surugadai hōgaku*, no. 2 (1988).

a foreign country could not file a lawsuit in a court of that country. Beijing criticized the acceptance of Taiwan's complaint by a Japanese court for violating the 1972 Japan-China Joint Communique and the 1978 Sino-Japanese Peace and Friendship Treaty. The Osaka High Court, however, acknowledged Taiwan's capacity to serve as a party to a court case in Japan based on the fact that even though diplomatic ties between Japan and Taiwan had been severed in 1972, Taiwan still effectively controlled and governed a specific region after that time. This legal view was based on the lack of provisions in Japan's Code of Civil Procedure addressing whether recognition of a government confers on it the capacity to participate in court actions in Japan.

On the second point, the Chinese side argued that based on international law, if a new government is recognized, the various state or public properties of the former government are also completely transferred to the ownership of the new government. The Kōkaryō case, said Beijing, involved exactly this kind of property. In response to this, the Osaka High Court offered the following interpretation from the standpoint of Japan's Code of Civil Procedure: Whenever the former government of a given state disappears completely, all of the property of that government is transferred to the new government, but since in the case of Taiwan the former government remained in control of a certain region, this fell under the category of an "incomplete transfer," and China could therefore not lay claim to the property in question. Moreover, the court held that based on the historical background of the dormitory, it was not possible to regard the Kōkaryō as "diplomatic property" or "property for the exercise of state power." In addition, in the course of the Osaka legal proceedings, the Taiwanese side cited the Taiwan Relations Act of the United States, noting that the ownership of various properties of Taiwan had been guaranteed both before and after the severing of diplomatic ties with Taipei by the United States.

In connection with the third point, as noted above, a series of key persons on the Chinese side including Deng Xiaoping repeatedly expressed the view that there must be some sort of practical action that the Japanese government and Prime Minister Nakasone could take with a view to settling the matter. In response, the Japanese government consistently cited the separation of powers, rejected the intervention of the administrative branch of government in the judicial one, and studiously avoided making comments on the case outcome. As noted above, Nakasone suggested that if the court requested it, he would state an opinion on behalf of the Japanese government, but he also immediately retracted that statement.

2. Why Did China Criticize Japan?

The Initial Chinese Nonresponse

Not including the most recent decision—the Supreme Court's 2007 remand—the Japanese courts have issued four decisions related to the Kōkaryō. Of these, only the initial 1977 decision by the Kyoto District Court recognized that the mainland Chinese government owned the dormitory, and all of the subsequent decisions determined that ownership lay with Taiwan. There is no record of a response by the Chinese side to the initial court decision. It is unclear whether this is because China thought that the decision was only reasonable or because it was not particularly interested in the case at the time.

The second decision was issued by the Osaka High Court in April 1982. As far as I know, the Chinese side did not publicly express any negative reaction to this decision. It was in response to the third decision, rendered by the Kyoto District Court in February 1986, that a councilor at the Chinese Embassy in Tokyo expressed his "feeling of regret." Even then, though, the Chinese did not express any further views. The 1986 court decision sparked next to no commentary about the Kōkaryō case in China, and it did not emerge as a major irritant in bilateral relations.

It was not until shortly before the final decision by the Osaka High Court in February 1987 that the Chinese began to raise this issue of their own accord. Prior to that decision, China had dispatched to Japan a delegation of six legal experts, led by Director General Wang Houli of the Department of Treaty and Law of the Ministry of Foreign Affairs, to exchange opinions about the Kōkaryō matter with the Japanese side. The January 23, 1987, overseas edition of the *People's Daily*, published just prior to this, carried an article by Li Haopei, a legal advisor to the Foreign Ministry, vehemently asserting the impropriety of the past judicial decisions on the case. These moves were undoubtedly part of a campaign of protest against the forthcoming decision by the Osaka High Court. I have already described above the harsh criticism unleashed by China after that February 26 decision was handed down.

This naturally raises the question of why China, which had said almost nothing about the previous three decisions, suddenly began to criticize Japan in February 1987, decades after the case had been set in motion. Below I cast light on this question by examining the structure of China's Japan policy at the time, considering this problem in the context of its connections with factors like China's relationship with Japan, international politics, and the Taiwan problem.

Precriticism Japan-China Ties

In November 1983, General Secretary Hu Yaobang visited Japan and announced that China would invite 3,000 Japanese youths to visit the country. In addition, Prime Minister Nakasone visited China in March 1984, and the bilateral mood became warmer thanks to the provision of the second round of yen loans, totaling as much as 470 billion yen, and the decision to establish the Japan-China Friendship Committee for the Twenty-First Century.

Pouring cold water on these warming relations was Nakasone Yasuhiro's visit to Yasukuni Shrine on August 15, 1985, in his official capacity as prime minister. This sparked an anti-Japanese demonstration by about 1,000 students from Peking University in Tiananmen Square in September 1985. (Ever since Nakasone has not visited the shrine again.) But until the October 1985 visit to China by Japanese Foreign Minister Abe Shintarō, the Chinese authorities were wary of triggering any adverse effects on China's relations with Japan, and thus they sought to eliminate irritants including the posters attacking Japan that had been put up by students on the Peking University campus. Furthermore, at a meeting of the Japan-China Friendship Committee for the Twenty-First Century that was held shortly thereafter, Hu presented a four-point proposal for the development of Sino-Japanese friendship, which he had put together himself.[16] Although other problems like China's trade deficit with Japan also arose, they did not cause any serious damage to overall relations between the countries.

A range of issues cropped up from the start of 1986 on, but they still posed no threat to the fundamental relationship between Japan and China, thanks in large part to the four principles of Japan-China friendship—peace and friendship, equality and mutual benefit, mutual trust, and long-term stability—that had been confirmed when Nakasone made another trip to China in November 1986. However, this one-year period did see frequent controversies arise, primarily in connection with historical awareness and the Taiwan problem, and frictions between the two countries began to increase. Taking the Japanese history textbook controversy in 1982 as the first instance, we might call the dispute sparked in June 1986 the second textbook controversy. This was followed in short order by two problematic statements made by Minister of Education Fujio Masayuki in July and September 1986. Also in September, the pro-Taiwan faction of the LDP held meetings honoring the posthumous influence of Chiang Kai-shek to commemorate the hundredth anniversary of his birth. Predictably, China reacted negatively to these occurrences.

The second textbook controversy refers to China's harsh criticism of the Japanese Ministry of Education's examination and approval of a senior high school Japanese history textbook that had been compiled by

---

16 Hu Yaobang, "Chū-Nichi yūkō kankei hatten ni tsuite no yon ten no iken" [Four Opinions about the Development of Friendly Relations between China and Japan], in *Nicchū kankei kihon shiryōshū 1970 nen–1992 nen* [Collection of Basic Materials on Japan-China Relations, 1970–92], China Division, Asia Bureau, Ministry of Foreign Affairs of Japan (Tokyo: Kazankai, 1993), 363–74.

a group calling itself the People's Council for the Protection of Japan. Fujio's statements, meanwhile, included his July rebuttal of criticisms by China and South Korea, which provoked a further backlash in those countries, and his September interview published in the magazine *Bungei shunjū*, in which he touched on the responsibility of Korea in the Japan-Korea Annexation Treaty and moreover criticized Prime Minister Nakasone's stance toward visits to Yasukuni Shrine, inciting harsh criticism from China and South Korea. As a consequence of these remarks, Nakasone dismissed Fujio from his cabinet post.

From late 1986 until the Osaka High Court decision in early 1987, several other disputes arose between Japan and China. One of these was touched off when Japanese defense spending exceeded the previously accepted limit of 1 percent of GNP; another erupted when the 11 crewmen of the North Korean ship *Zu-Dan* 9082, which came ashore in Fukui, Japan, were accompanied by a senior official of the Japanese Foreign Ministry and sent to Taiwan at their request (they subsequently went to South Korea). Many of these incidents from 1986 onward had roots in Japanese perspectives on historical, particularly wartime, truth; others were connected to Chinese fears about Japanese remilitarization or to the "two Chinas" and the Taiwan problem. Education Minister Fujio, meanwhile, was a pro-Taiwan member of the Japanese political elite. His involvement in the memorial meetings to honor Chiang Kai-shek and his previous membership in the conservative LDP group Seirankai, which had been formed amid moves to oppose the Japan-China Aviation Agreement, were viewed by the Chinese side as part of a series of intentional moves. As a result, China took an increasingly alarmed stance against developments in Japan.

Despite all of this, though, on the whole China exhibited a strong tendency to suppress criticism of Japan during this period. Indeed, the centripetal force between the two countries remained strong at this time, as was shown by Nakasone's visits to China. While the problems of historical awareness and Taiwan, which cropped up repeatedly, were indeed fundamental principles underpinning China's diplomatic approaches, the country was adept at managing domestic media coverage of these issues in terms of both journalistic quantity and quality. When the Kōkaryō problem arose, however, China found itself less able to apply the brakes to discussion of the problem, and the result was the rapid derailment of Sino-Japanese relations.

Anti-Japanese Criticism Operations

After the 1987 Osaka court decision, what specific actions did China take toward Japan in the course of raising the Kōkaryō issue? In charting its ties with Tokyo, China often adopts *gaiatsu* (external or foreign pressure) methods to provoke the Japanese government and arouse public opinion in Japan. This tendency was on display at the time of the textbook controversy in 1982, for instance. There are various ways for China to elicit the desired responses in Tokyo and among the Japanese public, one of which is to get the Japanese media to take up whatever it is that is being actively reported by China itself, in the expectation that articles sympathetic to China will be written. As noted later in this chapter, however, this backfired in the Kōkaryō case.

Another method taken by the Chinese involves approaching friendly persons or organizations, along with political heavyweights, in Japan to exercise influence in the Japanese political process. In the Kōkaryō case as well, China often engaged actively in lobbying along these lines. As noted above, in early May 1987, Deng Xiaoping met with House of Councilors member Utsunomiya Tokuma (chairman of the Japan-China Friendship Association), issuing his statement that linked a "revival of Japanese militarism" with the Kōkaryō issue. After returning to Japan Utsunomiya asked the government to resolve the dispute, going on also to proclaim the correctness of China's assertions in the July issue of *Gunshuku mondai shiryō* (Disarmament Review), a journal that he edited himself.[17]

---

17 Utsunomiya Tokuma, "Nicchū yūkō o samatageru futatsu no jiken: Kōkaryō to Zudan-gō [Two Incidents that Hinder Japan-China Friendship: The Kōkaryō Dormitory and the *Zu-Dan* 9082], *Gunshuku mondai shiryō* (July 1987). See in addition *People's Daily*, June 8, 1987.

In addition, Kōmeitō Secretary-General Yano Jun'ya, an "old friend" of China, harshly criticized the stance of the Japanese government and Foreign Ministry after his meeting with Deng described previously. Incidentally, Defense Agency Director-General Kurihara Yūkō, who had visited China immediately before that in May, was unable to secure a meeting with Deng, perhaps owing to the problem that Japan's defense expenditures had exceeded the 1 percent limit of GNP. Then on June 18, six groups for Japan-China friendship—the Japan-China Friendship Association, the Japanese Association for the Promotion of International Trade, the Japan-China Cultural Exchange Association, the Japan-China Friendship Parliamentarians' Union, the Japan-China Economic Association, and the Japan-China Society—held a meeting in Tokyo. Here they jointly urged the Japanese government to promptly resolve the Kōkaryō problem and to observe the principle of one China for the sake of Sino-Japanese friendship.

Connections with the Hu Yaobang Incident

Sino-Japanese relations in the era of General Secretary Hu Yaobang and Prime Minister Nakasone Yasuhiro had been sustained to no small extent by the personal trust between these two leaders. Conversely, this meant that bilateral relations would likely be put to the test once one or both of them had left the center stage of political life. As symbolized by the "Ron-Yasu relationship," Prime Minister Nakasone had forged a foundation for Japan-US relations based on a personal rapport with President Ronald Reagan. Similarly, Nakasone tried to craft harmonious ties founded on trust with China as well.[18] This was the basis for his personal relationship with Hu Yaobang.

The relationship between these two was formed through Hu's trip to Japan in November 1983 and Nakasone's visit to China in March 1984. On November 8, 1986, amid the lingering effects of Education

---

18 Yokoyama Hiroaki, "Chūgoku e no 'oime' to Nakasone gaikō" [The "Sense of Indebtedness" to China and Nakasone's Diplomacy], *Tō-A*, no. 304 (October 1992). Also see Laura Newby, *Sino-Japanese Relations: China's Perspective* (London: Routledge, 1988), 64–66.

Minister Fujio's intemperate statements, the friendship between the two men reached its peak when Hu personally invited Nakasone to the foundation-laying ceremony for the Japan-China Youth Exchange Center. As the *Yomiuri Shimbun* reported on November 9, at this summit meeting Hu Yaobang stated: "We praise the fact that the prime minister has contributed to the new development of Sino-Japanese relations. In my view, the prime minister and the citizens of Japan correctly understand the feelings of the Chinese people, and we also correctly understand the feelings of the Japanese people. There are no problems at all between the leaders of the two countries." In response, Nakasone stated that "The trust of leaders is crucial. I respect the fact that General Secretary Hu has considered the situation in Japan and made his best efforts….On this occasion, the purpose of the visit is to deepen our friendship."

The Hu Yaobang incident occurred immediately after this. Student demonstrations calling for democracy began in various regions of China in November and spread like wildfire to Shanghai and Beijing. Hu was viewed as having failed to adopt resolute measures in dealing with these protests, and he was removed from his post as general secretary at the enlarged meeting of the Politburo of the CCP Central Committee on January 16, 1987. Zhao Ziyang assumed the post of acting general secretary in his place. It goes without saying that the person who made the ultimate decision in this matter was Deng Xiaoping himself. Deng rejected the students' calls for democratization as "bourgeois liberalization" and decided to dismiss Hu, who had expressed a lenient attitude toward the students' demands and had incurred the hatred of the conservatives and party elders as a result.

Although the effects of the loss of Hu on Japan-China relations cannot be clearly measured, there is no question that China's policies toward Japan hardened on every front in the immediate aftermath of his fall from grace. It was reported after his purge, for instance, that among the charges leveled against him were the fact that he had invited to China 3,000 Japanese youths "based on his personal judgment" in the autumn of 1984 and that he had personally invited Prime Minister

Nakasone in November 1986 (although there is some doubt that this latter charge was actually brought against his character).[19] In addition, Party Secretary Deng Liqun, said to be one of the conservatives who drove Hu Yaobang to his downfall, reportedly made statements in connection with the criticism of Hu, such as "China is relying too much on Japan in economics and trade," "The quality of Japanese products is poor," and "Nakasone encouraged militarism, but Hu Yaobang joined hands with him," according to the *Asahi Shimbun* report on February 15, 1987. While the Kōkaryō decision was issued immediately after this by chance, it is by no means strange to view the aftereffects of Hu's fall from power as the background to China's sudden and vehement criticism of the Japanese court decision.

Moreover, in connection with the Kōkaryō decision, the Japanese government's repeated statements that it could not intervene due to the separation of powers also held a subtle meaning for China in connection with the Hu incident. Hu's ousting originated in Chinese students' calls for political democratization, and if Beijing were seen to acquiesce to the theory of the separation of powers in Japan, it could have undermined the legitimacy of Hu's banishment. As evidence for this, we can note that in this very period Deng Xiaoping became extremely sensitive about the theory of the separation of powers. When Deng met with members of the drafting committee for the Basic Law of Hong Kong in April 1987, he told them that China absolutely would not introduce the separation of powers as seen in Western-style democracy; he made a similar statement in June of the same year.[20]

---

19 *Yomiuri Shimbun*, January 23, 1987, and *Asahi Shimbun*, January 26, 1987. Also see Kojima Tomoyuki, "Tai-Nichi kōka no teiryū ni wa tōnai kattō" [Intraparty Conflicts are at the Undercurrent of China's Hardening Attitude toward Japan], *Tō-A*, no. 243 (September 1987): 49–59.

20 See *Selected Works*, vol. 3, 220 and 240–41, and Deng, *Gendai Chūgoku* (see chap. 1, n. 8), 323–24.

The Aftereffects of the Hu Yaobang Incident

This sensitive response by Deng Xiaoping may indeed have been closely related to the Hu situation, but we should not forget the international environment at the time, in which China found itself confronting a wave of democratization in the East and Southeast Asian regions. In February 1986, the Ferdinand Marcos regime in the Philippines was overthrown by the People's Power Movement, and in June 1987, the student movement for democratization also peaked in South Korea, resulting in an announcement of democratization by the South Korean government on June 29.

In China's foreign policy in the middle of the 1980s, decision-making authority was increasingly concentrated in the secretariat of the CCP Central Committee, whose key leader was General Secretary Hu Yaobang. The Chinese chair of the Japan-China Friendship Committee for the Twenty-First Century was the young Secretary Wang Zhaoguo, reportedly Hu's confidant; this suggests that the secretariat, which formally was coming to hold the most authority, played an important role with respect to bilateral relations under the direct leadership of Hu. However, as a result of Hu's ouster, Wang came in for sharp criticism for his complicity with Hu. He lost his key post in the party center and was transferred out of Beijing to serve as acting governor of Fujian Province. In that diminished capacity, Wang remained China's chair at the fourth meeting of the Japan-China Friendship Committee for the Twenty-First Century from late November to early December 1987. But starting from the fifth committee meeting the following year, Zhang Xiangshan—who, while well acquainted with Japan, was not a Central Committee member—became the Chinese head of that committee, thus marking Wang's removal. This clearly meant that the Chinese side had separated the Twenty-First Century Committee from the direct command of the Communist Party, a status that the committee had enjoyed in the Hu Yaobang era, and had essentially lowered its standing by placing it under the control of the Foreign Ministry. It was an indication that the secretariat could no longer play the key role it once had in China's policies toward Japan or in overall policy decisions.

In connection with the situation within the CCP, we can conclude that it was ultimately Deng Xiaoping's intentions that determined China's position with respect to the Kōkaryō case, too. As noted above, this was evident in the fact that when Deng met with Utsunomiya Tokuma and Yano Jun'ya after the problem arose and mentioned such things as the "revival of Japanese militarism" and the problem of Japan's compensation for China, these topics began to appear in the statements of other major Chinese figures immediately thereafter. After Yanagiya Kensuke's statement about a "man above the clouds" came to light, Sun Pinghua, chairman of the China-Japan Friendship Association, criticized the Foreign Ministry official's words and stated that "No matter what his formal position may be, China's top leader is Chief Deng Xiaoping, and the Deng system will continue no matter what else happens inside the party."[21] Moreover, when Premier Zhao Ziyang met with Foreign Minister Kuranari Tadashi during the Japan-China Ministerial Conference a short while later, he touched on Deng's words to Yano on Japan's "debt in the ledger book of history," noting that "Chief Deng Xiaoping's statement to the Kōmeitō representative is one that takes into consideration friendly relations between China and Japan and emphasizes the larger picture of Sino-Japanese friendship. It is a statement that represents the views of the government and people of China."[22]

In Connection with the Taiwan Issue

It goes without saying that the Kōkaryō court battle was deeply connected to the Taiwan issue. The political developments in Taiwan at the start of 1987 were behind China's growing concern about the disposition of the Kōkaryō dormitory. In the political sphere, the Third Plenum of the Kuomintang's Twelfth Central Committee was held under the leadership of Chiang Ching-kuo in Taiwan in March 1986.

---

21 *Yomiuri Shimbun*, June 8, 1987.
22 *Asahi Shimbun*, June 28, 1987.

Perhaps owing to the successful democratization movement in the Philippines immediately prior to that, this meeting passed a resolution on political reform and hinted at moves toward democratization. On September 28 of the same year the Democratic Progressive Party was formed, and in an ex post facto decision the Kuomintang abolished the ban on the creation of new political parties on October 7, thereby opening the way to a multiparty political system on the island. A week later, on October 15, the Kuomintang promised to enact a National Security Act lifting martial law, a step formally taken on July 15, 1987.

In the first multiparty elections, held in December 1986, the Democratic Progressive Party (DPP)—calling for "self-determination of Taiwan's inhabitants," a slogan that suggested independence as a part of Taiwan's future—achieved a breakthrough with the election of 12 new candidates to the Legislative Yuan out of 73 contested seats and 11 new candidates to the National Assembly, where 84 seats were up for re-election. Early in 1987 a delegation of DPP members visited the United States, where they met with former Vice President Walter Mondale and other figures in the Democratic Party to establish a partnership with that organization. On its way home in mid-February, this delegation also stopped in Japan, where it engaged in promotional activities.

In China, from June 1986 onward Deng Xiaoping himself took the lead in invoking the need for reform of the political system. This may have been prompted in large part by his awareness of the moves toward democratization in Taiwan. In 1987 China started paying more and more attention to developments on the island. On May 16, when Deng met the Nobel Prize laureates Professor Yuan Tseh Lee (Li Yuanzhe) of the University of California at Berkeley and Professor Tsung Dao Lee (Li Zhengdao) of Columbia University, he stated the following: "When it comes to the unification of the motherland, we are placing our hopes on the Taiwan authorities and on the people of Taiwan. Taiwan is a part of Chinese territory. If the unification of China is not achieved, Taiwan's position will be insecure, and it may at some point be seized by others."[23]

---

23 *Beijing Review* (Japanese edition) 25, no. 21 (1987): 6.

This remark suggested Deng's willingness to rely on the Kuomintang to put an end to the signs of Taiwanese independence.

Just when China was on the alert about Taiwan's trends toward democratization and independence, Japan's economic relationship with Taiwan progressed greatly within the single year of 1986. Starting in the middle of the year, Japan's trade with Taiwan exceeded its trade with China, supported in part by the island's strong economic growth. Moreover, when Toyota Motor decided to set up production facilities in Taiwan in February 1986, other Japanese automotive firms like Mitsubishi Motors also started investing in Taiwan. It is not hard to imagine that such developments as the aforementioned memorial meetings in honor of Chiang Kai-shek, which took place at around this time, strongly irritated the Chinese government. From China's standpoint, therefore, the Kōkaryō decision in February 1987 was timed so perfectly as to seem as though it had been intentionally engineered. It is no small wonder that the Chinese side thought that all of these developments in Japan were directed by the Japanese government, as if to project its own system on other countries.

3. Why Did China Moderate Its Criticism of Japan?

Deng Xiaoping's Orders and the CCP Situation

The polemic between Japan and China over the Kōkaryō situation advanced in an unexpected direction following Yanagiya's "man above the clouds" statement. Through the steps outlined above and exchanges of opinions at the Japan-China Ministerial Conference in late June 1987, the two sides began moving toward smoother relations once again. The Chinese media, however, appeared to be working in the other direction—while not directly related to the Kōkaryō case, media output involved aggressive written and photographic coverage of Japan's invasion of China, timed to coincide with the fiftieth anniversary of the Marco Polo Bridge Incident on July 7. It was frequently reiterated that

210

education of young Chinese was the chief purpose of this coverage; but given that in the wake of the Hu Yaobang incident, Deng Xiaoping felt most keenly the need for better historical education of the younger generation, it seems evident that these issues were closely associated.[24]

It was also Deng who ordered and guided the subsequent moderation of Chinese criticism of Japan. Clear signs of this were observed around the start of September 1987, just before the fifteenth anniversary of the normalization of Japan-China ties. For example, according to the September 5 evening editions of the *Mainichi Shimbun* and *Sankei Shimbun*, Deng stated in a meeting with the LDP's Nikaidō Susumu on that day that "Some unfortunate things have occurred in recent years between Japan and China" but avoided any direct mention of the Kōkaryō case. In addition, as the *Tokyo Shimbun* reported on September 12, when Deng met with Tsukamoto Saburō, chairman of the Democratic Socialist Party, on September 11, he stated the following in response to a question about the Kōkaryō: "[The Japanese side] believes that this is a matter of the law. We think this is a political issue." In response to a follow-up question, he replied: "I hope you will resolve the issue yourselves. I have said all that I have to say. I think you understand our point of view."

At this stage Deng had begun to recognize the basic differences in the standpoints of Japan and China and to grasp that resolving the dispute would be no easy matter. This essentially meant that he had prepared himself to shelve the problem until the final decision of the Japanese Supreme Court. Perhaps complying with Deng's intentions, as noted above, at his meeting with Foreign Minister Kuranari Tadashi in New York at the end of September, Foreign Minister Wu Xueqian did not say a single word about the Kōkaryō case. Chinese Ambassador to Japan Zhang Shu expressed his understanding for Japan's division of powers in a speech in October as well.

---

24 Deng, "Yong Zhongguo de lishi jiaoyu qingnian" [Use Chinese History to Educate the Youth], in *Selected Works*, vol. 3, 204–206.

What was the situation within the Chinese Communist Party while these moves were underway to clear away the problem? After the Hu Yaobang incident the so-called conservative faction, which remained loyal to socialist ideology, came to have greater say inside the CCP. The position of Premier Zhao Ziyang, who had originally been pro-reform, was by no means safe even though he had assumed the party office of acting general secretary. Fierce behind-the-scenes battles were waged again and again within the party from the spring to summer of 1987 in the run-up to the Thirteenth National Congress of the CCP that autumn.

These battles reached a peak at the Enlarged Meeting of the Politburo on May 13 and the National Party Rectification Work Meeting that was held from May 26. At the former meeting, Zhao asserted that the conservatives were obstructing China's economic reforms; at the latter gathering he called for reform and opening up, going on to state that the Four Cardinal Principles, including upholding the socialist road and the leadership of the Communist Party, "must not be understood by a rigid viewpoint."[25] Deng Xiaoping's intentions were reportedly at work here, but the reform-minded positions of Zhao and his circle began to prevail from this time on. In July 1987, reform of the political system, which had been shelved due to the Hu Yaobang incident, was resuscitated as well, and it became almost certain that Zhao would formally assume the post of general secretary at the Thirteenth National Congress of the CCP in August. The consolidation of the pro-reform camp's power base within the CCP occurred in step with a softening of China's policies toward Japan, and a clear correlation can be observed between the two.

---

25 *Sankei Shimbun*, May 25, 1987; *Mainichi Shimbun*, May 29, 1987; and *Nihon Keizai Shimbun*, May 31, 1987.

China's Intentions in Moderating the Criticism

What were the intentions of Deng Xiaoping and the rest of the Chinese leadership below him as they began working to efface the Kōkaryō problem, even though the dispute had not reached a final resolution and Japan had not yielded in any manner? I would like to consider this problem from the following three angles.

First, it can be noted that China had shown consistent concern for Japanese media reports and the trends of Japanese public opinion surrounding the Kōkaryō, making it aware that the overall Japanese reaction to this dispute was harsh toward the Chinese assertions. The Japanese media had long been relatively willing to take heed when Asian countries presented harsh takes on Japan's historical awareness about its wartime conduct. China, fully aware of this, had in the past effectively applied "external pressure," working through the "friendly persons" mentioned earlier to bring about favorable coverage. However, since the Kōkaryō issue went to the core of Japanese democracy, involving as it did the separation of powers, the Japanese media adopted different approaches than usual to covering it as an issue involving Chinese interests. For example, a March 2, 1987 editorial in the *Asahi Shimbun* asserted that the Osaka High Court's decision "cannot be viewed as representing a recognition of a new status for Taiwan, or as 'based on the argument that there are two Chinas.'" The same paper clearly stated in a subsequent editorial on September 27 that "It is unreasonable for China to ask the Japanese government to intervene in the judiciary in the Kōkaryō case." On its May 10 editorial page, the *Yomiuri Shimbun* also asserted, "If China is seeking interference by the Japanese government in this court case, that is a tall order....It is hard to understand the connection of the Kōkaryō issue with militarism." The *Mainichi Shimbun* followed suit in a May 13 editorial arguing that "China's assertions, which appear to be heavy handed, ignore the Japanese tradition of the independence of the judiciary." Confronted by such a monolithic stance in the Japanese media, China likely recognized that any deeper meddling than this would produce the opposite of the desired effect.

Second, in connection with the question of Japanese media attention, a debate about the third program of yen loans, to be implemented in 1990–95, was already being raised at the start of 1987. China was concerned about potential adverse effects on the yen loans due to the aggravation of Japan-China relations by the Kōkaryō issue. China's dialing down of its criticism of Japan, in early September 1987, more or less coincides with the period when Beijing requested that the Japanese government move up the starting time of the third yen loans and increase their amount. At the same time, though, in a speech delivered in Shanghai on September 2, Sun Pinghua—chairman of the China-Japan Friendship Association—claimed that Japanese aid to China was insufficient, hinting moreover that there was opposition in China to the country's renunciation of compensation from Japan.[26] As if in response to this sensitive phase of change in China's policy scene, the Japanese government marked the fifteenth anniversary of normalization of relations by deciding on a new special yen loan of 100 billion yen.

Third, around this time, relations between China and Taiwan had started to improve, and China may have determined that constant harping about the "two Chinas" problem and the Taiwan question was counterproductive in terms of developing relations across the Taiwan Strait and pursuing eventual unification. As noted above, China had remained watchfully vigilant about political developments in Taiwan from 1986 on, but changes in this stance became evident from the fall of 1987—perhaps in connection with circumstances inside the CCP— as a result of the lifting of martial law on Taiwan in July 1987. This was symbolized by the fact that China welcomed a visit in September 1987 by two reporters from Taiwan's *Independence Evening Post* to do direct reporting about the mainland. The Taiwan authorities initially issued a warning about the arrangement, but it subsequently took no harsh measures against the journalists. To the contrary, on October 14, the

---

26 *Asahi Shimbun* and *Sankei Shimbun*, September 3, 1987.

Kuomintang decided to permit visits by Taiwan residents to see their relatives on the mainland, implementing this change on November 2. China issued a statement welcoming this decision.

In Summary:
Elements Determining China's Japan Policy

In this chapter, I have used the example of the Kōkaryō case to elucidate empirically, to the extent possible, the factual details of the mechanisms of China's policy decisions toward Japan. Some parts of my account rest on conjecture, given the paucity of primary source materials; nonetheless, I would like to underscore several points that have become clear through the analysis above.

First, Deng Xiaoping played the paramount role in directing China's Japan policy. While the same may not be true of any number of relatively minor disputes, with respect to the Kōkaryō issue, a stance expressed by Deng was invariably the decisive factor, whether it was a trigger launching the campaign to criticize Japan or a factor prompting the moderation and winding down of that criticism. At the same time, though, the situation was made more complex to some extent by Deng's lack of an accurate grasp of the circumstances, as can be seen by his simplistic tying of the Kōkaryō case to a "revival of Japanese militarism."

Second, China's policies toward Japan are deeply intertwined with the situation within the CCP at any given time. The background to the Kōkaryō's growth into a major issue was the fall from power of Hu Yaobang, who had been close to Japan through his personal relationship with Prime Minister Nakasone Yasuhiro. Although the Chinese repeatedly stated that there would be no change in their policies toward Japan after Hu's ouster, in reality China's overall approach toward Japan became extremely harsh in a variety of areas going beyond the Kōkaryō issue. Japan may not have meant it as such, but its assertion of the separation of powers appears to have come across as a comment on the Hu situation. Additionally, the phases when China was softening its criticism of Japan mesh neatly with the emergence of pro-reform forces inside the party, such as when Zhao Ziyang assumed the powerful position of general secretary. We might go further and note that in Japan-China relations in the Hu Yaobang era, the key policies had been formulated and implemented under the direct leadership of Hu, with a central role played by the secretariat of the CCP Central Committee; after his fall from power, though, the overall role of the secretariat itself—not only the part it played in China's Japan policy—was diminished. In the aftermath of the Hu incident, the direct line that the Japan-China Friendship Committee for the Twenty-First Century had enjoyed to the party center was evidently cut, and control over the group shifted from the secretariat, where it had been during the Hu's era, to the Ministry of Foreign Affairs.

Third, the Taiwan question looms large indeed in China's foreign policy. No concessions at all were observed in China's diplomatic negotiations regarding the Kōkaryō situation—perhaps unsurprising, given that the dormitory case was itself connected to the Taiwan issue. This leads to the conclusion that the issue of the unification of China and Taiwan, or in other words the "one China" proposition, is the first principle of Chinese diplomacy. China has firmly reflected this truth in its domestic and foreign policies by closely following the development of politics and the economy in Taiwan, particularly since the introduction of democracy there, and the ties between Taiwan and other actors.

Fourth, in its policies toward Japan, China actively appeals to friendly persons and organizations and well-placed politicians on the Japanese side, thereby seeking to exert influence over public opinion and policymakers in Japan so that the situation will unfold to China's advantage. This was particularly evident as the Kōkaryō case developed into a major problem.

Fifth, in connection with this influence fostering, China pays extremely close attention to trends in Japanese public opinion as it crafts its policies toward Japan. When it saw that it faced a resolute

Japanese stance on the Kōkaryō issue, and in particular that this stance had been adopted in unison by all of the Japanese newspapers—and that moreover, there was little prospect for shifting conditions to its advantage—China started to exhibit a softer policy, opting instead to shelve the matter. The goal of effectively extracting more aid from Japan appears to have been another factor involved in China's reaction to the Kōkaryō case.

As indicated above, China's policies toward Japan involve highly complex factors intertwined with one another. It may not be wise to generalize about them on the basis of a single case like the Kōkaryō dormitory. At the very least, though, it is worth emphasizing one important point: China's Japan policies are, in the final analysis, an extension of its internal politics. But at the same time, we need to qualify this statement by noting that Japan-China relations in this era remained under the strong leadership of Deng Xiaoping. Insofar as his basic stance of friendship toward Japan was not shaken even by the Hu Yaobang incident, we can conclude that the countries and their relationship still remained within the strong framework of the 1972 System.

Chapter 8

The Escalation of Historical Issues and Jiang Zemin's Visit to Japan (1990s)

Although one can scarcely imagine it nowadays, in the Japan-China relationship under the 1972 System up through the 1990s, the leaders of each country made official visits to the other with a view toward enhancement of mutual understanding and institutionalization of stable ties. As part of these efforts President Jiang Zemin, China's paramount leader, made an official visit to Japan from November 25 to 30, 1998. The two countries marked this visit with a joint declaration that called for a "partnership of friendship and cooperation for peace and development."

Jiang's visit had originally been conceived with two significances in mind. The first was the commemoration of the twentieth anniversary of the conclusion of the Japan-China Treaty of Peace and Friendship; the other was the building of a Japan-China partnership, which would signify the achievement of bilateral partnership relations among the four countries of Japan, the United States, China, and Russia. Beijing had formed a "constructive and strategic partnership" with Washington through Jiang's visit to the United States in the autumn of 1997 and President Bill Clinton's visit to China in the summer of 1998, and a "strategic cooperative partnership" had been built with Russia following President Boris Yeltsin's visit to China in April 1996. China had also created similar relationships with Europe as a whole, and with Britain and France in particular.

The two countries' official assessment of the Chinese leader's visit to Japan was that it was a success.[1] But the actual post-visit evaluation was more complex than that. Prime Minister Obuchi Keizō visited China in July 1999, and at this time as well, the two sides offered positive assessments of Jiang's visit in the previous year. But in both countries there were many who described the Jiang visit as a failure due to a focus on historical issues that had rendered it impossible to clearly

---

1 "Gaozhan yuanzhu mianxiang weilai: Relie zhuhe Jiang Zemin zhuxi fangwen Eluosi he Riben yuanman chenggong" [Look Far Ahead from a High Place and Face the Future: Heartily Celebrating the Successful Visits by Chairman Jiang Zemin to Russia and Japan], *People's Daily*, December 1, 1998.

construct a more future-oriented relationship. Many Japanese criticized the attitude of the Chinese president for clinging to historical issues, along with Japan's decision to grant China two yen loans, totaling 390 billion yen, in 1999 and 2000.[2] Only abridged passages from the joint statement at issue appeared in China's official media, and in the end the full text was not made public.

Such facts are illustrative of the difficulties of the "performance diplomacy" involved in such summits. When it comes to these top-level meetings, the success stories—tricked out in pomp and splendor—tend to attract the most attention, but history is replete with summits that were anything but successes. Summitry is fraught with difficulty because it relies on the personalities of the leaders and it must produce results in a short period. And if these diplomatic efforts fail, their ripple effects may last a long time.

In light of the above, it is important to revisit Jiang's trip to Japan. It was precisely from this time on that China intensified its focus on historical issues, while Japan began to show increasingly less concern about such issues, a half-century since the end of the war. The limits of the 1972 System were becoming evident. Accordingly, in this chapter I undertake an objective reconstruction of the reasons why Jiang's visit to Japan produced results so poor as to be qualified as a failure, examining relevant public materials and newspaper articles as well as my own interviews of policymakers in both Japan and China.[3]

---

2 See, for example, Takubo Tadae, "Sore ni tsukete mo shitsurei senban, Kō Takumin" [The Incredibly Rude Jiang Zemin], *Shokun* (February 1999), and "Kekkyoku Kō Takumin ni 3,900 oku en o kenjō shita dake datta Gaimushō no 'munō'" [The "Incompetence" of the Ministry of Foreign Affairs, which Ultimately Just Gifted 390 Billion Yen to Jiang Zemin], *Shūkan Post* (December 18, 1998).

3 Outstanding studies like the following about Jiang Zemin's visit to Japan continue to be published in recent years: Eguchi Shingo, "Hashimoto shushō no Yūrashia gaikō to Kō Takumin shuseki no rainichi: 1997–98 nen" [Prime Minister Hashimoto's Eurasia Diplomacy and Jiang Zemin's Visit to Japan, 1997–98], in *Nicchū kankeishi 1972–2012*, vol. 1 (see chap. 7, n. 1).

1. The Circumstances Surrounding Jiang's Japan Visit

Jiang Zemin's visit to Japan had originally been scheduled for early September 1998. But the flooding of the Yangtze River valley in southern China and of the Songhua River valley in the north of the country became critical, and on August 21 China requested a postponement of the visit. At the same time, Beijing notified Moscow of a postponement of Jiang's trip to Russia, which he had also been scheduled to visit. President Kim Dae Jung of South Korea, who had originally been slated to visit Japan after Jiang, ended up arriving first. The inversion of this order subsequently had major significance.

President Kim, who came in the first part of October, had promised beforehand that if Japan presented clear apologies about the historical issues, he would never raise them again. There were various opinions within Japan's ruling Liberal Democratic Party about how to address this, but since Japan had never clearly expressed its attitude about the historical issues with South Korea in written form—and moreover, given Kim's pledge not to repeat this request in the future—Prime Minister Obuchi decided to incorporate a straightforward expression of Japan's regrets in his speech.

Thus, the following sentence was incorporated in the joint declaration: "Looking back on the relations between Japan and the Republic of Korea during this century, Prime Minister Obuchi regarded in a spirit of humility the fact of history that Japan caused, during a certain period in the past, tremendous damage and suffering to the people of the Republic of Korea through its colonial rule, and expressed his deep remorse and heartfelt apology for this fact."[4] On October 8, President Kim addressed the Japanese National Diet. In his speech, speaking of Japan's statement of remorse, Kim stated that he "accepted it as an

---

4 The Japan–Republic of Korea Joint Declaration was printed in the evening editions of various Japanese newspapers on October 8, 1998. The English translation is available at Ministry of Foreign Affairs of Japan (website), https://www.mofa.go.jp/region/asia-paci/korea/joint9810.html.

earnest expression"; moreover, he stressed that "Japan has changed" after World War II and praised the country for its "development of parliamentary democracy and economic growth."[5] Owing to such exchanges, assessments of Kim Dae Jung grew more positive in Japan, and relations between Japan and South Korea developed extremely smoothly thereafter.

At the time of Jiang Zemin's subsequent visit to Japan, the Chinese side requested a Japanese statement equivalent to or stronger still than that provided to South Korea. Prior to the postponement of Jiang's visit, both sides had more or less agreed on an expression along the lines that they had "reconfirmed the importance" of the statement by Prime Minister Murayama Tomiichi in 1995 (see Part 4 of this chapter). History, in other words, was no longer supposed to be a major stumbling block in Japan-China relations. But China, provoked by the straightforward expression incorporated in the Japan-South Korea joint declaration, began to strongly demand the insertion of the Japanese word for "apology" *owabi*, corresponding to the Chinese *daoqian*.[6] However, a majority of the General Council of the LDP opposed the inclusion of apologetic phrases in a joint statement, citing differences between Japan's relations with Korea and those with China. I present the relevant background specifics below, but in sum, the Chinese request met with staunch resistance from Prime Minister Obuchi and ultimately did not materialize.

---

5 *Asahi Shimbun*, October 9, 1998. English translation quoted from "Address by President Kim Dae-jung of the Republic of Korea before the Japanese Diet," Office of the President, Republic of Korea (website), October 8, 1998, http://15cwd.pa.go.kr/english/library/press/view.php?f_nseq_tot=25794.

6 These circumstances are discussed in the commentary section of the *Yomiuri Shimbun*, November 27, 1998, and in the *Asahi Shimbun*, November 29, 1998.

2. The Details of Jiang's Visit

On November 24, the day before Jiang arrived in Japan, final negotiations took place between Chinese Foreign Minister Tang Jiaxuan, who had come to Japan for the purpose of preparing for the presidential visit, and Japanese Foreign Minister Kōmura Masahiko. The final agreement was that the word "apology" would not be incorporated into the declaration, and that in its stead Prime Minister Obuchi would express an apology verbally to President Jiang. During these preliminary talks, Tang repeatedly noted that "Since President Jiang is of a different generation, I do not know if this will be acceptable to him."[7] The Japanese side did, however, agree to insert into an official document for the first time a clear expression about the "invasion of China," as had been requested by the Chinese side.

It is said that one sentence had originally been prepared in a form representing China's response to the desired apology. This was a passage to the effect that the Chinese side "appreciated that postwar Japan had built itself into a major economic power due to its having adhered to the path of a peaceful nation." It was a verbal formula clearly delineating between the Japan of the prewar and wartime era and postwar Japan, praising the "peaceful nation" in place since the end of World War II and aiming to build a future-oriented Sino-Japanese relationship. But since Japan's "apology" expression was not put into writing, this passage was deleted at the same time.[8]

On November 25, President Jiang arrived in Japan after completing his trip to Russia. An informal dinner hosted by Prime Minister Obuchi was held that night at the State Guest House. It was perhaps during this event that Jiang first learned from Chinese Foreign Ministry officials of the outcome of the diplomatic negotiations, and he is believed to have been sorely displeased by the compromise reached therein. Ac-

---

7 *Asahi Shimbun*, November 25, 1998.
8 *Asahi Shimbun*, November 29, 1998.

cording to a December 1998 interview with a Chinese source familiar with the matter, it was reported in China that at this time President Jiang harshly criticized both Foreign Minister Tang and the Foreign Ministry's people handling Japan relations who had been involved in these negotiations. On the morning of November 26, Jiang attended a breakfast meeting with former prime ministers including Nakasone Yasuhiro, after which he met with figures who had contributed to Japan-China friendship and their children. At these events, Jiang was already mentioning the importance of facing history squarely, but it was not until the official summit meeting with Prime Minister Obuchi that evening that the matter erupted in full public view. At the summit, Jiang allotted considerable time to the problem of historical awareness, calling for a more serious approach by Japan, including the launch of an "awareness program" aimed at the Japanese public.[9]

Jiang maintained his focus on historical issues during the state banquet at the Imperial Palace later that evening, where he sharply criticized Japan for its past militarism. Jiang's speech included the following lines, as reported by the *Asahi Shimbun* on November 27: "Unfortunately, in its modern history, militarism led Japan down the erroneous path of foreign invasion and expansion, causing great suffering for the Chinese people and the peoples of other Asian countries. The Japanese people themselves were deeply harmed by this too. There is a saying: 'Forget not the past, and let it be a warning about the future.' We must eternally take into consideration the lessons of this painful history." Jiang's emphatic recounting of historical issues in the presence of the Japanese emperor, a moment broadcast live on Japanese television, resulted in considerable distaste in Japan for Jiang for making such utterances at a state banquet.

Another matter that drew international attention at this time was the decision by both sides to not sign the joint declaration. The Japanese and Chinese governments have held that no signing had been planned

---

9 Various newspapers, November 27, 1998.

in the first place, but both the Japan-South Korea joint declaration and the Moscow declaration at the time of Prime Minister Obuchi's visit to Russia had been signed, and the mainstream view at this stage was that the failure to do so in this case was due to China's displeasure.[10]

On November 27, the visit schedule included such events as a breakfast meeting hosted by the speakers of both houses of the Diet and a reception hosted by the seven Japan-China friendship organizations; Jiang continued to devote considerable time to discussion of historical issues in these venues as well. A slight course correction in Jiang's statements was evident, though, from the welcoming dinner hosted by Prime Minister Obuchi on the evening of November 27. There, too, Jiang first touched on the historical issues, but then stated: "Japan has chosen the path of peaceful development in the postwar period, achieving great results on the economic front, and has become a key global economic power today. It will be favorable for Japan to continue to adhere to this correct path of development, as well as favorable for the peace and development of Asia and the world."[11] This appeared to be a clear resuscitation of the part that had been deleted from the joint declaration, indicating that at this point Jiang had begun to shift toward a softer stance. He had presumably sensed the negative reaction to his earlier comments.

What deserves attention on November 28 is the speech given by Jiang at Waseda University. Here, perhaps from his determination to convey his feelings to the young people of Japan, Jiang called himself a "witness of history" and stated that "35 million soldiers and civilians had died or been injured, and more than 600 billion dollars in economic losses had been suffered" in China due to Japan's invasion. In another section, though, he said: "The reason Japan has been able to become a major economic power is that it is indeed following the path of peace and development. This is the result of its getting along peacefully with neighboring countries." With this, he exhibited a stance distinguishing

10 *Sankei Shimbun*, November 26, 1998, evening edition.
11 Remarks by Jiang Zemin at the welcoming dinner hosted by Prime Minister Obuchi, materials of the Kantei (Prime Minister's Office).

between prewar and postwar Japan and struck a more balanced tone.[12]

That evening Jiang headed to Sendai, Miyagi Prefecture, in Japan's northeastern Tōhoku region, by Shinkansen. The next day he visited the monument to the Chinese author Lu Xun and Tohoku University, and in the afternoon, he traveled on to Sapporo, Hokkaido, where he did a tour of a farm. On November 30, he completed the official itinerary and returned to China. It is reported that Jiang appeared relaxed in Tōhoku and Hokkaido and that his mood was quite different from the oppressive atmosphere that surrounded him while he was in Tokyo.

3. Circumstances on the Chinese Side

It was the Japan-China relationship that generated the friction related above, but what specifically constituted the background to these events? Looking at the events of this visit, we can assume that some of the major causes lay on the Chinese side, and in particular with Jiang Zemin, but Japan and China doubtless have differing takes on the situation. Accordingly, I attempt an objective reconstruction here of the respective arguments and reasoning underpinning them, viewing matters from the standpoints of both countries. This is based on interviews that I conducted with policymakers in both countries. I will examine the Chinese side first.

Historical Issues

The most frequent observation on China's standpoint is that historical issues are core among the nation's principles. The way these issues were handled during Jiang's visit to Japan resulted in his loss of "face" (*mianzi*) as a leader. Put simply, the crux is the question of why China was accorded treatment less favorable than that given to South Korea. Viewed from the Chinese standpoint, it is hardly surprising that the

---

12 *Asahi Shimbun*, November 28, 1998, evening edition.

Chinese discerned some ill intention lurking behind Japan's inclusion of the word "apology" in an official document during Kim Dae Jung's visit, while it did not insert the same word in the joint declaration when Jiang came the following month.

In this connection, Japan asserted that when it came to its relations with China, it had taken many steps—including a visit by the Japanese emperor to China—that had no comparable equivalent in Japan's actions vis-à-vis South Korea. The Chinese response, though, was that if Japan were sincere about addressing its past, it should have felt no resistance to inserting the word "apology" on this occasion, and that Japan should settle the issue and build a future-oriented relationship with China through the word's inclusion. Moreover, in Japan there were some pointing out that Korea had been a Japanese colony, while in the case of China Japan had committed an invasion, a reason for the different responses to the two countries in the present day. Hearing such comments appears to have only further reinforced the Chinese sense of distrust about Japan's handling of the matter.

The Taiwan Issue

Another factor, also relating to the issue of "face," is the Taiwan issue. In its negotiations with the United States, China extracted from President Bill Clinton the "three noes": no support for "two Chinas" or "one China, one Taiwan"; no support for Taiwanese independence; and no support for Taiwan's membership in international organizations that are composed of sovereign states. Russia, too, made clear reference to these positions in its dealings with the Chinese. From Japan, though, during preliminary negotiations China only obtained the expression that "there is one China" in the joint declaration, ultimately failing to extract the "three noes" from Tokyo. This was reportedly due to strong resistance on the Japanese side.

Taiwan was in fact a more serious matter for China than the historical issues, as well as a source of lengthy disputes surrounding Jiang's visit to Japan. Ever since the victory by the Democratic Progressive

Party—which called for Taiwanese independence—in Taiwan's local elections in the autumn of 1997, China had been extremely vigilant about the political changes occurring on the island. In its efforts to improve its relations with the United States, China had made a number of concessions, including the release of political prisoners Wei Jingsheng and Wang Dan, and a promise to sign the United Nations' International Covenant on Economic, Social and Cultural Rights and International Covenant on Civil and Political Rights. What China had requested in return was chiefly US cooperation in stemming the trend toward Taiwan's independence. There is no question that from President Clinton's trip to China in late June 1998 through the rest of the year, the United States took many actions to inhibit the independence trend, such as encouraging Taiwan through various routes to engage in dialogue with China.

China sought the same from Japan at the time of Jiang's visit to that country. The visit took place immediately before the Legislative Yuan elections and the election of the mayor of Kaohsiung in Taiwan on December 5. China wanted the Kuomintang to come out victorious, no matter what, and sought to extract certain concessions from Japan to ratchet up the pressure on Taiwan. But these efforts encountered stiff Japanese resistance. As the Chinese authorities did not want to ruin the atmosphere of the semi-official Straits Exchange between China and Taiwan that had restarted in October with the Taiwanese business leader Koo Chen-fu's visit to China, they abandoned their insistence on the Taiwan question and redirected focus to historical issues. But the outcome was as described above. China was ultimately unable to extract anything from Japan on either Taiwan or historical matters. It is small wonder that Jiang felt that he had lost face.

Jiang Zemin's Personal Choices

The main actor in the problematic visit was, in the final analysis, Jiang Zemin himself. We must focus on the personal conduct and thinking of this leader in his stubborn adherence to the historical question. Jiang was born in Yangzhou in 1926. Jiang Shangqing—the younger brother of his father, Jiang Shijun—was a member of the Chinese Communist Party but was reportedly killed by a Chinese collaborator of Japan during the Sino-Japanese War in 1939. Since Shangqing had no sons, Shijun had his own son, Zemin, adopted by Shangqing's widow, Wang Zhelan. The Japanese military held strong sway over Yangzhou at that time, and this, combined with the death of his adoptive father, reportedly fostered in Jiang a strong antipathy toward Japan from this time on. In another widely known version of Jiang's background, his actual father, Shijun, was a cadre of the Wang Jingwei regime in Nanjing, which had built a close relationship with the Japanese military; moreover, Jiang Zemin had attended National Central University in Nanjing, where Japanese influence was strong, and studied Japanese there. This would have made him the son of a *hanjian* (Chinese traitor) and ineligible to join the CCP, so he allegedly entered it as the adopted son of his uncle instead.[13]

But it is unconvincing to claim that Jiang clung tightly to China's historical issues with Japan solely because of his personal experiences. It is more likely that there was a more recent impetus behind this. There are two turning points in particular worth exploring in this regard. The first is the fiftieth anniversary of the end of World War II in 1995. In May of that year, Jiang Zemin attended ceremonies commemorating the fiftieth anniversary of the victory in the Anti-Fascist War held in Moscow at the invitation of Russian President Boris Yeltsin. (Technically, of course, the People's Republic of China did not yet exist in 1945 when the war ended, and Russia itself was then the Soviet Union.) When Jiang returned to China after attending the celebrations, he switched in the direction of banning Japanese television dramas and films, which had been popular in China until then, and showing a large number of

---

13 See, for example, "Shiming jubao Jiang Zeming bei shoujian xuezhe huo baowai jiuyi" [The Scholar Who Reported Jiang Zemin by His Actual Name Obtains Compassionate Release for Medical Examination], *Duowei News*, February 19, 2015, http://china.dwnews.com/news/2015-02-19/59636722.html.

dramas and films with themes related to the Anti-Japanese War in their place. In the background, here was the rapid decline in interest in the Communist Party and socialism in China since the introduction of the socialist market economy in 1992. The CCP had fought these trends by strengthening patriotic education from 1994. Jiang's new 1995 direction reinforced this education and marked the start of the emphasis on the CCP's victory in the Anti-Japanese War as the source of its legitimacy in gaining power in China. By making the CCP the main subject of the Anti-Japanese War, in other words, Jiang was attempting to place the PRC among the ranks of the victorious powers. This runs counter to the facts, of course; it was the Kuomintang at the core of the Chinese war efforts during the Anti-Japanese War. Jiang was straining to provide an interpretation of history that placed the CCP at its center.

The second turning point was that Jiang reportedly read a Chinese translation of a Japanese book just before his visit to Japan, becoming enraged by its content. The original text was titled *Dai Tō-A sensō no sōkatsu* (A Summary of the Greater East Asia War). It had been compiled by the LDP's History Review Committee, and the Xinhua Publishing Company produced a Chinese edition for internal circulation in China.[14] The committee, with Yamanaka Sadanori as its chair and Itagaki Tadashi as secretary-general, was formed in August 1993 with more than 100 Diet members from the LDP. The roster of members included many cabinet ministers and members of mainstream LDP factions. Almost all of the articles collected in this book had been written by commentators and other nonpoliticians, but their titles included things like "The Fabricated 'Nanjing Massacre,'" and the undercurrent of the entire work was a critique of the historical view offered at the Tokyo Trials. It appears that Jiang read this book and determined that these were the firm historical views of many Diet members, including

---

14 "Guoji wenti cankao yichong" [Collection of Reference Translations on International Affairs], in *Da-Dongya zhanzheng de zongjie* [A Summary of the Greater East Asia War], ed. History Review Committee (Japan) (Beijing: Xinhua Publishing House, 1997), for internal distribution.

even mainstream LDP members, and came to believe that this represented the majority viewpoint in Japan.

It is frequently pointed out that Jiang's hardening attitude toward Japan was rooted in his own weakness in China's internal power struggles. But this is belied by many other developments at that time—for example, Jiang's success in improving relations with the United States, his establishment of strategic partnerships with Russia and various European countries, his skillful domestic leadership in devising measures to cope with flooding, a serious problem in China at the time, and his restoration of trust in and the morale of the Chinese military. On the basis of this evidence, it is clear that Jiang had already consolidated his power base to a fair extent. The actual circumstances may well have been that the people around Jiang were unable to restrain his personal feelings and the actions he based on them.

4. Circumstances on the Japanese Side

Fatigue over Historical Issues

Looking next at the situation on the Japanese side, the first thing to mention is that what might be termed "historical issue fatigue" had become widespread in Japan by this point. More than half a century had passed since the war's end, and generational change had been progressing. The generations that had actually experienced the war were well beyond the age of 60 by that time. Although there were of course some who justified Japan's actions in the war, the vast majority of the Japanese people felt a certain sense of remorse, even if they had not directly experienced the conflict, and acknowledged that their country had indeed been an invader. But when confronted with China's stubborn adherence to the historical issues and the repeated criticisms of their country by China, which seemed to treat the views of a revisionist minority in Japan as those of the majority, many Japanese gradually began to feel fatigue. Around the fiftieth anniversary of the war's end in 1995 in particular, China's repeated launch of fresh campaigns urging study of the Anti-Japanese War and stoking patriotism evoked considerable antipathy in Japan.

Japanese Apologies to China

In Japan, the perception that the country had already apologized to China for the historical issues was by that time firmly rooted. On this point, the Joint Communique of the Government of Japan and the Government of the People's Republic of China in 1972 stated the following: "The Japanese side is keenly conscious of the responsibility for the serious damage that Japan caused in the past to the Chinese people through war, and deeply reproaches itself."[15] Moreover, even though it was not an official statement by the Japanese government, in Emperor Akihito's address during his visit to China in 1992, he walked right up to the line of offering an apology with the following words: "In the long history of relationships between our two countries, there was an unfortunate period in which my country inflicted great suffering on the people of China. About this I feel deep sadness."[16] And although the August 15, 1995, statement by Prime Minister Murayama Tomiichi on the fiftieth anniversary of the end of World War II was not directed solely at China, it nonetheless included the following passage: "Japan …through its colonial rule and aggression, caused tremendous damage and suffering to the people of many countries, particularly to those of Asian nations….I regard, in a spirit of humility, these irrefutable facts of history, and express here once again my feelings of deep remorse and state my heartfelt apology."[17]

---

15 "Joint Communique," Ministry of Foreign Affairs of Japan (website) (see chap. 6, n. 13).
16 "Tennō heika no Yō Shōkon kokka shuseki shusai bansankai ni okeru tōji" [Remarks by the Emperor at the State Banquet Hosted by President Yang Shangkun], in *Kihon shiryōshū 1949–97*, 794. English translation quoted from "Japan's Apologies for World War II," *The New York Times* (online), updated August 14, 2015, https://www.nytimes.com/interactive/2015/08/13/world/asia/japan-ww2-shinzo-abe.html.
17 "Statement by Prime Minister Tomiichi Murayama 'On the Occasion of the 50th Anniversary of the War's End' (15 August 1995)," Ministry of Foreign Affairs of Japan (website), https://www.mofa.go.jp/announce/press/pm/murayama/9508.html.

To be sure, it was only in the Murayama statement directed at various countries of Asia, including China, that the word "apology" appeared. But Japan held that it had repeatedly expressed its feelings of regret through various opportunities in the past. When comparing China's case to that of Korea in particular, the Japanese had a strong sense that while their country had put such feelings into writing for China and had even arranged an imperial visit, nothing comparable had been done for South Korea.

Conditions Faced by Prime Minister Obuchi

The circumstances surrounding the Obuchi administration also need to be considered. Prime Minister Obuchi had assumed office on July 30, but his cabinet's support ratings had fallen owing to a combination of doubts about his leadership and the severity of Japan's economic stagnation. When on August 31, North Korea launched a Taepodong missile (North Korea claimed that it was placing a satellite in orbit), which reached Japanese territorial waters off the Sanriku coast, a sense of impending crisis regarding security issues suddenly gripped Japan. In this environment, criticisms grew stronger within the LDP about insufficient leadership capabilities and the failure of politics to play a more commanding role. This mood would end up driving the subsequent alliance between the LDP and the Liberal Party. The hardline stance opposing the inclusion of the word "apology" in a joint statement with China can be positioned in the context of these developments inside the LDP.

In Summary

How can we best sum up Jiang Zemin's visit to Japan in 1998? It resulted in a joint declaration whose keynote was a "partnership of friendship and cooperation for peace and development," and a concrete, future-oriented vision was offered. But this visit also left so bitter an aftertaste for both sides that these achievements were largely forgotten. As noted above, the two countries had their separate takes on the situation and reasons informing those takes, and these introduced distortions into the bilateral relationship. That said, the personal thinking of Jiang Zemin likely played a strong role in these events. The countries did not set out to damage their relationship intentionally, but miscommunication ultimately made the situation more convoluted.

After Jiang's visit, both countries maintained that the trip had been a success and continued coolheaded efforts to keep the relationship from deteriorating. Prime Minister Obuchi's visit to China on July 8–10, 1999, arranged in exchange for Jiang's tour of Japan, was a short stay of only three days, but it concluded in a harmonious atmosphere. Japan took a number of measures immediately before the visit to lay the groundwork for its success, such as announcing Japanese agreement to China's accession to the WTO. And while Obuchi was in China, the hosts strove to limit any mention of historical issues to an absolute minimum. During his discussions with Prime Minister Obuchi at the 1999 summit, President Jiang touched on them only to state that "We should draw lessons from history and look to the future."[18] This state of affairs had not changed as of the fiftieth anniversary of the establishment of the PRC on October 1, 1999, when no moves were seen to boost patriotism by tying it to the historical issues involving Japan. It seems reasonable to view this as indicating a certain amount of reflection in China in the aftermath of Jiang's Japan visit.

However, considering the subsequent development of Japan-China ties, this visit was a major turning point that stripped the 1972 System of its substance. The countries were confronted with a complex situation involving, on the Japanese side, the view that the historical issues had reached their final conclusion at the time of Emperor Akihito's visit to China; and, on the Chinese side, the nation's continued reliance

---

18 Various newspapers, July 10, 1999, and the op-ed column of *Sankei Shimbun*, July 11, 1999.

234

on the historical issues related to Japan, including the study of the Anti-Japanese War, and the personal circumstances of Jiang Zemin. Before long, the Sino-Japanese relationship was caught in a swirling vortex of mutual distrust.

Chapter 9

A Temporary Mending of Ties:
Toward a Mutually Beneficial Strategic Relationship (2000s)

1. From the 1972 System to a Strategic Relationship Benefiting Both Sides

From May 6 to 10, 2008, Chinese President Hu Jintao visited Japan as a state guest, successfully completing his entire itinerary. Hu's visit came on the heels of visits to China by Prime Minister Abe Shinzō in October 2006, to Japan by Premier Wen Jiabao in April 2007, and to China by Prime Minister Fukuda Yasuo in December 2007. As such, Hu's 2008 trip might well be called the capstone to this series of mutual visits by leaders, carried out to improve the damaged Japan-China relationship. From the start of the new century, bilateral relations had run aground on the shoals of historical issues, in particular the controversy surrounding Prime Minister Koizumi Jun'ichirō's visits to Yasukuni Shrine during his time in office (2001–2006). The images held by the two countries' peoples about the other country had also worsened, and anti-Japanese demonstrations had erupted in China in 2005.

Much of the world's media regarded Sino-Japanese ties as beyond improvement, issuing frequent commentaries depicting the bilateral relationship as suffering more serious rifts than the issues of Taiwan or North Korea. These commentaries argued that there was no strong will or capacity, in either Japan or China, to improve bilateral relations and that a third country would need to mediate as a consequence. At one point, the US government floated the idea of brokering an effort involving both Japan and China to conduct joint historical research.[1] The subsequent rapprochement soon made it clear that the two countries possessed the will and capacity to improve their ties, and simultaneously demonstrated that the problems of the region could be handled by the parties there.

Amid their warming ties, Japan and China acquired a specific vision for the new relationship that would replace the "Japan-China

1 One example is the remarks by Deputy Secretary of State Robert B. Zoellick on January 23, 2006 (reported in various Japanese newspapers on January 24).

friendship" slogan under the previous 1972 System. This was the "mutually beneficial strategic relationship" (*senryakuteki gokei kankei/ zhanlue huhui guanxi*), a new approach first proposed during Abe's "ice-breaking" October 2006 visit. After that, the Chinese avoided any sustained probing of historical issues or the Taiwan issue. China instead stressed the "peaceful development" that Japan had undergone in the postwar era as a means of prioritizing the new relationship, aiming to craft forward-looking long-term bilateral ties that took a broader view of the issues facing the nations.

Subsequently, during Premier Wen Jiabao's April 2007 visit to Japan, described as "ice melting," Tokyo and Beijing reached agreement on their mutually beneficial strategic relationship in a more concrete form. They first placed fresh importance on dialogue on all fronts and promoted exchanges between leaders, cabinet members and other high-level officials involved in economics and diplomacy, defense officials, the youth of both countries, and so forth. Mutual visits by the ships of the Chinese Navy and the Japanese Maritime Self-Defense Force were also incorporated into this framework. Japan and China further agreed on mutually beneficial cooperation in such areas as energy, the environment, agriculture, healthcare, intellectual property rights, information and communications technology, and crime, as well as on international cooperation on United Nations reform, North Korea, and other issues.[2]

Attracting the most attention during this visit to Japan was Wen Jiabao's address to the Japanese Diet on April 12, which was simulcast on Chinese media. In his speech Premier Wen praised Japan for its peaceful postwar development, stating that the Japanese government had on many previous occasions "admitted that Japan had committed aggression" and "expressed deep remorse and apologies to victimized countries," and further noting that China and its people "appreciate"

---

2 "Japan-China Joint Statement" (April 11, 2007), Ministry of Foreign Affairs of Japan (website), https://www.mofa.go.jp/region/asia-paci/china/pv0704/joint.html.

this.[3] To be sure, the Chinese put Japan on notice that they expected this stance to remain in evidence in the country's future behavior. That said, this was the first public statement in which the Chinese side basically acknowledged that Japan had expressed remorse and apologies in the past, and it broke through much of the resentment that had been smoldering in Japan to the effect that "no matter how many times we apologize, it will never be enough."

Prime Minister Fukuda, who took over following Prime Minister Abe's September 2007 resignation, visited China from December 28 to 30, 2007, in what he called a trip "that heralds and welcomes the spring." This trip made further progress toward putting the mutually beneficial strategic relationship into concrete form. The joint press statement that summarized the visit gave shape to the relationship as follows.[4] First, the two sides would strengthen mutually beneficial cooperation on the climate, environment, energy, and other key areas. Second, they would promote exchanges and mutual understanding in the field of security, as well as promoting youth, intellectual, and other exchanges. Third, cooperation would be enhanced in both regional and international security fields, covering issues like North Korea, anti-terrorism efforts, and reform of the United Nations. Fourth, the governments would pursue the resolution of issues related to resource development in the East China Sea. And fifth, they would find common ground by confirming the principles involved in historical problems and the question of Taiwan, such as by carrying out joint historical research. During this visit to China, Fukuda gave a speech at Peking University, which was also broadcast live throughout China.

3 *People's Daily*, April 13, 2007. English translation quoted from "Speech by Premier Wen Jiabao of the State Council of the People's Republic of China at the Japanese Diet: For Friendship and Cooperation" (April 13, 2007), Ministry of Foreign Affairs of the People's Republic of China (website), https://www.fmprc.gov.cn/mfa_eng/wjb_663304/zzjg_663340/yzs_663350/gjlb_663354/2721_663446/2725_663454/t311544.shtml.
4 "Visit by Prime Minister Yasuo Fukuda to the People's Republic of China (Overview and Evaluation)" (December 30, 2007), Ministry of Foreign Affairs of Japan (website), https://www.mofa.go.jp/region/asia-paci/china/pmv0712/overview.html.

President Hu Jintao's May 2008 visit to Japan took place in challenging circumstances that had arisen just before it. At the start of the year, an incident occurred involving the poisoning of *gyōza* dumplings produced in China, and the longer the facts of the incident were left unresolved regarding whether the poison had been introduced in China or later in Japan, the more public opinion in the two countries clashed. Moreover, protests by Tibetans along the route of the torch relay in various places in the world started in the run-up to the Beijing Olympics, resulting in tight security that distorted the relay route. In Japan as well, the torch relay was conducted in a bizarre atmosphere in Nagano Prefecture. But the Chinese government revived its dialogue with the fourteenth Dalai Lama a few days before Hu departed for Japan, thereby exhibiting a tentative stance of compromise with a view toward creating a positive atmosphere.

Hu Jintao's visit to Japan, christened a "warm spring" trip, included three meetings with Emperor Akihito—a welcoming ceremony, a state dinner at the Imperial Palace, and a farewell meeting—as well as multiple meetings with Prime Minister Fukuda. At the state dinner, Hu said almost nothing at all about the historical issues, as if to dispel the repeated mention of these issues by Jiang Zemin during his visit to Japan exactly one decade earlier, and lavishly praised the emperor's visit to China in 1992 by saying: "People of both of our two countries cherish fond memories of your historic visit.…It was an event greatly appreciated in the annals of China-Japan relations."[5]

As was noted briefly in Chapter 6, there was a background to this statement. Qian Qichen, who was Chinese foreign minister at the time of the imperial visit, stated in his memoirs (perhaps to emphasize his personal achievements) that he had targeted Japan as the "weakest link in the united front of the West's sanctions against China" and planned Emperor Akihito's visit to help China break out of its isolation following the

---

5 "Toast by President Hu Jintao of the People's Republic of China at Welcoming Banquet Hosted by the Emperor of Japan" (May 7, 2008), Imperial Household Agency (website), https://www.kunaicho.go.jp/e-okotoba/01/address/pdf/okotoba-h20-kokuhin-3.pdf.

Tiananmen Square Incident.[6] Seen in this context, Hu Jintao's statement essentially disavowed Qian's claim with his high praise for the 1992 visit.

During Hu's visit to Japan, the countries issued a new Joint Statement between the Government of Japan and the Government of the People's Republic of China, the fourth bilateral political document following the 1972 Joint Communique of the Government of Japan and the Government of the People's Republic of China, the 1978 Treaty of Peace and Friendship between Japan and the People's Republic of China, and the 1998 Japan-China Joint Declaration. As indicated by its title, which went on with "Comprehensive Promotion of a 'Mutually Beneficial Relationship Based on Common Strategic Interests,'" this 2008 statement established "mutually beneficial strategic relationship" as the expression symbolizing the future of the relationship. The document also clearly set forth the stances of avoidance of any mention of historical issues and the question of Taiwan, China's praise for Japan's peaceful postwar development, and Chinese approval of an enhanced Japanese status in the United Nations.

The content of the mutually beneficial relationship based on common strategic interests was enumerated as follows: (1) Enhancement of mutual trust in the political area, including exchanges of visits by leaders and security officials; (2) Promotion of people-to-people and cultural exchange, such as youth and intellectual exchanges; (3) Enhancement of mutually beneficial cooperation in energy, the environment, the economy, and the East China Sea; (4) Contribution to the Asia-Pacific region, including on the North Korea issue; and (5) Contribution to the resolution of climate change, energy security, poverty, contagious diseases, and other global issues.[7] All of these items represented nothing short of a stunning advance in bilateral ties. As if to symbolize this,

---

6 Qian Qishen, *Sen Kishin kaikoroku* (see chap. 6, n. 5), 185.
7 "Joint Statement between the Government of Japan and the Government of the People's Republic of China on Comprehensive Promotion of a 'Mutually Beneficial Relationship Based on Common Strategic Interests'" (May 7, 2008), Ministry of Foreign Affairs of Japan (website), https://www.mofa.go.jp/region/asia-paci/china/joint0805.html.

when a major earthquake occurred in Sichuan two days after Hu's return to China, the first request made by China for outside assistance in coping with it was to an international disaster relief team from Japan.

But this visit had still not put the Sino-Japanese relationship back on the right track. It certainly helped to thaw the ice somewhat, but that ice was nowhere close to melting away entirely. That said, if we look back over the bilateral relationship since normalization of relations, the importance of Prime Minster Abe's October 2006 visit stands out in clear relief. Without it, the subsequent mutual visits and the mutually beneficial strategic relationship, a concept central to Japan-China relations right up to the present day, could never have been achieved.

Japan-China relations prior to the Abe trip had remained frozen owing to the Yasukuni Shrine visits by Prime Minister Koizumi during his time in office. Shortly after Koizumi's resignation, Abe, the new prime minister, visited China. What made that possible? The background within Japan was of course important, but at the same time we must elucidate the even more important reasons that led President Hu Jintao to allow Abe's visit. Despite the fact that Beijing had made top-level exchanges conditional on an end to the Yasukuni visits, it accepted Abe's trip to China even though the question of whether such visits would end had been left unsettled. Naturally, the Chinese noted that it was their understanding that there would be no more visits. In Abe's own statements, though, he had merely repeated the formula: "Whether I have visited or will visit Yasukuni Shrine is not something I shall make clear."[8] Clearly this would have been impossible had there not been a tacit agreement and solid measure of trust between the two leaders supporting such resolve.

Accordingly, in this chapter I will elucidate empirically, in the context of the two countries' internal politics, the question of how bilateral relations, which had chilled in the Koizumi era to the point where

---

8 "Press Conference by Prime Minister Shinzo Abe Following His Visit to China" (October 8, 2006), Prime Minister of Japan and His Cabinet (website), https://japan.kantei.go.jp/abespeech/2006/10/08chinapress_e.html.

anti-Japanese demonstrations occurred in China, could be mended with the advent of the Abe government. My aim is to demonstrate anew the truth of the somewhat hackneyed theme that "foreign policy is an extension of domestic politics," with recent Japan-China relations as a case in point—underscoring the fact that domestic power struggles in China play a crucial role therein. The verification here involves a rough-hewn hypothesis and outline based on those materials available at present, information in my own possession, and inferences by analogy. I leave to future researchers the fuller inquiry into the historical evidence and its analysis.

2. The Realization of Abe's Visit and the Summit Meeting

Needless to say, the problems posed by Prime Minister Koizumi's visits to Yasukuni Shrine were the main factor in strained Japan-China relations. These visits were reportedly in response to the approximately 100,000 votes that Koizumi received from members of the Japan War-Bereaved Families Association when he opposed former Prime Minister Hashimoto Ryūtarō in the race for president of the Liberal Democratic Party in 2001, the stepping-stone to the premiership. In any event, though, he publicly pledged that he would visit Yasukuni Shrine on August 15, the anniversary of the end of World War II.[9] Koizumi emerged victorious in the contest and officially took office as prime minister on April 26. That summer he fulfilled his public pledge to visit the shrine, although the date of his visit was moved up from August 15 to August 13, perhaps owing in part to security concerns.

The Chinese reacted negatively to the visit as expected, but their response was rather restrained, and Koizumi visited China two months

---

9 Yomiuri Shimbun Political News Department, *Gaikō o kenka ni shita otoko: Koizumi gaikō 2000 nichi no shinjitsu* [The Man Who Turned Diplomacy into a Quarrel: The Truth about the 2,000 days of Koizumi's Diplomacy] (Tokyo: Shinchōsha, 2006), 223.

later, in October 2001. This was possible because the Yasukuni visits had been declared publicly and the foreign affairs authorities of both countries had engaged in behind-the-scenes negotiations, carefully laying the groundwork beforehand for a trip by the Japanese prime minister to China to readjust the relationship following the Yasukuni visit. While in China, Koizumi visited the Museum of the War of Chinese People's Anti-Japanese War at Marco Polo Bridge (Lugouqiao) outside Beijing, where he expressed his "feelings of heartfelt apology and mourning" for the Chinese victims of the war.[10]

China seems to have assumed that, as in the case of past prime ministers, Koizumi would end his visits to Yasukuni Shrine after a single trip there. Soon afterward, when an advisory group about a commemorative facility for Japan's war dead was established in December 2001, there was widespread speculation in and outside Japan that a facility that would substitute for Yasukuni would be created. Moreover, at the start of April 2002, Koizumi accepted an invitation to the Boao Forum for Asia on Hainan Island—positioned as a Chinese version of the Davos Forum—despite the fact that very few leaders of other countries were attending, thus making his second trip to China, albeit a single-day one, in rapid order. But on April 21, shortly after his return from this forum, Koizumi shocked many by paying a second visit to Yasukuni Shrine. Koizumi notified no one in advance, including the Ministry of Foreign Affairs. China had assumed that there would be no further visits and could not simply regard this as an unwelcome surprise. Beijing predictably reacted strongly against this development. While Koizumi must have felt that he had shown consideration by attending the Boao Forum, the Chinese likely harbored a sense of betrayal following this act. Indeed, as the controversy surrounding Yasukuni erupted once more, Japan-China relations soured.

However, Koizumi met with Premier Zhu Rongji at ASEM, the Asia-Europe Meeting, in September 2002, and with President Jiang

10 Yomiuri Shimbun Political News Department, *Koizumi gaikō,* 235.

Zemin during the APEC conference in Mexico in October. In 2003, President Hu Jintao and Premier Wen Jiabao took the reins in China. During this time, Koizumi's visits to Yasukuni Shrine continued, but summit meetings were maintained on the sidelines of various international meetings taking place in other countries. The end of such bilateral meetings came with the summit between Koizumi and Hu, held at the Asian-African Conference in Indonesia just after anti-Japanese demonstrations occurred across China in the spring of 2005. This marked the start of a year and a half during which no summitry took place; this period only came to an end with Abe's visit to China in October 2006. For what it is worth, although the anti-Japanese demonstrations in 2005 are generally described as a backlash against Koizumi's Yasukuni visits, the objective situation at this time made them out to be protests opposing Japan's inclusion on the United Nations Security Council.

During this time, the so-called Japan-China Strategic Dialogue (initially the Japan-China Comprehensive Policy Dialogue) served as the channel for substantive negotiations between the two countries. The Japanese side was represented by Vice Minister for Foreign Affairs Yachi Shōtarō, while the Chinese side was represented by Dai Bingguo, also a vice minister of foreign affairs. The first strategic dialogue began in May 2005, immediately after the anti-Japanese demonstrations; this was followed by a second one in June, a third in October, a fourth in February 2006, a fifth in May, and a sixth in September. The fourth meeting was held in Niigata, and the fifth one was held in Guiyang. These places were close to the hometowns of Yachi and Dai, respectively, illustrating how much attention was paid to creating a relationship of personal trust. The dialogue between these two individuals may be what ultimately led to a revival of leader exchanges.

It is commonly said that Abe deeply trusted Yachi and that Japan's China policy was discussed by the two in minute detail. Dai, meanwhile, was close to Hu Jintao. During the Jiang Zemin era, he held the key post of director of the International Liaison Department of the CCP Central Committee, and he was thereafter consistently active as a Hu confidant. A standard career arc should have taken him from his directorship to the foreign minister's seat, but in the end, he took office as executive vice minister, while Li Zhaoxing, who had been serving as China's ambassador to the United States, assumed the ministerial post. Li had presided over China's US policy during the Jiang Zemin era. Ultimately, though, while Dai technically ranked second at the Ministry of Foreign Affairs, he concurrently held the vital post of party secretary of the ministry, so it is no stretch to say that he was essentially the country's top diplomat.

In short, it is believed that Hu Jintao, who was primarily active in the party organization, sent his confidant Dai into the Foreign Ministry's government department but was unable to gain him the ministership. Dai instead grasped effective power by taking the top position of the party cell inside the ministry. During this phase, incidentally, the state councilor exercising control over overall foreign policy was former Foreign Minister Tang Jiaxuan—a figure who had held key posts in the Jiang Zemin era and may well have opposed the penetration of Hu's influence in the diplomatic establishment.

It was not until Hu Jintao finally succeeded to all of the major posts previously held by Jiang Zemin—assuming his position as chairman of the CCP Central Military Commission in 2004, and then as chairman of the State Central Military Commission in March 2005—that Dai Bingguo truly began to exert his influence in the foreign policy system. This was symbolized by his assumption of the directorships of the Central Office for Foreign Affairs of the CCP Central Committee and of the Foreign Affairs Office of the State Council on April 21, 2005.[11] Immediately before that, unprecedented anti-Japanese demonstrations had occurred in China. Foreign Minister Li Zhaoxing summoned 3,500 party, government, and military cadres to a briefing meeting on April 19, where he informed all present about the directive that

---

11 *Chūgoku soshiki betsu jinmeibo* [Directory of Names by Chinese Organization], 2006 edition (Tokyo: Radiopress, 2005), 31.

the demonstrations be stopped. Why did the Chinese have the foreign minister handle the problem of domestic protests? The answer may be that Hu Jintao, who had just grasped full power, was making Li take responsibility for the failure of his Japan policy. This could hardly have been unrelated to the fact that a mere two days later Dai Bingguo effectively became China's top foreign policy official. Li Zhaoxing was shortly thereafter relegated to unimportant tasks while still remaining minister of foreign affairs in name, a fact that was often observed in foreign policy circles at the time.

A power struggle surrounding foreign policy can be clearly observed here. The mending of Sino-Japanese relations ultimately owed to the creation of a policy line by Hu Jintao and Dai Bingguo in the course of waging this struggle—a line that took concrete shape in the Japan-China strategic dialogue between Yachi and Dai, which started a short time later in May 2005. The six sessions of dialogue produced the decision that Abe would visit China.

Prime Minister Abe visited China on October 8–9, 2006; he traveled to South Korea on October 9, and then returned home on October 10. During this period, several major developments occurred in the region. For example, the Sixth Plenum of the Sixteenth Central Committee of the CCP opened in China on October 8, and a nuclear test was conducted by North Korea as Abe was traveling to Seoul on October 9. I myself heard from a high-level official at the Japanese Ministry of Foreign Affairs that although Abe's trip to China had originally been envisaged to come after a stop in South Korea first, Abe ended up visiting Beijing prior to the Korea leg based on an insistent request from the Chinese.

The summit began on the afternoon of October 8 with a meeting between Prime Minister Abe and President Hu. During the meeting, Hu expressed the view that the "visits to Yasukuni Shrine have hurt the feelings of the peoples of China and Asia and damaged the political basis of Sino-Japanese relations." In response to this, Abe replied that "we shall look at past history squarely and shall continue to conduct itself as a peaceful nation"; the Chinese greeted this statement positively. As for the issue of visits to Yasukuni Shrine, Abe stated the following: "Whether I have visited or will visit Yasukuni Shrine is not something I shall make clear since this is a matter that has been turned into a diplomatic and political issue. I shall not elaborate on it. That said, from the viewpoint that both sides shall overcome political difficulties and promote the sound development of the two countries, I shall address this matter appropriately."[12]

The matters agreed to at this meeting were made public in the form of a joint press statement, suggesting a new orientation in Japan-China relations in many ways. First, the statement gave Japan-China relations the status of a "mutually beneficial relationship based on common strategic interests" for the first time in history: "Both sides shared the view that the two countries would strive to build a mutually beneficial relationship based on common strategic interests, and achieve the noble objectives of peaceful co-existence, friendship for generations, mutually beneficial cooperation, and common development."[13] Until that time the word used to characterize Sino-Japanese relations was "friendly." When China created strategic partnerships with major countries in the latter half of the 1990s, only Japan had been excluded. This reflected the will of the Japanese government at that time, which considered the military nuance included in the word "strategic" and remained mindful of the Japan-US alliance as a central axis of Japanese diplomacy.

The scope of the mutually beneficial strategic relationship ranged widely over such areas as politics, the economy, security, and regional cooperation in East Asia, and it was the first time that the two countries agreed clearly in writing, with respect to the issue of North Korea, to cooperate toward the denuclearization of the Korean Peninsula. North

---

12 "Press Conference by Prime Minister Shinzo Abe Following His Visit to China" (October 8, 2006), Prime Minister of Japan and His Cabinet (website), https://japan.kantei.go.jp/abespeech/2006/10/08chinapress_e.html.

13 "Japan-China Joint Press Statement" (October 8, 2006), Ministry of Foreign Affairs of Japan (website), https://www.mofa.go.jp/region/asia-paci/china/joint0610.html.

Korea then went ahead with its nuclear test while Abe was on his way to Seoul on the following day, October 9, essentially making the North Korea issue the first task for the new strategic relationship. In the immediate aftermath, China expressed its "understanding and sympathy" and offered its "necessary cooperation" to address the issue of Japanese nationals abducted from Japan by North Korea. This was perhaps out of particular consideration for Abe, given this issue's standing as a key theme of his administration.

Second, mention of historical issues greatly decreased, and instead there were many forward-looking statements. Not only was there no mention of Yasukuni, there was also no mention of "war" or "aggression," previously common terms that were replaced with positive evaluations of postwar Japan's "peaceful development." At the same time, the Japanese positively assessed the fact that China's peaceful development, along with its reforms and opening up, had provided a golden opportunity for Japan and the international community as a whole.

Third, this document did not mention the Taiwan issue. Certain conventional expressions are almost invariably included in the bilateral documents that China exchanges with other countries in the world, such as pledges that the other party will "respect the principle of 'one China'" or "does not support Taiwanese independence." The Chinese side did raise the Taiwan question at the meeting between Abe and Hu; at this time, Abe said verbally that Japan would adhere to the "one China" policy, offering no support for "two Chinas" or "one China, one Taiwan" or for independence for Taiwan, and that it would oppose any unilateral change to the status quo of the Taiwan Strait.[14] But none of this was included in the joint document resulting from the summit. Although some believe that the Taiwan issue made no appearance due to the time for negotiations running short, there is also the view that the Japanese opposed the unreasonable insertion of Taiwan in a bilateral document, and the Chinese ultimately had no choice but to swallow this.

14 *People's Daily*, October 9, 2006.

Perhaps because of the criticism this sparked in China, the joint press statement at the time of Premier Wen's visit to Japan half a year later did include this minimum wording: "Regarding the Taiwan issue, the Japanese side expressed its adherence to the position which was set forth in the Joint Communique of the Government of Japan and the Government of the People's Republic of China."[15] Why had such a development become possible? It is connected to the Chinese acceptance of Abe's visit without making the termination of the Yasukuni visits a precondition for it. The wishes of China's supreme leader Hu Jintao were likely the key factor in making this summit possible. I will bolster this view by examining this development based on the internal circumstances of Chinese politics at the time.

3. Circumstances on the Chinese Side

Considered from the perspective of China's internal politics at the time, these diplomatic moves vis-à-vis Japan were closely connected to the establishment and strengthening of President Hu Jintao's leadership. During the sudden improvement of relations with Japan, Hu said almost nothing about historical issues or Taiwan. The domestic response was a reported spread of criticism of Hu. Additionally, during this period China's relationship with North Korea had worsened, producing an undercurrent of criticism about Hu's North Korea policy.[16] With respect to Sino-Japanese relations in particular, Hu's concessions to Japan were painted as a serious problem by the forces arrayed against him—all the more since the end of the Yasukuni visits had been a precondition for restarting summit exchanges. Hu rapidly consolidated

---

15 "Japan-China Joint Press Statement" (April 11, 2007), Ministry of Foreign Affairs of Japan (website), https://www.mofa.go.jp/region/asia-paci/china/pv0704/joint.html. In addition, I also interviewed a senior official in the Japanese Foreign Ministry about the relevant circumstances.

16 Interviews conducted in October 2006 with senior Chinese bureaucrats in several regions immediately after Prime Minister Abe's visit.

his own power soon afterward, though, and these criticisms subsided before long. Abe's visit to China may have been a highly significant component of this power-consolidation process. In Chinese politics, activity that is visible not only domestically but also in the field of diplomacy, where the propaganda effect is high, occupies a key place in the overall establishment of power. When Hu was rising to power, China's largest diplomatic concern was its Japan policy. Given this, the stabilization that an Abe visit could bring to China's relationship with Japan may well have been one of the most important issues for the consolidation of power by Hu Jintao, whose base of political influence was still insufficient.[17]

Hu invited Prime Minister Abe to arrive in China on October 8, 2006. The Japanese side had initially scheduled a visit to South Korea first, but as noted above, at China's insistence it was decided that Abe would visit China first. Moreover, the Sixth Plenum of the Sixteenth Central Committee of the CCP opened on that same day. This is the Communist Party's most important meeting, and Hu harbored a special agenda in inviting Abe on the first day of this key event. His move was closely connected to both the power struggles inside the party that had occurred several weeks before this meeting and the arrest of Chen Liangyu, the party secretary of Shanghai.[18]

The latter incident was the turning point in the comeback engi-

---

17 A work that adopts the same viewpoint is Shimizu Yoshikazu, *"Chūgoku mondai" no uchimaku* [The Inner Workings of the "China Problem"] (Tokyo: Chikuma Shobō, 2008), see chaps. 2 and 3 of the book.

18 Details of the Chen Liangyu case are in the following books, among others: Zheng Yi, *Shanghai dafengbao: Chen Liangyu daotai yu Shanghaibang de mori* [The Tempest in Shanghai: The Fall of Chen Liangyu and the Final Days of the Shanghai Gang] (Hong Kong: Culture and Art Publishing House, 2006); Zi Ping, ed., *Jikui Shanghaibang* [Attacking and Crushing the Shanghai Gang] (Hong Kong: Transworld Publishers, 2006); Shi Weijian, *Shanghaibang mori hanjiang: Chen Liangyu chuanqi* [The Strong Leader of the Last Days of the Shanghai Gang: The Saga of Chen Liangyu] (Hong Kong: Culture and Art Publishing House, 2007); and Xiao Chong, ed., *Shanghaibang houzhuan* [An Account of the End of the Shanghai Gang] (Hong Kong: Ha Fai Yi International Publishing, 2008). My conjectures in this chapter about the facts of the case are based on these publications.

neered by Hu, who had been boxed in by the Jiang Zemin faction and had seen his position weakened. Chen Liangyu was one of the future leaders who had been carefully nurtured by Jiang Zemin; he had been expected to make a success of the Expo 2010 Shanghai China and join the ranks of China's top leaders at the Eighteenth National Congress of the CCP in 2012. Many rumors swirled around Chen, but in the end, he was arrested for amassing personal wealth by diverting Shanghai's social security funds. In that process, various scandals including mysterious stories of fatal illness swirled around Huang Ju, a member of the Standing Committee of the CCP Politburo who was one of the party's top leaders and who was close to Jiang Zemin. Moreover, problems inside the Beijing party committee were also exposed, leading to the arrest of the vice mayor of Beijing. In addition, scandals surfaced involving Jia Qinglin—another member of the Politburo's Standing Committee and a top leader with close ties to Beijing.

The outcome of all this was the swift erosion of the power base of the so-called Shanghai group close to Jiang Zemin. Zeng Qinghong, a leader of the Jiang faction, is alleged to have served as the mediator between the Hu and Jiang sides in this process.[19] It was on September 25 that the Xinhua News Agency reported the arrest of Chen Liangyu, and in the evening of September 28, just days later, Beijing sounded out Tokyo about a potential visit by Abe to China.[20]

The Sixth Plenum opened two weeks after these intense power struggles had sent their shock waves across China and to the outside world. The Chinese leadership received Abe on the first day of that meeting. Hu Jintao, who had subdued his biggest enemy in the Chen affair and made a large stride toward consolidation of power in the process, opened the party's most important meeting in the morning of October 8, boldly displaying his grip on power based on the Chen

---

19 *Sankei Shimbun*, September 26 and October 5, 2007.
20 Statement by former Vice Minister for Foreign Affairs Yachi Shōtarō, *Nihon Keizai Shimbun*, March 24, 2008.

affair. In the afternoon of the same day, Hu headed toward Tiananmen Square along with other Chinese leaders and received Abe as a state guest, after which he returned to the meeting, where it can be imagined that he flaunted another achievement—this time the mending of China's relations with Japan, which had been the country's single largest foreign policy concern—before the assembled members of the CCP's Central Committee. We can conclude that it was at this Sixth Plenum that Hu Jintao fundamentally secured his power inside the party, and thus over the country as a whole.

For Hu Jintao, the significance of this gathering was huge when we consider the subsequent political scene in China. This is connected to the Seventeenth National Congress of the CCP, which had been held in 2007. Hu assumed the office of party secretary in 2002, and his first term ended in 2007; a second term for him would place him in that office for another five years. This meant that the candidates for China's post-Hu leadership, who would be elected at the Eighteenth National Congress of the CCP to be held in 2012, needed at the very least to be included in the Politburo's Standing Committee at the 2007 Congress. Hu had to eliminate his political rivals as soon as possible; this set the stage for the significance of the Sixth Plenum.

Jiang Zemin had inherited the mantle of leadership from Deng Xiaoping in 1989, but it was only after the mid-1990s that he finally grasped power over the party, state, and military in a real sense. This may have been because Deng's stature was so commanding that Jiang could only take real control after Deng's death in February 1997. At the Fifteenth CCP National Congress, held in the fall of 1997, Jiang drove Qiao Shi, his biggest political rival, into retirement. This is the pattern of power succession in Chinese politics and is among the biggest encumbrances in the system of one-party communist rule, in which no mechanism for determining successors has been institutionalized.

Revisiting Hu Jintao's diplomacy, we see that from 2003 onward, he began to develop policies that differed from those of the Jiang era. One area where policies changed was the Taiwan issue; another was North

Korea. In sum, while Jiang had given Taiwan primacy among the various diplomatic policy issues facing China, Hu seems to have essentially lowered the issue's priority by redefining the Taiwan matter as one to be dealt with over the long term and maintaining the status quo. With respect to North Korea, meanwhile, Hu's policy approach began creating a certain distance between China and North Korea and drawing closer to the United States, such as by agreeing to chair the six-party denuclearization talks at Washington's request in the summer of 2003.

Prior to the March 2004 presidential election in Taiwan, President Chen Shui-bian gave impetus to the independence movement by raising matters including a change in the country's name and revision of the Taiwanese constitution starting in the summer of 2003. Hu Jintao, who had assumed the presidency and was now exercising full control over China's diplomacy, did not openly, forcefully oppose these moves, perhaps to head off views of China as a threat, but they were of course treated as serious issues by the Chinese leadership. It was actually the United States, though, that was most averse to Chen's radical moves at this time. As the Iraq War became more complex, the George W. Bush administration was absorbed with this conflict and the broader fight against terrorism. A high level of concern about further disputes that might entangle it erupting in Asia prompted the United States to entrust almost all authority in the six-party talks to China as the host country on the North Korea issue.

Taiwan, of course, provided one more potential element of crisis in Asia, and the situation at that time appeared fraught with the risk that China might launch a war if the Taiwanese continued to spur the trend toward independence. During this period, the Hu government refrained from commenting publicly about the Taiwan issue, but it is conjectured that behind the scenes Hu continued to ask the Bush administration to exercise restraint with respect to Taiwan. This may have been the cause of the Bush White House's repeated moves to inhibit pro-independence steps by Chen Shui-bian. One can imagine a barter where, in exchange for American constraints on the Chen government,

Beijing agreed to host the six-party talks and pursue resolution of the North Korea situation. There is no definite evidence on this score, but given the outcome, we can reason that the two countries were tacitly acting in concert.[21] If this hypothesis is valid, it means that the US-China relationship began to stabilize, ironically, thanks to Chen Shui-bian's promotion of Taiwanese independence. The six-party talks were the venue for dialogue on the denuclearization of North Korea, but for the United States it also functioned as a venue for confirmation of whether China would adequately fulfill the role of a "responsible stakeholder." This would also become the pillar of the United States' China policy in subsequent venues for such multinational discussions.

As described above, Hu Jintao made a public display of his consolidation of power over China's internal politics and foreign policy by inviting Prime Minister Abe to China on the date of the opening of the Sixth Plenum, in the immediate aftermath of the Chen Liangyu case. He aimed to distinguish himself from the Jiang Zemin era by refraining from any mention of historical issues at summit meetings, keeping quiet on the Taiwan issue, and actively offering Chinese cooperation on North Korea, and took significant steps to improve China's relations with Japan. A close linkage between the intraparty power struggles and foreign policies appears to have existed here.

4. Circumstances on the Japanese Side

As is widely known, Abe Shinzō had made many hawkish statements, including on the propriety of visits to Yasukuni Shrine, before becoming prime minister in 2006. He had also consistently argued that a very tough position should be adopted toward China. For those reasons

---

21 There were rumors to this effect at the time, and I repeatedly asked senior US government officials about it, but they invariably denied the possibility. They did confirm, though, that the Chinese side had frequently called on Washington to restrain Chen Shui-bian's aspirations for Taiwanese independence.

alone, Abe's prompt visit to China had a considerable impact. We cannot say definitively whether his hawkish statements before becoming prime minister were aimed at subsequent results by intentionally raising the stakes, but we can understand the consequences in this way. Abe's decision to visit China may perhaps have come during his final days as chief cabinet secretary to Prime Minister Koizumi, before he assumed the premiership. On August 3, just before taking the top office, Abe was a guest at the Tokyo-Beijing Forum hosted by the private Japanese think tank Genron NPO. There he set forth his own guidelines for Japan's China policy as follows: "I believe the Japan-China relationship is one of the most important bilateral relationships....In our relations, we must correctly recognize each other and constructively discuss what cooperation between the countries should be like through direct dialogue, with strong will, so that even if individual problems arise, these do not have any adverse effect on the development of Japan-China relations overall."[22]

Upon taking office on September 26, Prime Minister Abe quickly set about making preliminary arrangements for his visit to China. Previously, most Japanese prime ministers had made the United States their first destination after taking office, but for Abe this was China. Washington was of course consulted beforehand, and the US government is reported to have signed off on this. The improvement of and stability in Sino-Japanese relations were requests of the Bush administration, which was preoccupied with the Iraq conflict and the threat of terrorism.

During the period after he became prime minister and before he visited China, Abe ceased making hawkish statements and voiced a series of moderate positions in line with those of the previous government. First of all, Abe acknowledged the 1995 statement by Prime Minister Murayama Tomiichi that clearly rejected Japan's aggression and war in Asia in the past with an expression of remorse. He also recognized

---

22 *Nicchū taiwa* [Japan-China Dialogue] (Tokyo: Genron NPO, 2006), 8.

the 1993 statement by Chief Cabinet Secretary Kōno Yōhei about the involvement of the Japanese government in the issue of the comfort women during the war and even mentioned the war responsibility of Kishi Nobusuke (prime minister from 1957 to 1960), who was Abe's grandfather.[23] The new prime minister had revised his positions to ones completely different from his personal statements in the past, and he went so far as to declare that "I will take the criticism lying down."[24]

Abe's largest concern may have been that his China policy would appear to be a kind of kowtow diplomacy, involving major concessions to Beijing. There is little doubt that Hu and Abe were taking part in a summit fraught with serious risks for both of them. To minimize the domestic backlash in Japan, Abe, as noted above, resorted to vagueness about whether he had previously gone to Yasukuni, and whether he would visit the shrine again. Hu ultimately took the risk of accepting this vagueness and green-lighting Abe's visit; the trip would have been impossible but for Hu's strong desire to improve Sino-Japanese ties. Similarly for Abe, had his trip been viewed as involving unwarranted concessions to China, it would have meant a diplomatic blunder committed immediately after he took office. The serious risks that the visit potentially posed for both leaders had to be skillfully resolved at the same time. In a sense, Abe's tactic of a vague Yasukuni position may have worked to the mutual advantage of both parties as a result.

Ironically, North Korea emerged as another country giving its "blessings" to this improvement in Japan-China relations—in the form of the nuclear test that it conducted while Abe was en route to Seoul. In short, this only succeeded in further strengthening the rapprochement between Japan and China by positioning the North Korea issue as a common strategic challenge for them for the first time.

Abe's policy style differed considerably from that of his predecessor. Koizumi Jun'ichirō had asserted that his visits to Yasukuni Shrine were in the spirit of "denying war and desiring peace," projecting his

---

23 *Nihon Keizai Shimbun* and other newspapers, October 3, 4, 6, and 7, 2006.
24 *Nihon Keizai Shimbun*, October 11, 2006.

personal positions onto his diplomatic approach as prime minister. Abe's actions, by comparison, appear to have rested more on Japan's national interests or a strategic perspective than on his personal beliefs. I will leave to future historians the detailed topics surrounding these events, such as the question of what kind of moves were being made by the Kantei (the Prime Minister's Office), the Japanese Ministry of Foreign Affairs, foreign policy strategists, and other actors to bolster Abe's resolve. One way or another, though, the new prime minister's visit to China—which can rightly be called a Japanese version of the Nixon shock—had the effect of boosting his popularity right after he took office.[25] The Japanese public strongly approved of Abe's improvement of Japan-China relations.

In Summary

What lies at the heart of the worsening of Japan-China ties? A wide variety of analyses and viewpoints have sought to explain the deterioration of these relations. Some emphasize the differences in popular sentiments and sensitivities in Japan and China. Others hold that the reason lies in historical issues, foremost among which is Yasukuni Shrine, and seek Japan's remorse and apology. Still others argue that the source is China's political exploitation of history, calling for an end to this. Yet others attribute it to emotional conflict stemming from a power shift involving a rising China and a Japan whose international standing is weakening. Finally, there are those who interpret the worsening of bilateral ties in terms of opposing national interests involving economics, resources, or territory.

As I argued in Chapter 6 above, I have long focused on more structural aspects in Japan-China relations, such as the changes in the 1972 System. These aspects include the differences between the 1980s, when

---

25 *Nihon Keizai Shimbun*, October 30, 2006, and *Asahi Shimbun*, October 11, 2006.

conflict was minimized because bilateral political ties were firm even though interdependence had not yet been created, and the present day, when political ties have atrophied even though interdependence has deepened; and the fluid state that we see today, when the framework of a new relationship has not yet emerged in the face of great changes in the international environment, the generational composition of populations, public opinion, the Taiwan issue, and other factors that had informed the bilateral relationship from the Cold War onward.

However, as I argue in this chapter, Chinese politics—in particular the course of domestic power struggles—have been a major element, along with the personal factor of Jiang Zemin, in the ups and downs of the Japan-China relationship. During the formation of the mutually beneficial strategic relationship, the subject of this chapter, the key developments were the loss of the Jiang Zemin faction's influence, which was triggered by the fall of Chen Liangyu in September 2006, and Hu Jintao's consolidation of a power base in its place. There may not be conclusive evidence to support specific descriptions of the causal relationships in this process, but if we arrange those relationships based on input and output, the black box in between will point us in due course to a power struggle in Chinese politics.

Chapter 10

Japan-China Relations Face the Trial of the Senkaku Islands (2010s)

The eyes of the world are now riveted on Chinese economic trends. The reason is simple: As goes China, so goes the rest of the global economy. Recent years have seen lively discussion including positive assessments of the rise of China, and even arguments that in coming years the world would transition from the "Washington Consensus" to the "Beijing Consensus," in other words, to a Sinocentric world.[1] But such discussion has almost entirely vanished today. This is because the Chinese economy is clearly decelerating and the Chinese annual growth rate, far from maintaining the 8 percent level previously deemed the minimum standard (the so-called *baoba*, or "eight percent protection" policy), has now fallen below 7 percent. In addition, asset bubbles, nonperforming loans, and an underground economy involving shadow banking and the like are gradually becoming apparent as well. One does not have to peruse the "Panama Papers" to see that government corruption involving senior CCP cadres has become a routine affair; the wealth produced by the Chinese people continues to flow overseas in the form of illicit gains accumulated by such officials.

Debate about the "Beijing Consensus" first appeared in 2008, when China had successfully held the Beijing Olympics and then, while still basking in the Games' glow, provided 4 trillion yuan (approximately 57 billion US dollars) in financial assistance at the time of the global financial crisis that intensified shortly thereafter. China surpassed Japan in GDP in 2010 and became in both name and substance the world's number-two economic power, second only to the United States, in the same year successfully hosting the Expo 2010 Shanghai China. At around this time, China began espousing more egocentric views and attitudes in its dealings with other countries. While China did in fact demonstrate its economic prowess to the world in this period, though, its lax management ultimately resulted in a real estate bubble and widespread corruption, which helped to undermine its economic foundations.

---

1 See, for example, Stefan Halper, *The Beijing Consensus: How China's Authoritarian Model Will Dominate the Twenty-First Century* (New York: Basic Books, 2011).

How should we assess the current situation in China? Evaluations of the nation do not appear to differ so much by the nationality of those producing them, although they will vary depending on the individual China watcher or economist making his or her pronouncements. In Japan, one finds a wide variety of opinions, ranging from beliefs that China will continue to prosper to predictions of a collapse. The popular image of China has indeed fallen precipitously in Japan, as attested to by opinion polls across the spectrum, perhaps reflecting the worsening of bilateral ties. But bilateral relations are not necessarily strained to the point where things could explode. Rational approaches and concerted efforts on various fronts in the two countries aimed at avoiding conflict have proven effective for the moment, and the two sides continue to grope toward improved ties, albeit slowly. But the situation remains one where no major progress can be anticipated any time soon.

Why have Sino-Japanese relations reached such a pass? Many analysts in both China and Japan have offered commentaries on this focusing on Japan's policymaking. The bilateral relationship has frequently been discussed in the context of the successive changes of Japanese governments and the resulting political confusion since the beginning of the twenty-first century, a period that saw the formation of Liberal Democratic Party led administrations from Koizumi Jun'ichirō (2001–2006) to Abe Shinzō (2006–2007), Fukuda Yasuo (2007–2008), and Asō Tarō (2008–2009), and the subsequent Democratic Party of Japan administrations of Hatoyama Yukio (2009–2010), Kan Naoto (2010–2011), and Noda Yoshihiko (2011–2012).

Precisely because the Japanese policymaking process is transparent and there are many public statements by the parties concerned, it is easy to focus interest on Japan's China diplomacy, making it the central target of discussion. Conversely, on the Chinese side the policy process is opaque and the public statements of the persons involved are invariably the same, meaning that far less attention is paid to China's Japan policies. Perhaps reflecting this state of affairs, there is an unfortunate tendency for observers to think first and foremost about what Japan should do in order to improve bilateral ties. China, too, frequently holds that "all responsibility lies with Japan," painting a picture of a nation with no proactive stance on its ties with its neighbor.

But a one-sided analysis focused solely on Japan cannot offer a balanced perspective on the bilateral relationship. In the analysis below, I demonstrate that there are major variables on the Chinese side of the equation, too, when it comes to the causes of the deterioration of ties between the two countries. In this connection, though, we must approach this issue in an overall context encompassing China's domestic politics and foreign policy. The Chinese policy approach to Japan does not take form in a vacuum; we should understand it as rather as one part of the country's interwoven internal and external circumstances. While part of what follows overlaps with my account in Part I of this book, I would like to examine here the vicissitudes of Japan-China relations from 2010 onward from the standpoint of China's domestic politics.

1. China's Political Scene at the End of the Hu Jintao Era

The essence of Chinese politics is power struggles. This holds true whether we are talking about the Cultural Revolution or the Tiananmen Square Incident, and it remains true today. The conflicts that sway China's politics can be observed at all levels—not only at the higher levels of the central government, but at the regional and grassroots levels as well. But it is impossible to grasp the actual state of affairs from simple external observation. We must recognize that the power struggles starting in the late 1990s—when there were no charismatic figures left at the top, especially following Deng Xiaoping's death in 1997—transformed into a politics of compromise between leaders; into this confusion was added fierce special interest politics, due to the introduction of a market economy under the aegis of the country's one-party dictatorship. Thus, the power struggles have essentially evolved into contests revolving around personnel decisions and clashes between major interests. There is no room here for political reforms toward the creation of a system that takes heed of the popular will.

Roughly speaking, it is believed that three major factions existed among the Communist Party leadership as of the end of the Hu Jintao era at the start of the 2010s. These were the Shanghai faction led by Jiang Zemin; the Communist Youth League of China faction, whose leader was Hu Jintao; and the so-called Princeling Party, with Xi Jinping at its head. To the extent that special interest politics were involved, though, there was some fluidity in the memberships of these groupings. It may not be proper to speak of the groups of government bureaucrats on the State Council and the like as "factions" per se, but many such policy groups almost certainly exist.[2] For example, one policy lineage can be seen in Zhu Rongji, who held the post of premier during the latter half of the Jiang Zemin era, Premier Wen Jiabao, who succeeded Zhu, and Wang Qishan, who can be considered Zhu Rongji's protégén. Of these groupings, the network generally known as the Princeling Party does not have a solid organizational base in the party, army, or state, and its function and cohesion as a faction are thought to be relatively weak. Bo Xilai (see page 266) is the son of Bo Yibo, an erstwhile senior Chinese leader, but he still fell from power due to scandal, and Xi Jinping, reputedly a member of the same Princeling Party, joined the forces that pressed for Bo's ouster.

The Shanghai faction includes Jiang Zemin and Zeng Qinghong, also a Princeling whose father had served as a senior Chinese official. We must not forget that Xi Jinping was nominated for China's supreme lead-

---

2 A good deal of analysis and research has been done on factions and personal connections in China. In particular, the following works comprehensively cover the subject: Yang Zhongmei and Takahashi Hiroshi, *Chūgoku shidōsha sōkanzu* [Who's Connected to Who in the Chinese Leadership] (Tokyo: Sōsōsha, 2008); Takahashi and the Twenty-First Century China Research Institute, *Chūgoku jūyō jinbutsu jiten* [Encyclopedia of Key Chinese Figures] (Tokyo: Sōsōsha, 2009); and Takahashi and the Twenty-First Century China Research Institute, *Chūgoku saikō shidōsha who's who (2013–2018 nen ban)* [Who's Who in the Top Chinese Leadership (2013–2018 edition)] (Tokyo: Sōsōsha, 2013).

er by none other than Zeng, who held the post of vice-president during the first half of the Hu Jintao era. The chief power bases of the Shanghai faction are in the political and legal affairs (public security) departments and the propaganda and ideology departments, but this group has also seen its framework bolstered by strong support from the elders of the conservative faction. They provide robust support for the preservation of the current order to protect vested interests, and for that reason they are also deeply supported by the state-owned enterprise sector.

Since the Communist Youth League faction has a solid power base in the party organization, its tendrils spread all the way to China's regions. But this faction is not supported by the vested interests, given that in general its members are strongly pro-reform and have relatively weak ties with existing interest groups. It is disliked by the elders of the conservative faction but supported by pro-reform elders who feel antipathy toward the vested interests including the Jiang Zemin faction.

In addition to the simplified classifications outlined above, we must also consider the defense and public security organs including the People's Liberation Army and the People's Armed Police. In particular, the military is a huge organization, the human networks within it are complex, and the senior ranks have certain ties with the factions at the upper levels of the party. In retrospect, in the Hu Jintao era from 2002 to 2012, Hu lacked the secure power base necessary for advancing his own policies. The Jiang Zemin era prior to that saw a single-minded focus on growth, and Hu formulated the policy of "constructing a harmonious society" as the means for correcting the disparities and socioeconomic discrimination that this had produced. This approach itself was correct as a policy orientation, but gaps and discrimination had only burgeoned further by the end of Hu's era a decade later. This was because almost no specific policies were launched, and the line of emphasizing growth above all else continued unchanged as a result.

Why did this happen? Of the nine members of the CCP Politburo Standing Committee during the Hu era—Hu Jintao, Wu Bangguo, Wen Jiabao, Jia Qinlin, Li Changchun, Xi Jinping, Li Keqiang, He

Guoqiang, and Zhou Yongkang—five (Wu, Jia, Li Changchun, He, and Zhou) are regarded as members of the Jiang Zemin faction. Hu had managed with some difficulty to have Li Keqiang, one of his confidants, included among the nine Standing Committee members at the Seventeenth National Congress of the CCP in 2007. However, Xi Jinping, who was advanced by Zeng Qinghong among others, was chosen as the top candidate for China's next supreme leadership, and Hu was unable to position Li Keqiang as the top leader. As noted in the preceding chapter, although Hu Jintao did indeed enjoy a temporary ascendancy thanks to the Chen Liangyu scandal in 2006, he subsequently saw his star fall when the Jiang faction clawed back power. In sum, during Hu's decade as top leader, he saw powerful constraints imposed on him by the Jiang Zemin/Zeng Qinghong faction in the various arenas where political power was contested.[3]

The growth-first policy—which involved massive fixed asset investments that resulted in a land and housing bubble and overinvestment in major industries like energy and steel—caused serious deformations in Chinese society as well. In addition, under the "Three Represents" approach discussed in Chapters 3 and 4, which was continued from the Jiang era, matters had reached the point where vested interests called "special interest groups" were forming in the investment-dependent growth line. The key institutional bases in this process were the state-owned enterprises active in every major industry; they had formed a huge interest group in which politics and economics were inextricably interwoven, owing to the fact that cadres of the CCP and their relatives had "descended from heaven" to assume key management positions in them. These powerful figures did not disclose their assets, evaded taxes and moved funds overseas, and busied themselves with sending their children and relatives overseas to study or reside. What made this

---

3 While many works have been published on intraparty power analysis in this area, the following books by Shimizu Hirokazu are particularly illuminating: Shimizu, *Chūgoku mondai* (see chap. 9, n. 17), and Shimizu, *"Chūgoku mondai" no kakushin* [The Core of the "China Problem"] (Tokyo: Chikuma Shobō, 2009).

possible was, in fact, the socialist market economy under Communist Party dictatorship.

At the summit of these vested interest groups was the Shanghai faction, which was at the center of power at that time, along with the Princeling Party. As long as economic growth remained strong, there were no problems with this system where politics and economics intertwined. But after the onset of the global financial crisis in 2008, China, too, suffered the repercussions of global contraction, and deceleration gradually became evident in its economy. A partial collapse of the economic bubble fueled by excessive investment and the emergence of problems with nonperforming loans reverberated through the Chinese economy. In addition to these crises, investment and exports stagnated and upward pressure gradually grew on the employment and wage fronts. There is no use now in suggesting that income distribution policies such as tax system reforms should have been implemented while growth was being maintained. In a situation where desire dominated, reason was of no avail.

The Wang Lijun incident unfolded over the period from February through early spring 2012. Wang, the vice-mayor of Chongqing, took refuge in the US Consulate there, helping to trigger a scandal involving Bo Xilai and his wife Gu Kailai that ended in Bo's fall from power.[4] By repeatedly glorifying the memory of Mao Zedong, Bo had been calling for the maintenance of the status quo. His aim was to make inroads into the Politburo Standing Committee at the Eighteenth National Congress of the CCP, and this conservative position helped him to secure support from the Jiang Zemin faction. Zhou Yongkang, who had been close to Jiang and Zeng Qinghong and who was positioned at the top of the public security apparatus and the energy industry, and Li Changchun, who headed the propaganda organs, had supported him. Bo's fall resulted in the weakening of the Jiang faction, and in its aftermath the Hu Jintao

---

4 On the Bo Xilai case, see Takahashi and Twenty-First Century China Research Institute, *Who's Who 2013–2018*, pt. 1.

faction was expected to make great strides. At just this time, though, the son of Ling Jihua, a close ally of Hu's, died in a controversial traffic accident, and Ling's conduct in disposing of the matter was regarded as problematic. This dealt a blow to the Hu faction as well.

The result was a reversal in the factional struggles at the Beidaihe Meeting, or "summer summit" in the summer of 2012; and at the CCP's Eighteenth National Congress that autumn, the Hu faction was routed across the board, handing Jiang Zemin and Zeng Qinghong a resounding victory. Of the seven members of the Politburo Standing Committee that was newly elected at the Congress, held in November 2012—Xi Jinping, Li Keqiang, Zhang Dejiang, Yu Zhengsheng, Liu Yunshan, Wang Qishan, and Zhang Gaoli—four (Zhang Dejiang, Yu, Liu, and Zhang Gaoli) were clearly close to Jiang and Zeng, while only one, Li Keqiang, was a member of the Hu faction. There was also only one person regarded as close to Xi Jinping, namely Wang Qishan, a member of the Princeling Party.[5] Hu Jintao retired completely and ceded all of his posts to Xi Jinping, in a marked contrast with the way Jiang had retained his post on the Central Military Commission for a few years after ceding power to Hu. In any case, though, the Xi Jinping era was formally inaugurated on the occasion of this Eighteenth National Congress of the CCP.

2. The Senkaku Islands Issue Intensifies

During this period, Japan-China relations saw turmoil to match that seen in the domestic Chinese political scene, confronting the mutually beneficial strategic relationship that had been in place since 2006 with difficulties. The two main events were, first, the 2010 collisions between a Chinese fishing trawler and Japan Coast Guard patrol boats

---

5 Takahashi and Twenty-First Century China Research Institute, *Who's Who 2013–2018*, pt. 1.

in the waters off the Senkaku (Ch. Diaoyu) Islands, and second, the vehement campaign of criticism launched by China in response to the Japanese government's decision to purchase the Senkakus from their private owner in 2012.

In the 2010 collisions, a fishing vessel from Fujian Province operating in Japanese territorial waters off the Senkakus received warnings from patrol boats of the Japan Coast Guard. After the Chinese trawler collided with them, the JCG arrested its captain. Online discussion in China reacted strongly against the Japanese handling of the incident, and the Chinese government also adopted a tough stance. Various exchanges ensued between the two sides, and in the end Sengoku Yoshito, chief cabinet secretary to Prime Minister Kan Naoto of the Democratic Party of Japan (DPJ), arranged for the release and repatriation of the Chinese captain. In the interim, Chinese rare earth exports to Japan ground to a halt, and four employees of a Japanese corporation were detained in China, ostensibly for entering an off-limits area. Anti-Chinese demonstrations in response to these arrests occurred in Japan in October 2010, and in retaliation, thousands took part in anti-Japanese demonstrations in China, chiefly in Sichuan Province. Prime Minister Kan and Premier Wen Jiabao met at international conferences including the East Asia Summit. Thereafter, at a summit meeting between Kan and President Hu Jintao on the occasion of the APEC Economic Leaders' Meeting, the parties agreed to return to the mutually beneficial strategic relationship, whereupon the tensions subsided.

The incident in 2012 proved to be thornier. In April, Ishihara Shintarō, the governor of Tokyo, suddenly announced that his government would purchase three islands in the Senkaku chain, namely Uotsurishima, Kitakojima, and Minamikojima, and actually launched fundraising activities to that end. This caused a huge uproar within Japan and was blasted by China as a reckless, unilateral measure; for the time being, though, the affair did not expand beyond that. Then in July, in an effort to address the simmering issue, the DPJ administration of Noda Yoshihiko agreed in principle to the so-called nationalization of the islands—their purchase by the state.[6] In response, a spokesman of the US State Department issued a declaration indicating that the Senkakus fell within the scope of application of the Japan-US Security Treaty.

Around this time, such diversionary actions as Russian Prime Minister Dmitry Medvedev's visit to Kunashiri Island and South Korean President Lee Myung-bak's visit to Takeshima (Kr. Dokdo)—both areas subject to territorial claims by Japan—also took place, but the Chinese government did not exhibit an overly sensitive reaction to these incidents. At this stage, the Japanese side explained that the "nationalization" of the Senkakus would contribute to stabilizing the situation, and the Chinese response was far from harsh. But on August 12 a boat carrying members of a Hong Kong organization, the Action Committee for Defending the Diaoyu Islands set sail for the islands. When they reached the area on August 15 they ignored a warning from the Japan Coast Guard and landed on one of the islands. They were detained by the Japanese authorities and forcibly deported shortly thereafter, a move triggering a sudden intensification in the backlash in China. Anti-Japanese attacks launched on the Internet were matched by anti-Japanese demonstrations that took place in various cities in China. In some cases, the demonstrators ran amok and vandalized Japanese supermarkets and restaurants. But the public security organs only quelled particularly radical action and did nothing to stop the riots themselves.

Prime Minister Noda sent a personal letter to President Hu in which he called for a defusing of the situation. On September 9, Noda and Hu held a brief meeting on the sidelines of the APEC summit in Vladivostok; on the following day, September 10, Japan formally decided on the purchase of the three islands. From that time until September 18,

---

6 A detailed account of the actual circumstances at this time can be found in Sunohara Tsuyoshi, *Antō Senkaku kokuyūka* (Tokyo: Shinchōsha, 2013), published in English as *Fencing in the Dark: Japan, China, and the Senkakus* (Tokyo: Japan Publishing Industry Foundation for Culture, 2020).

the anniversary of the 1931 Manchurian Incident, the anti-Japanese demonstrations in China continued to expand. Rioters destroyed stores related to Japan throughout China and called for a boycott of Japanese products. From September 19 onward, the protests suddenly abated, but intimidating acts by Chinese public vessels became more frequent in the Senkaku Islands region.

In the 2012 incident, the Chinese response became particularly harsh in mid-August, immediately after the Hong Kong activists landed on the Senkakus and were arrested. Although there had already been considerable discussion about the "nationalization" of the Senkakus, not many Chinese public vessels were active in the waters near the islands, and scrambles of Japanese Self-Defense Force aircraft were infrequent. Why did China's attitude suddenly harden from the middle of August? The change coincided with the above-described power struggles in China. From the time of the summer 2012 Beidaihe Meeting onward, the Jiang Zemin faction suddenly seized the high ground in intraparty power struggles, which had been held by the Hu Jintao faction until then. Mention decreased of the mutually beneficial strategic relationship with Japan, which had been promoted by Hu, while historical issues suddenly took center stage.

The nature of the intraparty struggles related to the anti-Japanese demonstrations in September 2012 has gradually become clearer in recent years. A good deal of information has recently come to light, principally in Hong Kong, indicating that the mastermind of the protests was none other than Zhou Yongkang, the Politburo Standing Committee member with a grip over the public security apparatus at the time. Zhou reportedly mobilized shadow organizations and other groups, fomenting anti-Japanese demonstrations with the aim of plunging the Hu leadership into chaos.[7] At the time, the Chinese media

---

7 There have been various reports about this, primarily out of Hong Kong. The initial report was the article, "Zhou Yongkang jie fanri dao Xi" [Zhou Yongkang Is Seeking to Overthrow Xi Jinping by Using Opposition to Japan], *Oriental Daily News*, December 9, 2013, http://orientaldaily.on.cc/cnt/news/20131209/00174_001.html.

was also overflowing with anti-Japanese invective, and it can well be imagined that both Li Changchun, the Politburo Standing Committee member who superintended the propaganda apparatus, and Liu Yunshan, the head of the Central Publicity Department, were involved in this plot as well; both men were core figures in the Jiang Zemin faction. For what it is worth, almost all of the anti-Japanese protests two years earlier, in 2010, occurred in various cities in Sichuan Province; Zhou Yongkang was previously the party secretary of Sichuan and was known as a key power holder in the province. His role and the eruption of demonstrations there appear to be related.

In May 2013, perhaps in order to assert that the Senkakus were Chinese territory, a discourse holding that Okinawa was originally a vassal state of Qing-dynasty China was published in *People's Daily* by researchers at the Chinese Academy of Social Sciences. This was reportedly done on direct personal orders from Jiang Zemin.[8]

3. The Roll-Out of Xi Jinping Politics

In retrospect, Xi Jinping squarely positioned his anti-corruption campaign as a key issue from the outset. Xi's biggest ally in this effort was Wang Qishan, who had assumed the office of secretary of the Central Commission for Discipline Inspection. Xi, who had taken office as general secretary at the CCP's Eighteenth National Congress, exhibited a resolute stance against corruption, stating at a meeting of that commission in January 2013: "We must uphold the fighting of tigers and flies at the same time, resolutely investigating law-breaking cases of leading officials and also earnestly resolving the unhealthy tendencies

---

8 Zhang Haipeng and Li Guoqiang, "Lun 'Maguan Tiaoyue' yu Diaoyudao wenti" [On the "Treaty of Shimonoseki" and the Issue of the Diaoyu Islands], *People's Daily*, May 8, 2013. The information about Jiang Zemin's orders was widely circulated in Beijing at the time.

and corruption problems which happen all around people."[9] Perhaps owing to the fact that the target of this campaign was the party itself, Xi advanced the concept of "governing the country according to the law" (*yifa zhiguo*), or law-based governance, at the same time.

This concept had already been put forward chiefly by Chairman Qiao Shi of the NPC in the 1990s. Qiao was a rival of Jiang Zemin, and the two were reportedly candidates for China's supreme leadership post following the Tiananmen Square Incident. Ultimately Qiao, who had not been enthusiastic about suppressing the student movement, lost out when Jiang Zemin was elevated; he thereafter took the post of NPC chairman. This is, naturally, a legislative body, and Qiao advanced the establishment of a legal framework under the banner of law-based governance, working to create such a framework against the backdrop of China's fledgling policy of reform and opening up. But Jiang forced Qiao to withdraw from the political stage in 1997 at the Fifteenth National Congress of the CCP; after this the concept of law-based governance gradually disappeared from Chinese political discourse as well.

Xi's anti-corruption campaign required tackling the sources of the rights and interests that generated corruption. These were the state-owned enterprises. The interweaving of politics and economics was a problem inherent in the socialist market economy—namely, a market economy under Communist Party leadership—from the outset, and the "construction of a harmonious society" as advocated by Hu Jintao was forced to yield before the "Three Represents" and the like advanced by Jiang Zemin. As a result, the party bureaucrats and their relatives who "descended from heaven" (*amakudari*) to take high posts in state-owned enterprises came to use these businesses to accumulate huge amounts of wealth behind the scenes and then send these illicit gains overseas. Efforts to reform state-owned enterprises ran into opposition from

9 Xi Jinping, *Shū Kinpei kokusei un'ei o kataru* [Xi Jinping Discusses Statecraft] (Beijing: Foreign Languages Press, 2014), 432; also published in English as *Xi Jinping: The Governance of China*.

the Jiang faction, naturally, but also from the massive group of vested interests, which included retired cadres and cadres still on active duty.

Both the anti-corruption campaign and law-based governance were just parts of Xi Jinping's struggle to acquire power, as discussed in detail in Chapter 5. Although Hu Jintao put a collective leadership system in place, the majority of high-level posts were ultimately held by members of the Jiang faction, and Hu was rendered impotent when the "construction of a harmonious society" and other policies he championed were blocked by vested interests. Based on the lessons learned from this experience, Xi first took on and toppled Bo Xilai, who had aimed at entering the central leadership by repeating leftist sloganeering that lionized Mao Zedong, and then set about extirpating the big "tigers," major figures involved in corrupt activities. These were Zhou Yongkang, who held sway over the public security apparatus (thereby making him a key figure in the political and legal realms), Sichuan Province, and many state-owned enterprises including the energy sector; and Xu Caihou and Guo Boxiong, two military men who had been vice chairs of the Central Military Commission during the Hu era. Needless to add, all of them were close to Jiang Zemin, from whose faction Xi sought to seize power as his ultimate goal.

This power struggle was settled in the months from the spring to June or July of 2014. First, Xu Caihou was stripped of his party membership on charges including the acceptance of massive bribes and accumulation of vast wealth through abuse of his military position and his improper relationships with women. Xu was reportedly detained and investigated in March 2014.[10] He died of cancer in March 2015; it seems that he was detained at right around the time that his terminal illness was discovered. The next person to be arrested was Zhou Yongkang, reputedly the kingmaker behind the scenes during the Hu era and a figure who had publicly sung the praises of Bo Xilai. A probe was

---

10 "Zhonggong Zhongyang jueding jiyu Xu Caihou kaichu dangji chufen" [The Central Committee of the Communist Party of China Has Punished Xu Caihou by Expulsion from the CCP], *People's Daily*, July 1, 2014.

reportedly launched into the "Zhou Yongkang matter" in 2013, and cadres in Sichuan Province and in the energy sector with close ties to Zhou were arrested one after another by the first half of 2014. On July 29 that year, the Central Commission for Discipline Inspection decided to assemble a case against Zhou for acceptance of massive bribes and improper relationships with women, and it was then decided at the Politburo meeting held on December 5 that he would be stripped of his party membership and the case would be referred to the judicial organs for prosecution.[11] As for Guo Boxiong, first his son and then himself were taken into custody in the first part of 2015, and Guo was expelled from the CCP at the Politburo meeting on July 30, 2015.

In this manner, the Xi Jinping regime laid waste to the nucleus of the Jiang faction in the course of the power struggle. An objective examination of the situation shows that it was also around this time that various kinds of social instability began setting in. On the economic front, a deceleration trend owing to overinvestment, overproduction, and falling exports had grown clear, and the risks posed by the spread of shadow banking (which might rightly be called black market lending) became evident. It was increasingly plain that China's economic problems were mounting.

In addition, even though the new Xi administration had promoted unification with Taiwan in its early days, the Sunflower Student Movement, which occupied Taiwan's Legislative Yuan in opposition to this policy, emerged in March 2014, and the Ma Ying-jeou administration on the island had no choice but to halt further integration with the mainland. Then on August 31, 2014, the NPC Standing Committee took a decision aimed at strengthening the central government's supervision of the election for the next chief executive of Hong Kong. This prompted students in that territory opposed to this to launch the so-called Umbrella Movement; soon young people were engaged in

11 "Zhonggong Zhongyang jueding jiyu Zhou Yongkang kaichu dangji chufen" [The Central Committee of the Communist Party of China Has Punished Zhou Yongkang by Expulsion from the CCP], *People's Daily*, December 6, 2014.

repeated anti-government demonstrations all over Hong Kong. Finally, it was during this period that numerous riots by Uighurs erupted in the Xinjiang Uighur Autonomous Region, and incidents in which many people were killed or injured also occurred.

All these developments convinced the conservative faction—centered on the vested interests—from around August 2014 to emphasize the need for stronger leadership by the party center, a message delivered through such organs as the Central Publicity Department. Although decisions related to the rule of law were issued at the Fourth Plenum of the Eighteenth Central Committee of the CCP held in October 2014, the strengthening of party leadership was stressed throughout, it being noted that the party's leadership was fundamental to law-based governance.[12] Subsequently, the Xi administration's stance on the reform of state-owned enterprises grew vague. Thus, while Xi's government achieved its desired goals in the anti-corruption campaign by taking down the targeted "tigers" and defanging the Jiang faction, then working toward a compromise with the massive vested interest layer, it also focused on stabilization of the system and continued to strengthen its authoritarian character on various fronts.

4. The Xi Administration's Japan Policy

During this time, the pendulum of Xi Jinping's Japan policy oscillated wildly, apparently at the mercy of internal politics. On January 30, 2013, shortly after the inauguration of the new administration, a frigate of the Chinese navy locked its fire-control radar on a patrol helicopter aboard a naval escort of Japan's Maritime Self-Defense Force. In July,

---

12 Xi Jinping, "Guanyu 'Zhonggong Zhongyang guanyu quanmian tuijin yifa zhiguo ruogan zhongda wenti de jueding' de shuoming" [Explanation about the "Decision of the Central Committee of the Communist Party of China on Some Serious Issues in All-Around Promotion of Governance of the Country with Law"], *People's Daily*, October 29, 2014.

the Chinese maritime law enforcement authorities, which had been dispersed among various government agencies, were integrated into the China Coast Guard; from that time on, Chinese encroachments inside the territorial waters of the Senkaku Islands and Japan's exclusive economic zone became more frequent. The Chinese navy also expanded its activities to include military exercises in the western Pacific.

In November 2013, China declared that the airspace of the East China Sea over a broad area encompassing the Senkakus would henceforth be a Chinese ADIZ, or Air Defense Identification Zone. In response to this, Japanese SDF aircraft were scrambled with increasing frequency. These measures were basically developments that occurred after the advent of the Xi administration, and they appear to have been expressions of the will of the top leader. Taking into consideration the power struggle underway at that time, we can surmise that this may have involved a compromise by the new leadership in order to gain the support of the military and the public security organs.

Prime Minister Abe Shinzō of the LDP, who had returned to power in December 2012, and President Xi engaged in a brief face-to-face exchange just before the G20 Summit Meeting in Saint Petersburg, Russia, on September 5, 2013. While this first contact between the leaders was not a formal summit meeting, they agreed to promote the mutually beneficial strategic relationship. No further advances were observed in the bilateral relationship after that, though, and Abe suddenly visited Yasukuni Shrine on December 26, 2013, one year after he reassumed the post of prime minister. The Chinese naturally criticized this officially, but there were no anti-Japanese demonstrations, and the criticisms did not last long. On the global diplomatic stage, meanwhile, China—particularly the Ministry of Foreign Affairs—continued to strongly criticize Japan's stance regarding historical issues.

From the start of 2014, discussion concentrated on whether a Japan-China summit meeting would take place at the Beijing APEC Economic Leaders' Meeting in November that year. It was the Japanese side that displayed a proactive stance on such a meeting, and between

May and June LDP Vice President Kōmura Masahiko, Noda Takeshi of the opposition DPJ, and Minister of Land, Infrastructure, Transport, and Tourism Ōta Akihiro of the Kōmeitō—all of whom have a wide range of personal connections in China—visited the country and met with the Chinese leadership. In fact, though, Hu Deping had already visited Japan prior to that in April. This figure, believed to have been Xi Jinping's secret emissary, is a son of Hu Yaobang, a leading Japanophile. Hu Yaobang in turn had enjoyed an extremely close relationship with Xi Zhongxun, Xi Jinping's father, and Xi and Hu Deping reportedly are very close as well. It is thought that Hu met with Prime Minister Abe during his trip to Japan, thereby playing a key role in establishing a channel of communication between Abe and Xi.

On July 27–29, former Prime Minister Fukuda Yasuo, sensing that the Chinese were seeking to improve bilateral relations, made a secret visit to China along with Secretary General of the National Security Secretariat Yachi Shōtarō, a close confidant of Abe's. On July 28 Fukuda met with Xi and gave him a personal letter from Abe, and detailed negotiations began around this time between Yachi and State Councilor Yang Jiechi with a view toward a summit at the APEC conference in November, as the *Nihon Keizai Shimbun* reported on November 18. The leading actors in the creation of the mutually beneficial strategic relationship in 2006 had been Yachi and Dai Bingguo, and Yachi, who enjoyed the trust of the Chinese, represented the Japanese side this time as well.

In October 2014, Li Xiaolin—chair of the Chinese People's Association for Friendship with Foreign Countries and a daughter of Li Xiannian who is also close to Xi—visited Japan and met with Abe, increasing the momentum toward a summit conference. Yachi visited China just prior to the Beijing APEC Leaders' Meeting and made the final arrangements with Yang. The two sides reached agreement on four items with a view toward improving Japan-China ties: (1) development of the mutually beneficial strategic relationship; (2) surmounting the historical issues and other political difficulties; (3) constructing a crisis management mechanism in the East China Sea and preventing the appearance of unforeseen circumstances there; and (4) restarting political, diplomatic, and security dialogue and building a relationship of political trust.[13]

The outcome of this sequence of events was a summit meeting between Abe and Xi prior to the opening of the Beijing APEC Leaders' Meeting. The summit lasted 25 minutes, and while observers speculated about potential friction because Xi, perhaps worried about the cameras, did not look Abe in the eye, there is little doubt that this meeting was a crucial breakthrough in the improvement of bilateral ties. Abe and Xi met next on April 22, 2015, at an event commemorating the sixtieth anniversary of the Asian-African Conference.[14] At this time the two leaders confirmed in a harmonious atmosphere their mutual desire to promote the mutually beneficial strategic relationship.

The seventieth anniversary of the end of World War II arrived in 2015, and it was also a year when three important events occurred between Japan and China. The first was the statement by Prime Minister Abe about the seventy-year anniversary in August. The second was the passage of a series of peace- and security-related bills in Japan that acknowledged the country's right of collective self-defense. The third was the memorial ceremony and military parade in China on the seventieth anniversary of the victory in the Anti-Japanese War on September 3. One could argue that the official Chinese response to the first two of these was more muted than the sensation that these events generated in Japan. And although there was of course discussion of the past during the Chinese commemoration of the 1945 victory, the proceedings did not include anything in particular that directly depicted contemporary Japan in a hostile light.

---

13 "Regarding Discussions toward Improving Japan-China Relations" (November 7, 2014), Ministry of Foreign Affairs of Japan (website), https://www.mofa.go.jp/a_o/c_m1/cn/page4e_000150.html.

14 "Japan-China Summit Meeting" (April 23, 2015), Ministry of Foreign Affairs of Japan (website), https://www.mofa.go.jp/a_o/c_m1/cn/page1e_000041.html.

The latest developments in the Sino-Japanese relationship show a clear tendency toward improvement of China's ties with Japan since the advent of Xi Jinping's government. This was especially evident in the developments from 2014 on, with a particularly conspicuous movement toward warmer ties through the good offices of former Prime Minister Fukuda in the summer of that year. What brought about this thaw? Observers frequently cite the economic necessity for China of friendlier ties with its neighbor, or a Chinese policy of driving a wedge between Japan and the United States; but such factors had been present all along and cannot account for the sudden emergence of these changes at this juncture. Accordingly, I would like to consider once again the possibility that the answer lies in the dynamics of Chinese domestic politics.

To start with my conclusion, we can see that China's rapprochement with Japan advanced in tandem with the consolidation of the Xi Jinping regime. Xi agreed to an unofficial meeting with Abe at the G20 meeting in Saint Petersburg in September 2013, and China's protests against Abe's visit to Yasukuni Shrine at the end of the year did not last long. Xi then used his close confidant Hu Deping as his personal emissary in response to the overture that Japan made at the start of 2014.

The major advance in Xi's Japan policy came after the end of July 2014, when he met former Prime Minister Fukuda and Secretary General Yachi in China. This coincides exactly with the settlement of the power struggles in China. The investigation of Xu Caihou concluded with his expulsion from the party at the end of June, and the bribery case against Zhou Yongkang was opened at the end of July. This was when Xi achieved his decisive victory over the Jiang Zemin faction, and it was indeed at this juncture that he responded positively to the Japanese approach. A similar alignment between domestic drama and the Japan relationship was seen at the time of the Chen Liangyu scandal in 2006; it is hard to believe that such power struggles, namely the waning fortunes of the Jiang faction, coincided by chance with the changes in China's Japan policy. In sum, this decade's shift in the Chinese policy approach to Japan occurred at exactly the moment when the internal power struggles had been settled.

China's relationship with Japan indeed began to improve with the advent of the Xi era, but events also took place running counter to this trend. On February 27, 2014, just when Xi was making his moves to enhance Japan-China ties, China suddenly decided that September 3 would henceforth be the day for commemorating the victory in the Anti-Japanese War and that December 13 would be a day of national mourning for the Rape of Nanjing.[15] As noted above, a ceremony and a military parade commemorating the seventieth anniversary of China's victory over Japan were held on September 3, 2015. It is commonly believed that this decision reflected Xi's will, but he was concurrently seeking warmer bilateral ties, which raises the question of why these two national memorial days were designated out of the blue, without any discussion of potential memorial events up to that point.

One hypothesis, which I examined in Chapter 5, is that Xi may not have been directly involved in this decision. The body that declared the two memorial days was the Standing Committee of the NPC, with some 200 members. Xi, who held no post in the NPC, did not attend the relevant meeting. The NPC Standing Committee chairman was Zhang Dejiang, who ranked third in the party, making it likely that he played the key role in this decision. Zhang was an atypical member of the Chinese leadership, being a graduate of Kim Il Sung University in North Korea; he had also long had close ties to Jiang Zemin. The epidemic of SARS, a new kind of pneumonia, had occurred in Guangdong Province in 2002–2003, when Zhang was the province's party secretary. While his slow response to the epidemic was regarded as problematic, he nonetheless eluded responsibility thanks to Jiang's pro-

---

15 "Queding Zhongguo renmin kangri zhanzheng shengli jinian ri, sheli Nanjing datusha sinanzhe guojia gongji ri" [Deciding on a Day for Commemorating the Victory of the Chinese People in the War of Resistance against Japan and Establishing a National Memorial Day for the Victims of the Nanjing Massacre], *People's Daily*, February 28, 2014.

tection. Moreover, when it came to "governing the country according to the law" as advocated by Xi Jinping, this was in fact an area where Zhang, who chaired the Standing Committee of the NPC, a legislative organ, should have taken the initiative. Zhang mentioned this relatively infrequently in his speeches and statements, though, and he appeared too passive about it to be considered a true advocate of this line.

In short, the fact that Zhang Dejiang had a close relationship with Jiang Zemin could hardly have been unrelated to the sudden establishment of these two national memorial days. For what it is worth, it was also the NPC Standing Committee, with Zhang as its chair, that on August 31, 2014, decided to introduce measures to control the election of Hong Kong's next chief executive, a step that triggered the Umbrella Movement.

In Summary

In this chapter, I traced the complicated power politics inside the Chinese Communist Party that occurred during the transition from the Hu Jintao era to the Xi Jinping era, examining their impact on China's Japan policy.

At the end of the Hu era, China's presence on the world stage waxed with the Beijing Olympics, the global financial crisis of 2008, Expo 2010 in Shanghai, and China's rise as the world's second largest national economy. Intraparty struggles intensified against this backdrop in advance of the post-Hu era, and the Jiang Zemin faction, including Zhou Yongkang, injected chaos into China's new Japan policy under the mutually beneficial strategic relationship by fomenting radical anti-Japanese demonstrations in the wake of the 2012 Senkaku Islands incident as part of its attacks against Hu's mainstream faction.

With the advent of the Xi Jinping era, the new leader gradually consolidated his power base, and Zhou Yongkang, Xu Caihou, Guo Boxiong, and others who may rightly be called the ringleaders of the

Jiang faction were taken into custody and expelled from the party one after another. Xi took steps at the same time to improve Sino-Japanese ties, engineering a bilateral summit at the Beijing APEC meeting in 2014 and resuscitating the mutually beneficial strategic relationship, though it remained in a fragile state.

That said, many human networks believed to be part of the Jiang faction remain among the leadership, and many former and current cadres outside these networks have already formed a vested interest bloc reaping great benefits from the status quo. It therefore seems both premature and wrong to conclude that Xi Jinping, China's supreme leader, is promoting improvement of Japan-China relations in a linear fashion. As the paramount leader Xi must constantly strive to create a balance within the party, after all, and it is unthinkable that he would abandon the nationalism deriving from the Anti-Japanese War as the basis of the CCP's legitimacy.

Conclusion

Chinese Politics and Japan-China Relations

I would like to conclude this book by summarizing the results of my analysis offered above. I will first reorganize recent Japan-China relations into the three periods indicated below and then, based on my analysis thus far, attempt to summarize the major causes of the fluctuations in Sino-Japanese ties in connection with Chinese domestic politics.

To state my conclusions first, as indicated by my hypothesis set forth at the beginning of this volume, the power balance inside the Chinese Communist Party in domestic politics has played a major role in determining Japan-China relations. In particular, the presence of the Jiang Zemin faction, which was a powerful supporter of maintaining the existing system, and the presence of Jiang Zemin as an individual were major causes of the deterioration in bilateral ties. China's Japan policy has largely been at the mercy of Jiang himself and the calculations and private interests of the vested interests represented by him.

1. Period I: The 1972 System (1972–95)

The first of the three periods was the two-plus decades from the normalization of Japan-China relations in 1972 until 1995, which marked the fiftieth anniversary of the end of World War II. This phase was essentially an era of Sino-Japanese friendship. China was still in the latter stages of the Cultural Revolution when diplomatic ties were normalized, and it was at this time that moderate policies focused on the economy were gradually introduced, with Zhou Enlai playing the lead role. The end of the Cultural Revolution came in 1976 with Mao's death and the fall from power of the Gang of Four close to Mao, after which a transition from the previous revolutionary line to a modernization line spearheaded by Deng Xiaoping began in 1978.

Within the year, a Treaty of Peace and Friendship was concluded between Japan and China. China looked to Japan's modernization as its own development model, and economic exchanges between the two countries expanded as well. It was also at this time that Japan's yen loans (in the form of official development assistance) to China began. During the 1980s, Hu Yaobang became the supreme leader in China. Hu attached utmost importance to China's relations with Japan and strengthened the friendly relationship that he enjoyed with Prime Minister Nakasone Yasuhiro. When Nakasone made an official visit to Yasukuni Shrine in 1985, however, he faced intense criticism both in Japan and abroad, China included. Nakasone subsequently refrained from visiting the shrine after learning that Hu was under assault from the conservatives owing to his actions. But in 1987 Hu was dismissed from office due to his lenient attitude on the issue of China's democratization.

When Hu died in 1989, a democracy movement seeking his rehabilitation arose, but that movement was eventually suppressed in the Tiananmen Square Incident. The incident led Western countries to enforce economic sanctions against China, and Japan froze its yen loans to its neighbor as well. Based on a policy of not isolating China, though, the Japanese government unfroze those loans before long and urged China's reintegration into the international community. And Deng Xiaoping, who had witnessed the collapse of the Soviet Union in 1991, decided to fully adopt the market economy line in 1992 and, from there, embarked on a growth strategy of boldly attracting foreign corporations into the Chinese market.

That same year, the Japanese emperor made an official visit to China, and the sentiment spread in Japan that the issues of history had fundamentally ended. From around this time, meanwhile, the Japanese economy entered a prolonged period of stagnation in the wake of the economic bubble's collapse. In 1993 the Liberal Democratic Party lost its grip on government, and although it returned to power the following year, this was at the cost of forming a coalition government with the Japan Socialist Party (JSP), its erstwhile political foe. In 1995 Prime Minister Murayama Tomiichi, a JSP veteran, issued his so-called Murayama Statement addressed to Japan's Asian neighbors on the occasion of the fiftieth anniversary of the end of World War II, in which he expressed a clear stance on historical issues.

This phase of Sino-Japanese relations can be called the 1972 System. It was basically an era of "Japan-China friendship," during which a certain agreement existed between the two nations concerning the two fundamental issues of history and Taiwan. With regard to history, the agreement was that Japan would express a feeling of apology for its past actions based on acknowledgment of and remorse for its invasion of China, while China would waive war reparations and make peace with Japan by differentiating between the country's wartime leaders and its people. The understanding on the Taiwan issue was that the Japanese government would sever diplomatic relations with the Republic of China and recognize the People's Republic of China as the sole legitimate government of China.

Several conditions made the 1972 System possible. The first was on the international front. Thanks to rapprochement between the United States and China based on their view of the Soviet Union as a common threat, China no longer viewed the US-Japan Security Treaty as a threat. The second involved the domestic situations in the two countries. In Japan, the LDP's long dominance meant that it could maintain policy consistency, while in China a series of leaders including Mao Zedong, Zhou Enlai, Deng Xiaoping, and Hu Yaobang consistently prioritized friendship with Japan.

But while the international and domestic circumstances surrounding Japan and China changed greatly starting in the 1990s, bilateral relations remained static, entrenched in the same old framework based on an outworn premise of "friendship" that did not extend beyond the two countries. As the power balance between Japan and China shifted amid such a state of paradox, many frictions subsequently arose between the two countries, and their relationship morphed into a more complex one that could no longer be contained within the existing framework.

2. Period II: The Surfacing of Frictions (1995–2006)

The second period of Japan-China relations lasted roughly a decade, from 1995 to 2006. This was a time of growing bilateral discord, primarily over issues of history, in the context of a sea change in the power balance between the two countries as China's ascent became clearer, on the one hand, while Japan lingered in the economic doldrums, on the other.

In May 1995, prior to the Murayama Statement, President Jiang Zemin visited Moscow to participate in celebrations marking the fiftieth anniversary of the Soviet victory in World War II at the invitation of Russian President Boris Yeltsin. The People's Republic of China did not yet exist when the war ended in 1945, and China was then known as the Republic of China. Nonetheless, Jiang Zemin asserted during the visit that the PRC was among the victorious powers. For what it is worth, neither did the Russian Federation exist in 1945, the government of Russia at the time being the Soviet Union. As justification for his claim, Jiang argued that the core of the anti-Japanese struggle was the Chinese Communist Party. Perhaps for that reason, on returning to China he put a stop on broadcasts of Japanese television programs, which had been aired frequently until then, and increased the number of programs related to the Anti-Japanese War for the purpose of historical education and study of the CCP.

There was one more reason behind this, namely the issue of Taiwan. In the mid-1990s, discussions on the Guidelines for Japan-US Defense Cooperation were being pursued between Japan and the United States with an eye to strengthening cooperation in the post–Cold War era. China reacted strongly against this, viewing it as a scheme for the joint defense of Taiwan by the two countries. Moreover, when a presidential election was held for the first time on the island in March 1996 and President Lee Teng-hui was elected to serve a second term, he further strengthened Taiwan's tendency for self-reliance. Lee also continually glorified the bygone days of Japanese colonial rule in Taiwan. And so, for China, the Taiwan issue developed into yet another historical issue between itself and Japan.

At the time of the 1996 presidential election, a crisis erupted in the Taiwan Strait when China undertook military exercises there, straining Sino-American relations. This served as a turning point between the United States and China. In 1997 the two countries embarked on dialogue aimed at avoiding conflict, and a strategic partnership was established by US President Bill Clinton and Chinese President Jiang Zemin. By contrast, Japan and China hit a rough patch owing to the dual historical issues of the Anti-Japanese War and Taiwan. This came to the fore during Jiang's 1998 visit to Japan, when he repeatedly criticized past Japanese militarism, including in his remarks at the state banquet held in his honor by Emperor Akihito. Japanese public opinion of Jiang turned sharply negative, and on that score his visit to Japan has been remembered by the people of both countries as an unambiguous failure. Judging from Jiang's subsequent actions, this experience was hugely traumatic for him.

When George W. Bush became president at the start of the twenty-first century, US relations with China also grew difficult. Soon after the September 11, 2001 terrorist attacks, though, the two countries revived their cooperative relationship under the banner of anti-terrorism. While the Japanese economy remained sluggish at the time, Japan had recovered some of its dynamism on the political front. This was best represented by the advent of the Koizumi Jun'ichirō government. Koizumi called for an end to factionalism in the LDP and pushed through with such bold moves as fighting political corruption and implementing postal service reforms. Koizumi had listed official visits to Yasukuni Shrine among his campaign pledges prior to the LDP presidential election, and once elected, he visited the shrine annually for a total of six times until he stepped down in 2006. Bilateral ties deteriorated on this point alone, even though Japan-China relations were otherwise basically good, economic relations included. Sino-Japanese relations in this era have been characterized as "cold politics, hot economics" (*zhengleng jingre*).

Hu Jintao, who replaced Jiang Zemin as China's paramount leader in 2002, sought to repair relations with Japan. But in 2005 protests arose in China to oppose Japan's permanent membership in the United Nations Security Council. Hu attempted to contain anti-Japanese movements and met with Koizumi at international venues; Koizumi, for his part, continued to insist that his visits to Yasukuni Shrine did not negate Japan-China friendship. Nonetheless, national sentiments toward each other's country steadily worsened.

3. Period III: Groping for a Mutually Beneficial Strategic Relationship (2006–Present)

The third period spans the time from the formation of a mutually beneficial strategic relationship between Japan and China to the present. Despite this milestone, unstable relations continued during this period due to the dispute over the Senkaku Islands, until signs of compromise were finally seen at the APEC Economic Leaders' Meeting held in Beijing in November 2014. Still, the bilateral relationship overall has continued to grow more volatile, mainly due to security concerns in the East China Sea and South China Sea.

It was in October 2006, soon after the Koizumi administration gave way to the Abe administration, that Japan and China finally met each other halfway, easing the frictions that defined the second period. Although originally regarded as a hawk, Prime Minister Abe Shinzō refrained from visiting Yasukuni Shrine and concluded a "mutually beneficial relationship based on common strategic interests" with Hu Jintao, the contents of which could be regarded as a transformation of the 1972 System. Whereas the 1972 System had been founded on Sino-Japanese friendship based on agreement about the issues of history and Taiwan, the mutually beneficial strategic relationship reconfigured bilateral relations into a more comprehensive and future-oriented framework. With respect to history, under the new relationship China made the positive assessment that Japan—unlike before and during World War II—had built its present prosperity based on peace and development. Departing from the bilateralism of the 1972 System, moreover, the new framework placed Sino-Japanese ties in the global context, such that the two countries would cooperate with each other in tackling common regional problems in areas including the environment, resources, crime, and natural disasters.

The following year, Premier Wen Jiabao visited Japan and addressed the Diet. "Since the normalization of diplomatic ties between China and Japan," he remarked, "the Japanese Government and leaders have on many occasions stated their position on the historical issues, admitted that Japan had committed aggression and expressed deep remorse and apology to the victimized countries. The Chinese Government and people appreciate the position they have taken." When Hu Jintao subsequently visited Japan as a state guest in 2008, he confirmed the strengthening of the mutually beneficial strategic relationship and agreed to the joint development of the East China Sea. The Chinese conservatives, though, who clung to their vested interests, reacted strongly against such policy initiatives by the Hu leadership.

Sino-Japanese ties had taken a turn for the better, but they worsened again in 2010. In Japan the Democratic Party of Japan had just replaced the LDP as the ruling party, and China, which was becoming more self-assertive as its national power increased, openly promoted its maritime expansion. In China's relations with Japan, these changes were epitomized by an incident in which a Chinese fishing boat collided with patrol ships of the Japan Coast Guard near the Senkaku Islands and the Chinese captain and crew members were detained. Anti-Japanese riots broke out in China, and the Japanese government ultimately calmed the situation by relenting and releasing the captain.

In 2012 Japan and China once again found themselves at odds over the Senkaku Islands. When Tokyo Governor Ishihara Shintarō announced that the city would purchase the privately held Senkakus, Prime Minister Noda Yoshihiko countered the move by proceeding to "nationalize" the islands. Although China initially did not object to Japan's explanation that nationalization was desirable in the interest of stabilizing the Senkaku situation, it reacted strongly after a while, claiming that this entailed a change in the status quo. The Chinese subsequently intensified activities in the vicinity of the Senkakus, and with this as the turning point, China came to strongly assert sovereignty over the islands.

Japan-China ties were frayed even further when Prime Minister Abe visited Yasukuni Shrine in December 2013. The atmosphere between the two countries changed greatly after a summit meeting between Prime Minister Abe and President Xi Jinping was finally held in November 2014 on the sidelines of the APEC Economic Leaders' Meeting in Beijing. A four-point agreement was announced, and the mutually beneficial strategic relationship was revived. Regarding the Senkakus, the agreement did not spell out the existence of a territorial dispute, stating only that both sides had different views. The Xi Jinping government had clearly adopted a conciliatory policy toward Japan. Discussions soon began about establishing a contact mechanism to ensure security in the East China Sea, and various other exchanges were also quickly resumed. In this manner, Sino-Japanese relations began to slowly move toward improvement. These were superficial developments, though, and there has been no fundamental improvement in the relationship based on mutual trust.

4. Factors Affecting Bilateral Relations: Past Discourse

As I have noted above, the 1972 System premised on Japan-China friendship, which prevailed from the 1970s to the mid-1990s, came to suffer from repeated tensions surrounding historical issues from the mid-1990s on. While the two sides subsequently reached a common ground with the formation of a "mutually beneficial strategic relationship" in 2006, establishing such a relationship has proven difficult due to the intensification of the Senkaku Islands issue. Why have Japan-China relations encountered such repeated frictions from the mid-1990s onward?

There is a general tendency to interpret this in terms of a power shift or power transition involving China's emergence and Japan's decline. It is true that the Chinese economy took off thanks to the introduction of market economics and the attendant entry of global corporations into the Chinese market, while Japan was obliged to endure a lengthy period of stagnation due to the collapse of the economic bubble and the subsequent vicissitudes of domestic politics. And there is no denying that this has led the peoples of both countries to harbor a keener sense of mutual competition. However, this interpretation only serves to describe the facts, and does not provide a persuasive argument.

In previous works, I drew on the changes in the fabric of the 1972 System and the failure to establish a mutually beneficial strategic relationship in explaining the repeated tensions. Once the Cold War paradigm that had supported the 1972 System collapsed and the war generations withdrew from the political stage, the system's past-oriented framework could no longer support bilateral ties. With the rapid democratization of Taiwan, meanwhile, the nature of the "Taiwan issue" underwent partial change. I have further argued that despite the changing fabric of the 1972 System, the specific objectives and policies of the mutually beneficial strategic relationship as an alternative framework have remained unclear, rendering the Japan-China relationship unstable.

However, this interpretation is still insufficient. Other researchers have argued that the historical issues are critical and have blamed the Japanese government's stance by holding that bilateral relations are aggravated by Japanese actions that provoke the Chinese, such as the Yasukuni controversy. To be sure, cabinet officials in Japan have caused a furor from time to time by making provocative statements about historical issues, at times resulting in their resignation. But such offensive statements by cabinet officials were actually more common in the 1970s and 1980s than they have been in recent years, and yet in those decades relations between the two countries remained amicable.

5. Factors Affecting Bilateral Relations: Domestic Chinese Politics

I believe that the main cause of the deteriorations and improvements in Japan-China relations may in fact lie more with the Chinese side than with the Japanese side. A trend for the power struggles and factional warfare being waged in Chinese politics to be directly reflected in China's Japan policy has become particularly evident since the mid-1990s. That is to say, as marketization led to greater social diversity in China, and as popular mistrust of the Communist Party and the socialist system grew, the CCP party center became apt to rely on nationalism, and anti-Japanese education was reinforced as the basis of the party's historical legitimacy. Such tendencies were few in the past. The reason is that China had absolute leaders like Mao Zedong, Zhou Enlai, and Deng Xiaoping, who were able to contain from above any complicated problems that arose in Sino-Japanese relations in the greater interest of "friendship."

For instance, while Japan and China were negotiating the Treaty of Peace and Friendship in 1978, more than 100 armed fishing vessels suddenly converged on the waters off the Senkaku Islands, causing tension. As soon as Deng Xiaoping learned of the state of affairs, though, all of the fishing boats turned back. As to the background to this incident, the widely accepted theory in recent years is that top leaders in the Chinese navy were at odds with Deng over another incident and that they mobilized the fishing boats to disorient the mainstream faction just as the peace treaty negotiations hit a snag.

To give another example, at the time of Hu Yaobang's fall from power in 1987, the conservative faction criticized Hu for having leaned toward Japan by using his personal rapport with Prime Minister Nakasone Yasuhiro, as evidenced in the invitation that he extended to 3,000 Japanese youths in 1984. Yet this was not made public at the time, and Deng Xiaoping, who took a broader perspective, did not reconsider China's relations with Japan.

Once such major figures had passed from the scene and it became the eras of Jiang Zemin and Hu Jintao, though, Japan-China relations quickly began to falter. During the Jiang Zemin era, education on the Anti-Japanese War was thoroughly implemented by order of Jiang, and the Taiwan issue was recast as a historical issue with Japan. During his visit to Japan in 1998, Jiang persistently criticized past Japanese militarism and became a persona non grata in the country.

As I noted in Chapter 8, there is an inside story about Jiang Zemin that is well known in China. Although Jiang's official personal history claims that he was adopted by his uncle Jiang Shangqing, this history is said to have been falsified in order for Jiang to join the CCP. Jiang's real father was a cadre in the intelligence organ of the Nanjing-based Wang Jingwei regime, which was regarded as a puppet government of the Japanese; in other words, his father was a *hanjian* (traitor to the Chinese) in the eyes of the CCP. Furthermore, Jiang Zemin himself is said to have studied Japanese at National Central University in Nanjing. The story goes that since the son of a traitor could not join the CCP, Jiang's personal history was revised to make it seem as though he had been adopted by his uncle, who was a party member. It could be that Jiang strengthened his anti-Japanese bent to conceal his complicated personal history. The commentator who was arrested after revealing this inside story, Lü Jiaping, was suddenly released in February 2015, possibly in connection with the decline in the Jiang Zemin faction's influence.

There is a fact that is even more intriguing than this inside story: In the course of formulating the mutually beneficial strategic relationship in 2006, as well as in preparing for the Japan-China summit at the Beijing APEC meeting in 2014, it was the Chinese side that actively approached the Japanese side. In both cases, moreover, the Chinese did so precisely when first Hu Jintao and then Xi Jinping had curbed

Jiang Zemin's power in domestic politics. According to my interviews of persons who were involved in policymaking at the time, the Chinese side did not present any conditions to the Japanese during either of these negotiations. It was generally reported that in 2006 China had demanded an end to the Yasukuni visits, while in 2014 it had called on Japan to acknowledge the existence of a territorial dispute over the Senkaku Islands, as well as to stop the Yasukuni visits. My interviewees informed me, though, that in fact no such conditions were stipulated.

Allow me to explain how this is connected with power struggles. In the 2006 case, Hu Jintao had until then been obstructed at every point by the Jiang Zemin faction, which was the majority faction in the CCP. Five or six members of the nine-member Politburo Standing Committee belonged to the Jiang Zemin faction, among whom Zeng Qinghong, the faction's leader, had an overwhelming say in policy matters. According to recent information, Zhou Yongkang and Liu Yunshan, who held sway over the public security and propaganda organs, mobilized and organized the anti-Japanese demonstrations in 2005.

At the time Chen Liangyu, the party secretary of Shanghai, was Jiang Zemin's favorite and regarded as one of the up-and-coming top leaders. But in September 2006 Chen was arrested by the Hu Jintao faction on charges of corruption, and he was replaced as Shanghai party secretary by Xi Jinping, a personnel decision that was reportedly a compromise between Hu and Zeng Qinghong. In this way, Xi was able to make a bid for the post of next top leader. In the immediate aftermath of the Chen Liangyu scandal, Dai Bingguo, a key figure in Hu's foreign policy brain trust, allegedly contacted Japanese Vice Minister for Foreign Affairs Yachi Shōtarō and requested that Prime Minister Abe, who had just succeeded Prime Minister Koizumi, make an unconditional visit to China. In October 2006 Abe visited China as his first overseas destination since his inauguration, thus thawing the bilateral relationship that had been deadlocked over the Yasukuni issue.

In sum, China's policy toward Japan changed at Hu Jintao's initiative precisely when a close associate of Jiang Zemin fell from power.

Hu Jintao and Li Keqiang are leaders with deep ties to Japan. Under the aegis of Hu Yaobang in the mid-1980s, Hu Jintao oversaw youth exchanges between Japan and China as head of the Communist Youth League. The individuals who played secretarial roles under Hu Jintao were Li Keqiang and Li Yuanchao, currently China's premier and national vice president respectively, both of whom are Japan experts who frequently visited Japan at the time.

The circumstances before and after the Japan-China summit meeting at the Beijing APEC meeting in 2014 were extremely similar to those of the 2006 case. In 2010 the collision incident off the Senkaku Islands occurred between a Chinese fishing boat and Japan Coast Guard patrol vessels, and in 2012 the nationalization of the Senkakus by the Japanese government prompted violent anti-Japanese demonstrations in China. In the wake of these developments, bilateral relations had run aground.

The Xi Jinping government was subsequently launched in China in November 2012; in the following month the LDP returned to power in Japan, and Abe began his second term as prime minister. Abe called for a dialogue with China, but received almost no response. He visited Yasukuni Shrine a year later in December 2013. This time around, though, no demonstrations took place in China, and what criticism arose ceased after a short while. Looking back from today's vantage point, this was a time when Xi Jinping was waging fierce struggles to secure his power base. In March 2012 Bo Xilai, Xi's greatest rival, fell from power. Shortly thereafter, Zhou Yongkang, the head of the Central Political and Legal Affairs Commission, and Xu Caihou, a top military leader, are said to have planned a coup d'état in an effort to restore Bo to power. All three were key members of the Jiang Zemin faction.

In 2014, the world's attention focused on whether or not a meeting would happen between Prime Minister Abe and President Xi, who were attending the Beijing APEC summit that fall. The action offstage started in the spring. Hu Deping, a son of Hu Yaobang and a confidant of Xi Jinping, visited Japan in April, as did Li Xiaolin, a daughter of Li Xiannian who was also close to Xi, in October; both of them met secretly with Prime Minister Abe. They were presumably acting as private emissaries for Xi. In June, the Chinese approached former Prime Minister Fukuda Yasuo, who enjoyed good relations with China. It would appear that he accepted the role of interlocutor with China and also consulted with Abe on a number of occasions. In late July Fukuda made a secret trip to China and met with Xi. He was accompanied on this visit by Secretary General of the National Security Secretariat Yachi, the same man who had established the mutually beneficial strategic relationship with China in 2006 in his capacity as vice minister for foreign affairs.

Chinese politics underwent major change during this period, the outcome of which was the rapid consolidation of the Xi Jinping regime. The mainstream and Jiang Zemin factions had been locked in battle behind the scenes since the Bo Xilai scandal in 2012, but the Xi Jinping side was able to fully constrain Xu Caihou in late June and Zhou Yongkang in late July. This gave Xi control over the top levels of both the military and the police, and the power balance in domestic politics was reversed. The easing of China's policy toward Japan coincided exactly with these developments in domestic Chinese politics.

In Summary

I will wrap up this chapter by summarizing the above. First, the presence of Jiang Zemin was a major driver of the shifts that have occurred in China's Japan policy in recent years. While a series of top Chinese leaders including Mao Zedong, Zhou Enlai, Deng Xiaoping, Hu Jintao, and Xi Jinping refrained from openly expressing hostility toward Japan in the interest of the bigger picture, Jiang stands out as the exception. He bolstered his anti-Japanese credentials instead, perhaps to conceal his background. This anti-Japanese bent became pronounced from the late 1990s, when study of the Anti-Japanese War was strengthened in the wake of the issues of history and Taiwan. Even after the advent of the Hu Jintao era, Jiang still enjoyed immense political power, and his close allies held strong power bases in the public security, propaganda, and military apparatuses. Bo Xilai, Zhou Yongkang, Xu Caihou, and Guo Boxiong are some cases in point.

Second, anti-Japanism not only served to satisfy Jiang's personal sentiments but was used by his faction as fodder for attacking the mainstream faction. After the start of the twenty-first century, in particular, the former persistently attacked Hu Jintao's policy of reconciliation with Japan as well as the mutually beneficial strategic relationship, which was the vehicle for this policy. The anti-Japanese demonstrations of 2005, aimed at blocking Japan's permanent membership in the UN Security Council, took place just as Hu Jintao took full control over the party, state, and military, while the 2010 and 2012 anti-Japanese protests over the Senkaku Islands coincided with the transition from Hu Jintao to Xi Jinping.

Third, in connection with the above, anti-Japanism transcended the level of Jiang Zemin as an individual and grew into an ideology that served to maintain the status quo for the vested interests constituted by collusion between the Communist Party and state corporations. This meant opposing further reforms of the existing system and reinforcing autocracy under the CCP. To that end, nationalism was stoked by promoting study of the Anti-Japanese War as the source of the CCP's historical legitimacy. At its essence, however, all this amounts to nothing more than an attempt to preserve the individual vested interests of the leaders. Japan was the easiest country to bash in the light of history, and no one stood to lose anything by slamming Japan. It goes without saying that this approach was spearheaded by Jiang Zemin and his group.

It has become abundantly clear that the true target of the anti-corruption campaign being pursued so vigorously by the Xi Jinping leadership is the Jiang Zemin faction, the symbol of the vested interests.

In that respect, it would come as no surprise if China were to move toward a major rapprochement with Japan. But regardless of a successful transition to a mutually beneficial strategic relationship with Japan, it will be no easy feat to undo the weight of the decades, particularly the twenty-odd years since the mid-1990s, of singling out Japan as the scapegoat and allowing this view to permeate Chinese society.

At the same time, even if Xi Jinping were to fully triumph in this power struggle, he cannot afford to reject the major premise of Communist Party leadership. In fact, Xi is conducting the anti-corruption campaign in order to strengthen CCP leadership; and even if the Jiang Zemin faction were to collapse entirely, the massive layer of vested interests within the CCP—the largest force resisting Xi's campaign—is unlikely to negate party leadership. Depending on the circumstances in the coming years, therefore, it is entirely possible that Japan, being a convenient vehicle for bolstering Chinese nationalism, will be unduly exploited once again as a means of achieving national cohesion, even if the leadership is aware that such a tactic cannot penetrate effectively into Chinese society.

The greatest vigilance is needed in regard to the waters of the East China Sea and the air space over it. Judging from the status quo, China has no intention of halting the expansion of military operations by its navy and air force. This is probably not a new policy that was introduced by the Xi Jinping government but part of a long-term military strategy that has been gradually promoted by China over many years since the Deng Xiaoping era, given that military buildup is a key pillar in China's vision of achieving great-power status. Although China may continue to adopt a flexible diplomatic stance toward Japan under the Xi government, then, there will likely be no end to this upward trend in China's military and security prowess. If that is so, Japan and China need to prepare in advance for potential contingencies between them in the East China Sea, including unintentional accidents, by creating rules and mechanisms to prevent such eventualities—or, should one occur, to minimize its impact.

It goes without saying that China's disclosure of even a small amount of information regarding its military and security would be enough to significantly ease tensions. But China is one of the most closed and secretive countries when it comes to such matters. While we have become accustomed to dealing with China on that premise, that in itself is abnormal. In particular, such secrecy by a huge and influential country like China is inevitably disturbing to the rest of the world. As things are now, though, transparency of information in China is but a pipe dream, for this can be achieved only when the Chinese political system itself is democratized.

The Chinese political system—that is the greatest and most crucial problem.

Afterword

This is my first monograph in many years since I finished my study titled *Gendai Chūgoku no seiji to kanryōsei* (Politics and Bureaucracy in Contemporary China), which was published by Keio University Press in 2004. In April 2012 I left Keio University, where I had worked for 31 years as a faculty member, and almost 9 years have now passed since I took up my current post as president of the National Defense Academy (NDA) of Japan. While I have published several edited volumes in the interim, all of them were work that I had carried over from my time at Keio University, and none of them were authored solely by me.

My work as president of the NDA has kept me busy. What is expected of this position is not scholarship but rather education. The president cannot tackle with a half-hearted attitude questions of how to nurture students who will come to protect the nation and its citizens and contribute to world peace 20 or 30 years from now. Whereas I was able to focus rather freely on research during my years at Keio, this has been impossible since I moved to the NDA—and rightly so. I am humbled when I think about the fact that the students will one day be devoting their lives as senior officials of the Japan Self-Defense Forces, the last bastion of the people's safety and security.

That said, even after becoming president of the NDA, I have continued my in-depth research as a scholar who resolved to devote my life to scholarship from the time I entered graduate school many years ago. My area of expertise being Chinese politics and foreign relations, which are subjects of decisive significance for the diplomacy and security of Japan today, there have fortunately been ongoing requests and demand for my analyses from both Japan and overseas. I also find it soothing to look through China-related books and materials when I have spare time from work.

Around the autumn of 2015, I was contacted by Baba Kimihiko of Iwanami Shoten, who wanted to assemble a special issue of the journal *Shisō* (Thoughts) to mark the fiftieth anniversary of the start of the Cultural Revolution in 2016. Would I submit an article as part of that effort, he asked. I wondered whether I could find the time for the research involved, but the Cultural Revolution was my life's work since my younger days, and I felt strongly compelled to write a piece on the subject. I accepted Mr. Baba's request. I somehow managed to find the time to produce a draft article, and when it was published in the January 2016 issue of *Shisō*, my scholarly sensibilities were aroused for the first time in many years. This was a blissful moment for me.

At that time, Mr. Baba suggested that I rework some of my previous articles and publish them as a book. I was frankly delighted. Although finding the time to write would be difficult, I wanted to face the challenge, even if it was a slow process. With that thought, I gladly took on the offer. As my time constraints prevented me from producing a completely new work, I reread some of my previously published papers and decided to reorganize them under the theme of "Japan-China relations as viewed from the perspective of Chinese politics." Even though the oldest of these articles date back 20–25 years, when I read over them again I felt confident that they still held up well today; the Chinese political system has not changed in its essence.

This book is the product of making each of these papers, which I completely reworked over the course of about a year, converge on a single theme. As is clear from how the book came to be, I owe a special debt of gratitude to Baba Kimihiko, the editorial director of Iwanami Shoten, for rekindling the fire of my scholarly soul, which had dampened down a bit in recent years.

As noted above, the chapters of this work are based on articles previously published in various outlets, which I have substantially reedited in line with the subject of this book. I indicate below the original material for each of these chapters and where they first appeared.

Introduction: "Chiiki kenkyū to shite no Chūgoku seiji kenkyū: Rekishi, genjō, kadai" [The Study of Chinese Politics as Area Studies: History, Current State, and Issues), in *Ajia Afurika kenkyū: Genzai to kako no taiwa* [Asian and African Studies: A Dialogue between the

Present and the Past], ed. Keio Institute of East Asian Studies (Tokyo: Keio University Press, 2015).

Chapter 1: "Seiji taisei kaikaku to minshuka undō" [Political System Reforms and the Democracy Movement], in *Iwanami kōza gendai Chūgoku bekkan 1: Minshuka undō to Chūgoku shakai shugi* [Iwanami Lectures on Contemporary China, supplementary vol. 1: The Democracy Movement and Chinese Socialism], eds. Nomura Kōichi et al. (Tokyo: Iwanami Shoten, 1990). A revised version of this essay was reprinted in my book, *Chūgoku seiji to minshuka* [Chinese Politics and Democratization] (Tokyo: Simul Press, 1992).

Chapter 2: "Ten'anmon jiken to Soren kaitai" [The Tiananmen Square Incident and the Dissolution of the Soviet Union], in *Iwanami kōza sekai rekishi 27: Posuto reisen kara 21-seiki e* [Iwanami Lectures on World History, vol. 27: From the Post-Cold War Period to the Twenty-First Century], eds. Kabayama Kōichi et al. (Tokyo: Iwanami Shoten, 2000).

Chapter 3: "Chūgoku Kyōsantō no seisaku kōsō: Seiji, keizai, gaikō no sōgo renkan" [The Policy Platform of the Chinese Communist Party: Interrelationships between Politics, Economy, and Diplomacy], in *Chūgoku seiji to Higashi Ajia* [Chinese Politics and East Asia], ed. Kokubun Ryosei (Tokyo: Keio University Press, 2004).

Chapter 4: "Chūgoku ni okeru katoki no seiji taisei: 'Mittsu no daihyō' to 'tōkoku kōporatizumu'" [The Political System of the Transitional Period in China: The "Three Represents" and "Party-state Corporatism"], in *Keiō Gijuku sōritsu 150-nen kinen hōgakubu ronbunshū: Keiō no seijigaku, chiiki kenkyū* [Collected Essays of the Faculty of Law on the 150th Anniversary of the Founding of Keio University: Political Science and Area Studies at Keio University], ed. Faculty of Law, Keio University (Tokyo: Keio University Press, 2008).

Chapter 5: "Rekishi izen to shite no bunka daikakumei" [The Cultural Revolution as Prehistory], *Shisō*, no. 1101 (January 2016), with newly added material.

Chapter 6: "Reisen shūketsugo no Nicchū kankei: '72 nen taisei' no tenkan" [Japan-China Relations after the End of the Cold War: Transformation of the "1972 System"], *Kokusai mondai*, no. 490 (January 2001).

Chapter 7: "Tai-Nichi seisaku kettei no mekanizumu: Kōkaryō mondai no baai" [The Mechanisms for Determining China's Japan Policy: The Case of the Kōkaryō Dormitory], in *Ajia jidai no Nicchū kankei: Kako to mirai* [Japan-China Relations in the Asian Age: Past and Future], ed. Kojima Tomoyuki (Tokyo: Simul Press, 1995).

Chapter 8: "Shiren no jidai no Nicchū kankei: Kō Takumin hō-Nichi kijitsu" [Japan-China Relations in an Age of Trial: An Account of Jiang Zemin's Visit to Japan], *Hōgaku kenkyū* 82, no. 1 (January 2009).

Chapter 9: "Nicchū kankei to kokunai seiji no sōgo renkan: Kinnen no kankei kaizen o megutte" [The Interrelationships between Japan-China Relations and Domestic Politics: The Improvement of Japan-China Relations in Recent Years], *Hōgaku kenkyū* 81, no. 6 (June 2008).

Chapter 10: Revised text of guest lectures given at the John Goodwin Tower Center for Public Policy and International Affairs, Southern Methodist University, in September 2013 and the Ministry of Foreign Affairs of Singapore in October 2013.

Conclusion: Revised text of guest lectures given at the Henry M. Jackson School of International Studies, University of Washington, in May 2015 and at the Program on US-Japan Relations, Harvard University, in April 2016.

Viewed from the outside, the NDA tends to be misunderstood as a straitlaced place. To be sure, discipline and guidance are strict in the daily lives of the cadets, who are expected to become high-ranking officers of the SDF. Once you look inside, though, you find that it is a human space animated by a warm sense of fellowship and a shared purpose. The cadets are truly fine and likable. In my many interactions with SDF officers, I find that under their uniforms most of them are full of character and humanity. Those who devote their lives to the peace and security of the country and its people are utterly sincere and genuine.

At the NDA, I have been supported by many kindhearted souls. I am deeply grateful for the daily support and consideration of the successive vice-presidents and other members of the administration, as well as of everyone involved in secretarial work. These individuals constantly pay close attention to my work environment in my capacity as academy president, while at the same time they greatly respect my other facet as a scholar.

On a personal note, on March 31, 2017, I retired from the Faculty of Law at Keio University, an institution that I cannot thank enough for its help and support over the four decades from my student years until my move to the NDA. Most of the pieces composing this book were written during my time at Keio. Accordingly, I would like to offer this book as a "graduation thesis" to Keio University, the alma mater that nurtured me over the years.

Kokubun Ryosei
January 2021

Index

A

Abe, Shintarō 199

Abe, Shinzō

diplomatic visit/summit meeting (2006) 236, 237, 241, 242–58, 295

Japan-China relations 277, 278, 279, 296–7

Yasukuni Shrine 241, 247, 248, 249–50, 254–5, 276, 279, 289, 291, 296

Action Committee for Defending the Diaoyu Islands 269, 270

ADIZ *see* Air Defense Identification Zones

Afghanistan 111

Air Defense Identification Zones (ADIZ) 276

Akihito, Emperor (Japan) 166–7, 231, 233, 239–40, 285, 288

Allied Occupation 189

"allowing some people to become rich first" (*Xian fuqilai*) 98–9, 102

Alma-Ata Protocol (1991) 75

American studies 23–4

anti-bourgeois-liberalization campaign (1980s) 47, 49

anti-Chinese demonstrations 268

Anti-Fascist War (Russia) 142, 228

Anti-Japanese War *see* Second Sino-Japanese War (1937–45)

anti-Japanism 228–9, 236, 242, 244, 245–6, 289, 295, 298

Kōkaryō dormitory court case (1987) (Japan) 199–200, 202–3

Senkaku (Diaoyu) Islands 268, 269, 270, 271, 281, 290–1, 296

Anti-Rightist (*Fanyou*) campaign (1957) 89, 113

anti-spiritual-pollution campaign (1983) 47, 96

anti-terrorist solidarity 110–11

APEC *see* Asia-Pacific Economic Cooperation

area studies 17–26

Asahi Shimbun 205, 212, 223

ASEAN *see* Association of Southeast Asian Nations

Asia Research Institute (Keio University) 23

Asia-Pacific Economic Cooperation (APEC) 109–10, 110–11, 268, 269, 291, 294, 296

Asian financial crisis (1997) 100, 123

Asian-African Conference (Indonesia) (2005) 244

Association of Southeast Asian Nations (ASEAN) 112

authoritarianism 29, 67, 128, 135

party-state system 116–21

pro-democracy movement 57–8, 59, 60, 61, 62

B

Bai, Hua 47

Baltic States 74, 75

Bao, Tong 53, 62

Baoshan Steel Works (Shanghai) 180

Beidaihe Meeting (2012) 267, 270

"Beijing Consensus" 260

Beijing Normal University 69, 71

Beijing Spring 42, 45, 51, 90

Beijing Students' Autonomous Federation 69

Beijing Wanbao 147

M

About the Author

Dr. Kokubun Ryosei has served as president of National Defense Academy (NDA) of Japan since April 2012. He is also professor emeritus at Keio University since 2019. After completing his undergraduate and graduate degrees at Keio University, he began teaching there as an assistant professor in 1981. Kokubun became an associate professor in 1985 and a professor in 1992, and served as director of Keio's Institute of East Asian Studies from 1999 to 2007 and dean of the university's Faculty of Law and Politics from 2007 to 2011. He has been a visiting scholar at Harvard University, the University of Michigan, Fudan University, Peking University, and National Taiwan University. Kokubun's research interests encompass Chinese politics and international relations in East Asia. He is a former president of the Japan Association of International Relations and the Japan Association for Asian Studies. Kokubun has edited and published numerous English publications as well as Japanese, including: *Japan-China Relations in the Modern Era* (Routledge, 2017); *Sino-Japanese Relations: Rivals or Partners in Regional Cooperation?* (World Scientific, 2013); *Getting the Triangle Straight: Managing China-Japan-US Relations* (Japan Center for International Exchange [JCIE], 2010); *Sino-Japanese Relations: The Need for Conflict Prevention and Management* (Cambridge Scholars Publishing, 2008); *The Rise of China and a Changing East Asian Order* (JCIE, 2004); and *Challenges for China-Japan-US Cooperation* (JCIE, 1998). He was awarded the Asia-Pacific Prize (Mainichi Shimbun) in 1997, the Suntory Prize(Suntory Foundation) in 2004 and the Kashiyama Prize (Kashiyama Foundation) in 2017.

（英文版）中国政治からみた日中関係
Japan-China Relations through the Lens of Chinese Politics

2021年3月27日　第1刷発行

著　者　　国分 良成
英　訳　　公益財団法人日本国際問題研究所
発行所　　一般財団法人出版文化産業振興財団
　　　　　〒101-0051 東京都千代田区神田神保町2-2-30
　　　　　電話　03-5211-7283
ホームページ　https://www.jpic.or.jp/

印刷・製本所　大日本印刷株式会社

© 2017 Kokubun Ryosei
Printed in Japan
ISBN 978-4-86658-127-9